MURDER MOST LOCAL

Historic Murders of

NORTH CORK

PETER O'SHEA

D1337864

Murder Most Local
Historic Murders of North Cork by Peter O'Shea
ISBN: Soft Cover 978-1-9163796-1-9
ISBN: Hard Cover
Copyright©2019 Peter O'Shea
ALL RIGHTS RESERVED. International copyright secured.

Published by Most Local Press

Printed in Poland by Totem

Acknowledgements

First of all, I would like to say thank you to all the people who came out and supported me with 'Murder Most Local, East Cork Historical Murders'. The feedback I received at the time was amazing and inspired me to keep researching and writing.

It's hard to write acknowledgements for a local true crime book when people are reluctant to talk. The few that do talk rarely want to be mentioned at all, the opposite in fact. Thank you to the those few.

I have met many along the way who have pointed me in the right direction quietly and for that I am grateful. I have got plenty of "we don't talk about that around here, you know yourself" and that's fine too. It makes the readers all the more keen to find out for themselves, especially the younger generations that don't hear the stories anymore.

Thanks to my family for putting up with me. There was little mentioned in our house except North Cork. We had a lovely summer holidaying there. It is a place that we hadn't spent enough time in. We all loved it and we will definitely be visiting more. Thanks to Gemma Kelleher for pointing me in the direction of the Mallow Field Club Journals.

Again I can't thank the proofreaders and editors enough. It's a hard ask, thanks to Karen Casey, Kathleen Forrest, Catherine Casey and Nessa O'Shea.

Contents

Murder Map

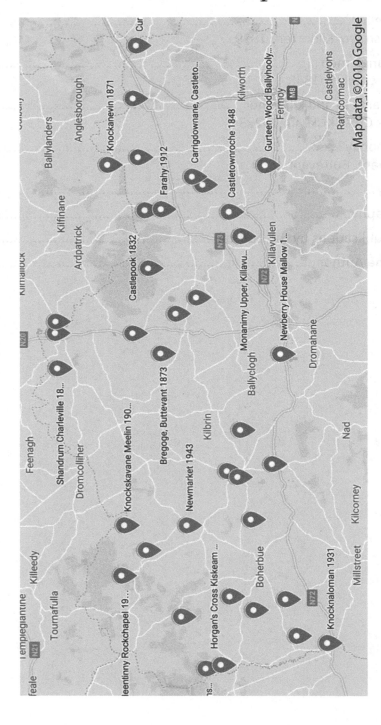

Introduction

Following on from my last book, 'Murder Most Local, Historical Murders of East Cork' in 2018, I found I was drawn into the interesting cases further North in the county. After researching and writing the first few stories, I wanted more. Often cases are long forgotten especially amongst the families involved. When visiting North Cork I got "we don't talk about that here" while researching and this spurred me on even more.

Just for clarity I have defined an area of North Cork as being north of the N72. Historical murders seem to be far easier to find in this area than in East Cork so I had to stop somewhere. There are fewer murders in this book than in the East Cork version but some are far more complicated and therefore longer. I have left out some obvious murders than many people will ask about but felt they have been covered well elsewhere. I found myself having to stop somewhere before it became an unmanageable tome, that couldn't be read in bed.

I didn't struggle to find content, however some villages in the area are devoid of murder while others there are many but unconnected. Certainly it is clear North Cork suffered its share of agrarian unrest which led to death. In Ireland generally we do get more than our share of murders about land, many people often reference John B Keane's The Field. North Cork features cases much more complicated and gruesome than The Field.

There are other motives besides agrarian unrest; love, lust and money are also at play. Where ever you go in Ireland though the same motives are there land, money, love/women, jealousy, drink and insanity. Most of these motives are still similar to those in today's society. One extreme case in this book the actual murder is the motive.

Each story is different and unique, there are times when you think you know who did it and others remain unsolved. Some it is obvious from the very start who committed the murder, but the question in each case, will they get away with it? Comparing the different cases there are times when the chief suspect can't be proven guilty. While in other cases a suspect ends up paying with their life when less evidence is produced.

All the murders are actual real events that have taken place in the last 200 years.

For many years in Ireland being found guilty, meant the murderers paid for their crime with their lives. In the early 1800's executions were held in public and served as a grim warning to others not to do likewise. Any lesser crime such as manslaughter would see the person transported to a far flung colony; petty crimes were punished similarly back then. Those found guilty of murder but insane generally meant life imprisonment. Despite the severe punishment people were still driven to killing for many reasons as we shall see.

With the foundation of the Irish Free State murder seems to become more uncommon in the 1920's and 30's but not in North Cork. The cases in this period generated a huge amount of public interest at the time. Some are still talked about to this day but there are others that are long forgotten.

In modern Ireland we sometimes think crime is a modern problem. After reading these pages you can't but be convinced there was always serious crime

A cold death
Meenroe Meelin Newmarket 1902

On the 11th of February 1902 before sunrise, farmer Daniel Collins from Gooseberry Hill was on his way to the wedding of a neighbour. There was no sign of winter coming to an end that year and the weather was still very cold. The day was bleak with snow falling and ice on the roads. People would normally have stayed indoors but it was Shrove Tuesday and there was a wedding to get to.

Back then in Ireland nobody could get married during lent. So anyone needing to get married in a hurry (if you know what I mean) did it on that day. Therefore many people were getting married on that day.

As Collins was on the way to the wedding he came across the body of a local well known farmer known as Ben Charles. The farmer's body bore all the signs of a violent death and robbery. The pockets had been turned out and his head had several marks on it. The snow was blood soaked from his head injuries. The blood had congealed due to the cold.

Collins alerted a farmer living nearby then ran off to the village of Meelin where he alerted the police. Sergeant Patrick Madden led a party of constables to the scene as quickly as they could. It was obvious that foul play had occurred sometime during the night. The Sergeant thought the body was there for some time as it was stiff and cold. Madden did not have to go far to tell the relations as the farmer lived close by in the next townland Knockskavane.

Many theories were suggested some said he was attacked on the roadside. Others however said he may have fallen and died of exposure and was later robbed by an opportunistic passerby.

The man found on the road was Benjamin Charles O'Connor a comfortable farmer aged about sixty. He had been married to his wife for over thirty years and they had a large family of nine children. O'Connor was an inoffensive man and nobody could think of a motive for the crime except robbery.

It did not take long for the Police to figure out the last movements of Benjamin O'Connor. The day before he had been to Newmarket Fair

3

but did not carry out much business there. He had not bought or sold any cattle so it was thought he would not have had much money on him. Instead he had hired a young labourer named Michael Leonard at the fair. After some drink they set off for O'Connor's farm a distance of about six miles a considerable distance given the cold weather. The pair however stopped off at Meelin at a pub before continuing their journey.

The police obviously tracked down Leonard and arrested him to question him. He was most likely not hard to find as he only lived in Knockskehy the townland to the east of Knockskavane. Leonard claimed that Ben Charles was beaten up on the road home and he ran off to get help nearby. But it seemed he did not actually tell anyone until the morning after.

Not long after three more were arrested. Jeremiah Tobin a thirty year old labourer from the village of Meelin and farmers Cornelius Connors and Daniel Keeffe from the locality.

At noon on the 14th of February an inquest was held by Coroner James Byrne into the details surrounding the suspicious death. District Inspector Francis O'Neill Newmarket was there for police and County Inspector Gamble also attended. The foreman of the jury was a retired farmer from the area, Cornelius McAuliffe.

Daniel Collins the old farmer from Gooseberry Hill was called to tell of finding the body on Tuesday morning. Collins said he was walking along the road after seven but before sunrise when he spotted a man lying on the road. He called out to him but receiving no answer ran off to get help. He knew the man lying there was Benjamin O'Connor so he went to his cousin Patrick O'Connor nearby. The two then returned to the scene and found that he was in fact dead. Collins thought at the time he must have been there all night as there was frost on his coat. Collins then went on to Meelin to the police while Pat O'Connor remained at the roadside with the body.

Close to the place where Benjamin O'Connor was found.

Patrick O'Connor son of the deceased man, aged just fourteen identified the body of his father. The last time he saw him alive was Monday the 10th when his father headed off to Newmarket fair at ten in the morning. It was the next morning before he saw him again on the side of the road dead with a bloody face.

Doctor William Dodd gave medical evidence. He examined the body on the 12th and performed the post mortem. The doctor immediately ruled out an accidental death and described injuries to the left and right temples. During the post mortem he found the skull fractured on the left hand side. There were several injuries to the arms and around the wrists. Two ribs had been fractured and they punctured the lungs. The doctor concluded that death was a result of the skull and rib fractures and Benjamin might have lived longer but for the exposure. Dr Verling who had assisted in the post mortem agreed with Dodd's account.

After a very technical testimony from Doctor Dodd the Coroner asked him "In your opinion doctor in what manner or by what weapon was the fracture inflicted". The doctor replied a blunt instrument. Coroner enquired again "such as a stick" but the doctor thought more like a stone or a heavy blunt object. The coroner then summed up what had been heard saying the injuries were enough to result in death.

The jury's verdict was "That the said Benjamin Charles O'Connor of Knockskavane was found dead at Meenroe on the 11th of February 1902. We believe the causes of death was fracture of the skull and ribs inflicted by some person or persons unknown on the night of the 10th or morning of the 11th and that we desire to convey to the widow and family of the deceased our sincerest sympathy and condolence in their great affliction and that we fervently hope that the perpetrators of the foul deed will be speedily brought to justice."

Not long after the inquest was finished the funeral took place. It was well attended by many from all over the area and Benjamin O'Connor's remains were taken to Tullylease Graveyard.

One week later the four men were brought before a magistrate and charged with having killed Benjamin O'Connor. The district inspector Francis O'Neill said he was still making inquires and not yet ready for a court hearing. The four were remanded back into custody for a further eight days.

It turned out the eight days was nowhere near enough, several more applications were made and the four remained in jail without any evidence produced against them. By mid April they had got legal representation, HH Barry and Sons Solicitors, Kanturk who now argued their case.

District Inspector Francis O'Neill was still confident his police would uncover something to prove their involvement. He asked Barry to trust that he would soon make progress in the matter. Barry however argued that his clients were being punished without actually being tried; they were now in jail for over two months. He saw no progress at all in the case saying there was not a shred of evidence against them. Barry asked that if no evidence was found in the next eight days then the men should be discharged.

The application for another remand was granted but the case it seemed was now on very thin ice and about to fall apart.

One week later the court sat again, the district inspector knew he would struggle to get yet another remand so witnesses were called to begin the proceedings. Before magistrate Hardy the four were again charged.

The first witness was David Allen who worked at his father's shop in Newmarket. He told how he attended Benjamin O'Connor on the 10th February and Michael Leonard was also with him. Benjamin had purchased a handle for a shovel and other items costing 1s 10d paying with a pound note.

Publican and farmer in Meelin Jeremiah Quinlan was called to the stand and he admitted to knowing the accused men. Tobin he said was actually related to him and he recalled him being in the pub several times that day. Tobin entered the pub at seven in the evening, Daniel Keeffe and Dan Curtin arrived shortly afterwards. The publican recalled that Michael Leonard and Benjamin O'Connor were also there at the same time. He was surprised when Daniel Keeffe paid for drink he had 10 or 12 shillings which he thought was an awful lot of money. In the pub also at the same time was Cornelius Connors better known as Con Bawn, Denis McAuliffe and Cornelius Hannon.

He saw Benjamin O'Connor and Leonard leave the pub twenty minutes before ten. Not long after just before ten Cornelius Connors and Daniel Keeffe left the pub.

The morning after he said Jeremiah Tobin came in at nine and Cornelius Connors arrived an hour later.

After hearing from the witnesses and with still no evidence against the accused the prosecution applied for another remand. Francis O'Neill again said he would soon have more evidence and the application was granted.

It was over two weeks later on the 8th of May when the four men were again charged in court. Now the prosecution had lined up several more witnesses but were still investigating the case.

Widow Deborah O'Connor now took the stand and told how she saw her husband on the roadside that morning with his pockets pulled out. He lay on the road a half mile from their house but only a few feet from his own boundary ditch she said. She also told that leaving that day for Newmarket her husband carried two purses, a yellow one for money, silver coins and notes. He also carried a black leather purse for keeping receipts and papers. Three days after her husband was killed she heard a spade which he had bought at the fair had been found nearby. Deborah said her husband was sixty four years old and was in good health, they had been married for almost thirty five years.

Another publican Mary Sullivan in Meelin was called to give evidence. Mary told how she was married to Michael Sullivan and her husband was the publican. On the morning of the 11th February four men approached her house about nine. One of them Con Connors knocked and asked for porter. She let them in and served four glasses of porter which Connors paid for but she didn't know the other three. She noticed a mark of blood on Connors chin and another on his shirt, what she described as a writing pen full, he also had black eyes. Connors followed her to the hall while the others were drinking. Mrs Sullivan said to him "by gonneys Con it is not right for anyone to be about the village today as there is no knowing who the police will arrest, as Ben Charlie is dead". She then took her apron and wiped the spot of blood from his face but Con gave nothing away.

Farmer John Lenihan from Scarteen Upper a townland between Newmarket and Meelin was the next witness. He told how on the night of 10th of February Ben Charlie as he called him and Michael Leonard stopped at his house on their way home from the fair.

It was sometime around seven, taking shelter from the snow shower. They only stayed fifteen minutes smoking their pipes while waiting for the snow to stop.

Daniel Barry from Knockduff was called as a witness having met Daniel Keeffe on the day of the fair. Barry recalled meeting Keeffe going to the fair with a cow and calf. Before the day was over he had bought the cow and calf from him and Keeffe bought another cow. The witness told how he ended up driving all the animals home and Keeffe told him he would call later for his cow. Daniel Keeffe did call to him later that night with a man called Curtin but that was all the farmer had to say.

After hearing these witnesses the accused were further remanded into custody. The district inspector knew he was clearly running out of time and would need something better soon or else his case was over.

Two weeks later they were brought up again at the police office in Cork.

Now Francis O'Neill district inspector gave in saying the Crown Solicitor ordered the men to be discharged. They still had not found any evidence against them despite all the effort they had put into investigating the case.

The magistrate Mr Horne then discharged the men leaving them free to go after over three months in jail. One of the men said they had no money and no means to get home. O'Neill was harsh and said there was no money available for such circumstances; he even went so far to say he believed some of them were reasonably well off.

The magistrate disagreed with the Police saying it wasn't right to discharge them so far from home, he asked the room "what is the train fare" O'Neill replied he believed it was 4s 3d to which the magistrate said he would see the men's train fare paid. So the four men walked free and had their fare paid to get home.

We are still no closer to finding out who killed Ben Charlie on that dreadful cold night in February. Why didn't the Police get a statement from Leonard as to where he was when it all happened? Did he become separated from Ben Charlie at some point? Leonard lived further east than the O'Connor farm so he should have been with him all the way. Either way Michael Leonard must have known more.

The district Inspector was not happy with the outcome of the case or with the performance of his officers. Months later he initiated a police inquiry against Meelin Sergeant Patrick Madden and Constable Michael Sullivan.

The inquiry was held over several days by other District Inspectors. The men were accused with not being on patrol on 10th February when the station log says they were. They were also accused of not proceeding to the scene of the crime on the morning of the 11th with due haste having heard about it at eight that morning. Sergeant Madden was also charged under code 1855 of not examining the scene of the crime with due care and attention. He apparently ignored certain items pointed out to him by a constable.

Michael Sullivan was discharged on all counts against him. Madden however was found guilty on not investigating the scene correctly and demoted to the rank of Constable.

Village of Meelin and the road Benjamin took that night.

Begorra he's dead
Thomas Street Mitchelstown 1913

According to the census of 1911, James Walsh Senior was a boot maker who lived alone in Thomas Street, Mitchelstown. Ten years before the house had been a busy one with five almost adult children at home with him and his wife Julia. In 1911 his eldest son David had long since left Ireland for Boston. Next eldest Denis and William were postmen in the town. Two daughters Mary Anne and Julia probably left to marry, as had youngest son James.

Mathematics was not one of the boot maker's skills as between the census 1901 to 1911 he had aged seventeen years! Now his occupation is given as bill poster.

He was not alone for long though, youngest son James better known as Jumbo had married a local woman Ellen Barrett in 1909. He worked as a labourer and in no time at all they had two young children, Julia, named after James mother and James born in 1912.

The young family moved back in with his father on Thomas Street. An arrangement that has become so common again in recent years with rising house prices. The arrangement however had its drawbacks, especially when James Senior arrived home drunk there were rows in the house. It was even worse when both father and son came home drunk together. James senior was said to have been a hard worker and had raised his family over the years. Now though he was back supporting his youngest son who had not taken after him as a hard worker.

On the Sunday night of 9th November 1913 Jim Walsh (James Senior) came home drunk from a funeral about half five. He was so drunk that he went upstairs and fell against the corner of something.

He came down to his daughter in law Ellen and asked had he cut himself. He had a deep cut over the left eye. She was preparing the supper at the time. Her husband arrived home just before six. He was equally as intoxicated as his father was, having been out all day.

The whole family had supper together around the kitchen table. Ellen's husband went back out again after dinner and Ellen had had enough of it. Despite the lashing rain outside she hurriedly took the two children and left for the workhouse. She didn't want to be there when he came home later after even more drink. She often went to the workhouse as a threat to him to stop drinking and he would go off the drink for a while but it didn't last. She needed to do something more drastic. He would be so drunk when he came home later and wouldn't notice she was wasn't there till the following morning.

The next morning Ellen left the workhouse after nine and made her way towards home at Thomas Street with her two young children. She was cautious about going home and what her husband would say to her for making the point. Would he be at home waiting for her nursing his hangover ready to pick an argument with her?

She made a few inquiries from neighbours before going in. She had nothing to worry about her husband James was up and gone, he was seen leaving at half eight.

Ellen took the kids home and settled in with no one at home. She made some tea but something didn't feel right. About 11 that morning Ellen crept up stairs as she had heard no sound from her father-in-law yet.

She found her father-in-law kneeling with his head pressing against the window sill. His hands were under his chest. It looked at first like he had come out of bed but had all his clothes and boots on. She knew immediately he was dead and had been for some time. Ellen ran to her neighbour John Wiley.

Wiley a neighbour from Robert Street, went upstairs to verify what Ellen had said. It seemed she was right Jim Walsh had all the signs of being dead. Wiley's young lad then ran off to find James Walsh and inform him his father had died.

It didn't take a detective to find Walsh; he was located in Finn's public house on Baldwin Street which was close by.

James immediately came running up Thomas Street to see his father. By the time he arrived home the priest, Fr O'Connell was there with John Wiley. Young Walsh enquired of his father "is he dead"; Wiley replied "begorra he is dead and well dead". Walsh then asked the priest had he given his father the sacraments". When he learned that it had been done the son remarked that now there was no need for an inquest. He was keen to move the body into a bedroom downstairs but Wiley said it should not be moved until the police arrived. Wiley himself had already moved the body without thinking about it.

Walsh seemed upset and was crying when he heard his father was dead. It was by now well into the afternoon and Walsh agreed he would go for the police. On his way there though he met a neighbour and made arrangements to have the body moved as soon as possible. He told her he wanted his father washed and setup in the bed downstairs.

He led the police to believe at first that the old man had just died with the priest. Walsh told the constable that he was out drinking all morning and implied his father had died during this time.

Thomas Street Mitchelstown close to the scene.

The police suspected foul play when they saw marks on the old man. Despite the fact James Walsh had informed them of his father's death suspicion fell on him. Before the end of the day he had been arrested and everyone awaited the findings of the inquest.

On Tuesday the 11th of November an inquest was held in Mitchelstown Courthouse by Coroner Richard Rice. District Inspector Lewis represented the police while solicitor Patrick Murphy was for James Walsh who had been arrested. The jury was led by foreman Mr P Farrell.

Ellen was the first witness called, she detailed the events leading up to her father-in-laws death and discovering the body on Monday morning. She had never seen her husband come to blows with his father but they often argued bitterly. Ellen denied they rowed about the money the old man had in the post office. When asked by a juror Ellen detailed the injuries. She said on Sunday evening he had a cut over his left eye but on Monday morning there were four marks on the left side of his face.

John Wiley was then called to describe how he had found the body. A woman had frantically come to him that morning saying," run John Wiley, old Jim Walsh is dead". When he found the body it was kneeling with right side of head firmly against the wall. He was kneeling forward in such a way that his boots were off the ground.

Wiley told the inquest how he then turned the body over onto his back and confirmed he was dead, thinking it must have been with a good while. There was no signs of a struggle, it looked like the old man had gotten out of bed but had clothes and boots on. The witness was asked again was he sure he had marks on the left side of his face because it was the other side that was against the wall.

Dr Edmond Walsh gave medical evidence after completing the post mortem the day before at the house on Thomas Street. He had found the wounds over the left eye, one of which was deep and another bruise under the eye. In the chest he found one of the cavities of the heart thickened and enlarged as a result of heart disease otherwise the organs were healthy. This defect of the heart the doctor said could cause sudden death. But the doctor thought if this had occurred he would not have been found in the cramped up position he was.

A juror asked "would that mean that he was killed or had been dead for some considerable time and that he was placed in that position". It was the District Inspector Lewis who relied first saying "exactly". When the doctor got the chance to reply he could not be so sure. The wounds were not enough to cause death and there were no fractures. The doctor felt it was the condition of his heart and the injuries which resulted in death.

The doctor had treated Jim Walsh before in the local hospital saying he was bad then. The doctor clarified to district inspector Lewis that the heart alone could easily have resulted in death. Dr Walsh said again that the position he was found in was not consistent to with a position he would expect to find a body after heart failure.

John Wiley was recalled again to describe one more time the position he found the body in. Lewis interrupted saying "his evidence is that he must have been placed there after rigor mortis set in".

After hearing the evidence the coroner went back over it all before allowing the jury to leave. With only five minutes deliberating the foreman returned with the verdict. They agreed with the medical evidence found that death was caused by heart failure brought on by violence. The jury felt they had no evidence to make comment on the violence that had occurred.

Directly after the inquest there was a special sitting of Mitchelstown Court. James Walsh Junior was charged that he wilfully and feloniously and with malice aforethought killed and murdered James Walsh his father of Thomas Street Mitchelstown.

Head Constable applied for a remand for eight days so that police could proceed with their investigations. Solicitor Murphy reserved his defence but pleaded for bail for his client. The funeral of his father was to be tomorrow and he should attend it. His client also had a very young family.

Head Constable Ralph was completely opposed to bail for the accused. Murphy relented but replied "well I would not be so persistent your worship but when all the facts are known it will be seen that there is really nothing in the case".

No matter bail was refused and Walsh was remanded into custody and taken to Cork Gaol later that day. The funeral occurred the following day and not only was James Walsh junior not present. He was locked up and under suspicion for his father's death.

Walsh was remanded in custody several times as the police made their inquiries and built their case against him. The best they would be able to provide would be circumstantial evidence and was it ever going to be enough to convict.

In late December the case came before a special sitting of Mitchelstown Court on Saturday the 27th. The courtroom was filled to capacity with people desperate to hear details of the case. Magistrate Dickson presided over the hearing while District Inspector Lewis prosecuted and solicitor Murphy defended.

When the charge was read to him, James Walsh appeared obviously worried looking and very aware of the position he was in. His wife and two young children were also in the courtroom. The children were too young to know what was going on but his wife Ellen was visibly upset with the proceeding and at times burst out crying.

Head Constable Ralph was the first witness and read a statement James Walsh told him in the barracks that day. "I don't know anything about him, I'm out all the morning since half eight. I was drinking a bottle of porter at Mr Finn's when I was called. Father O'Connell was with him before he died and I went in as the priest was leaving and my father was dead then and I came straight up to you". Ralph then described going to the house in Thomas Street and finding the body in a bed downstairs. He examined the bedroom upstairs and had questioned Ellen Walsh. Ellen had led him to believe she had stayed at Thomas Street that Sunday night with her husband. She also told him her father-in-law had gone to bed after supper about half six.

John Wiley was called and again gave testimony of the position and time he had seen the body. The exact position now seemed more critical to the case and may prove how he had died. Wiley said the body was cold when he moved it and he felt it had been dead for quite a while.

Dr Edmund Walsh also repeated the evidence from the inquest and was questioned by defence. The exact position of the body and how the legs were off the ground was discussed. The doctor felt the body could have been moved after rigor mortis had set in. He told how normally rigidity occurred five or six hours after death and lasted for several hours. He came to the conclusion James Walsh had died at least twelve hours before Wiley had seen the body. That would make the time of death at eleven or twelve on Sunday night.

The next witness was a neighbour who lived off George's Street, Mrs Elizabeth Dolan. She told how she had passed by Walsh's house on Thomas

Street at about half six on Sunday 9th of November. As she did James Walsh senior came out shouting "come out we'll have it outside, the place is too small, come out you hungry crew yourself wife and children".

After this Lewis said that completed the evidence that day and he would need more time in court at a later date. Murphy objected to how long the case was taking saying his client was already in jail for over six weeks. Lewis explained that before Christmas he had been engaged with other cases at the Assizes and not able to devote himself to this case.

It was a week later before it was back in court again. James Walsh was now said to be looking the worse for wear the longer he spent in jail. There were many more witnesses to be called. Thomas Street was in the middle of the busy town where many people lived and worked.

John Daly who lived right opposite the Walsh's house was sworn in. That Sunday evening he heard a loud voice he recognised as James Walsh senior. He came out onto the street and said "come out now, you murdering ruffian, you bloody get, I supported both you and your wife and two children". Daly told how it was usual to hear the loud voices of father and son arguing. Recently though it had become even more frequent.

Later that night Daly heard footsteps nearby and he assumed it was James Walsh junior. He also heard him greeting someone on the street.

Later John Daly was lying in bed when he noticed a bright light coming from the street outside. He got up thinking it was about twenty past eleven, outside the Walsh residence there was a fire on the street. Daly could not tell what was burning but could smell paraffin oil. At that time there was a light coming from James Walsh Junior's bedroom.

Kate O'Keeffe who lived on Robert Street recalled half eleven on Sunday the 9th of November. She heard a knock on her door. It was James Walsh junior who she knew as Jumbo. He told her that he was out looking for his wife, children and father. She could tell he was very annoyed that nobody was home but never told her why his wife was out so late with the children. Walsh threatened to go down and burn down the house but she warned him not to do anything he may regret later.

Was it already too late for this advice?

Several more witnesses from the area were produced and gave evidence of meeting Jumbo on the streets Sunday evening. He was seen staggering yet some said he was neither drunk nor sober. Slowly the prosecution were building a case against James Walsh but it all remained to be circumstantial evidence.

Richard Meade, porter from the Mitchelstown Union Workhouse took the stand. He told how he admitted Ellen Walsh and her two children about eight on the 9th of November. It wasn't the first time she stayed there. She had been three or four times in the past. Lewis questioned the witness asking, what was the reason she gave for going to the workhouse. Murphy objected to the question and the question was not allowed.

James Walsh knocked on Thomas Ryan's house on Robert Street saying "let me in, let me in, I must go if you don't let me in". Ryan did not answer but knew exactly who was outside. It was about half eleven on that Sunday night.

Constable McCarthy was called to give evidence of having been called to Thomas Street last October. He said it was Ellen Walsh who called him accusing her husband of assaulting her. Old Jim Walsh was also there and he described his son as "the greatest murdered unhung". He claimed his son often beat his wife and was willing to give evidence against him.

In total it took four days in court hearing evidence during the month of January before the prosecution ended on the 17th. When asked had he anything to say in reply to the charges against him he merely replied "not guilty".

District Inspector Lewis applied to have the case returned for trial at the next Assizes in Cork and the judge granted it. The defence Mr Murphy asked on what charge was he to be tried -manslaughter or murder. Judge Dickson replied that the charge was the capital one of murder and must remain so. James Walsh was then removed for the courtroom and taken back to Cork Gaol for at least another two months.

It was now completely out of Walsh's control, nothing he could do or say would save him. His wife's attempt in telling the police she spent the night at Thomas Street had also been foiled.

On Thursday the 19th March in the county court Justice Dodd heard the case at the Cork Spring Assizes. The attorney General had arrived to conduct the prosecution while solicitor Murphy still defended James Walsh.

The Attorney General opened the case going over all the details. He said it was a horrendous case where a father was killed and called it parricide. There was in his opinion enough evidence to find against Walsh. Both the husband and wife had tried to conceal the facts and get him away with it. Blatant lies had been told by them both. This fact alone he said was evidence of the guilt of James Walsh. He said there was now suspicion on Ellen Walsh as she lied to cover for him.

It was a case he said where there was no deadly weapon but the old man had been beaten and it resulted in death. He asked the jury to decide on the charge of murder but finding him not guilty he must be found guilty of manslaughter. It all depended he said on whether they believed he was intent on killing his father or just beat him and didn't consider the consequences.

Witnesses were called and it was a rerun of the evidence already heard. When the prosecution finished though Walsh knew he was done for. He now decided to change his plead and admitted his guilt but on the charge of manslaughter. His defence counsel begged for mercy for their client saying had the father not suffered from heart disease there would not have been such serious consequences.

The judge when sentencing said had Walsh reported the death when it occurred and told the truth it may never have gone this far. By trying to conceal it and also dragging his wife into it had made it much worse for him. Now though he was found guilty of manslaughter and must serve a custodial sentence. Justice Dodd gave him just twelve months and said the time already served may be considered.

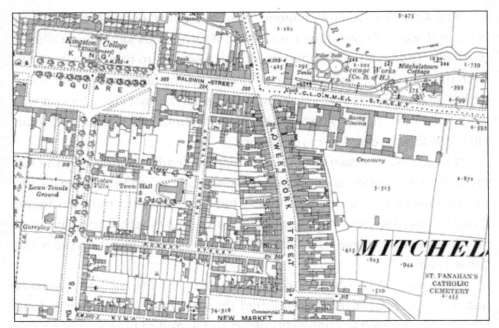

Map of Mitchelstown and Thomas Street.

They will have to prove it
Knocknaloman (near Rathmore) Cork 1931

In the small village of Rathmore Co. Kerry close to the Cork border, quiet crowds were gathered on the streets. For hours they remained in shock, February showers of sleet came and went but they remained. The crowds were there waiting for a funeral procession and to pay their respects to the family.

Inside a building at the back of Hassett's Hotel doctors performed a post mortem on a young woman. They struggled to come to a straight forward conclusion. Eventually word was received that a result would not happen today. As a result the inquest was to be postponed. For the family and friends it came as another blow. At this point nothing worse could happen.

On Sunday the 8th of February 1931 Ellen O'Sullivan had disappeared returning home from her aunts in the village of Rathmore. It was however days later before it was reported to the guards. Her father thought she had stayed at her aunts in Rathmore. It was her work colleagues at the creamery found it strange she had not turned up for work for several days. Therefore it was Wednesday or Thursday before the guards got word and initiated a massive search of the area.

Ellen O'Sullivan was from the townland of Knocknaloman on the Cork side of Rathmore. She was twenty five years old and had worked at the Duncannon creamery for six years where she was now the head butter maker. She lived at home with her father Denis, 2 sisters and a brother who worked the farm. One of her sisters also worked in a creamery. Her mother had died not too long before. There was another brother and 2 more sisters. Hannah was married and living in Millstreet. Hannah had only married Timothy Buckley two weeks before her sister disappeared. She had returned from the honeymoon days before Ellen went missing. Her other sister was training to be a teacher in England.

It was not until the following Saturday, Valentine's Day of all days, that a body was found concealed under furze bushes in a bog. Suspicions were raised immediately that foul play was involved as her clothes were torn and missing and she had wounds to her head.

Such was the desolated area where the body was found that the guards held out little hope for witnesses. The nearest house to the place was occupied by a single elderly farmer called Patrick Creedon. He told the guards he had passed by the road at half seven on Sunday night. He met a man on the road but the night was dark. The man saluted him and he thought he also saw a bicycle and thought he had heard a woman's voice.

Despite the terrible weather the guards continued their search of the area hoping to find some clues to the crime. The cause of death was not clear and they did not initially see injuries sufficient to the cause of death so waited to learn more from the post mortem.

That very Saturday night though the guards wasted no time and made an arrest of a local man they believed was with Ellen that night when she was returning home.

It was not until Monday that the arrest became public when he appeared in court. That day at Killarney district court before Judge Gallagher, Jeremiah Cronin a farmer near Rathmore stood accused.

Details of the arrest were read out in court; Superintendent Gantley said how Cronin had made no statement. He was however represented by a solicitor Mr Ferguson from Kanturk. Gantley applied for a remand for a further eight days to allow his men investigate further. Ferguson merely asked that the sitting be in Mallow and the judge agreed to sit again in Mallow on the 23rd.

The case was such a brutal murder without motive that it attracted huge attention of the press. This put the guards under immense pressure to find the killer. All the top brass of the Garda Síochána, Superintendents and Chief Superintendents arrived in Rathmore to oversee the investigation. Even the Garda Commissioner Eoin O'Duffy arrived.

Over the next few days the guards continued the search of the area. The bicycle had been discovered near the main road and nearby the cover of the book Ellen had borrowed from her aunt Mrs Moynihan. The book was "The Gamblers" by William Le Queux. Bizarrely it was a crime novel set in the south of France. Little did Ellen know she was about to become a murder victim and her own story would turn out to be a mystery like the book.

Ellen had only stopped at her aunt's for a few minutes that evening, but sometimes she stayed there. She collected the book and headed to the village saying how she had no light on her bike and wanted to be home before dark.

Now almost half a mile away near where the body was found but on the Cork side of the river the remains of the book were discovered. She had gone to her aunts that night to borrow it. Also discovered near the bike was a bundle of clothes. These were believed to not be connected with the case and had been stolen some time before.

The guards now believed that Ellen was attacked on the road and a struggle took place. Her body was then dragged a few hundred yards to the Awnaskirtaun River. Here the river marked the boundary between Cork and Kerry. The killer then crossed the river and concealed the body on the Kerry side. Yet the bicycle was found nearer to the village of Rathmore.

Everything still hung on the outcome of the inquest. Local doctors knew the case was complicated and requested the help of a pathologist. As the investigation went on the guards remained tight lipped, revealing little to the press who were all over Rathmore watching them. The search continued looking for more clues. They excavated several places excavated. It was obvious that something was not adding up.

The inquest was finally held on Tuesday the 17th of February in Rathmore by coroner Dr O'Sullivan after being postponed the day before. The coroner only wanted to identify the body that day and reveal little else while the investigation was ongoing. Dr O'Sullivan regretted having to be there saying he hoped the perpetrator would get justice soon.

He told the crowd "if the full facts could be disclosed here you would be profoundly shocked". He admitted being shocked himself when he had read the pathologists report. Ellen's father Denis O'Sullivan identified his daughter's remains before the inquest finished that day. Afterwards the funeral took place to Millstreet with a huge crowd present.

So now the inquest was adjourned, the funeral had taken place and yet no medical evidence had been given. The coroner had seen the pathologists report but it was not for public consumption until the guards knew more. Jeremiah Cronin was still in jail awaiting another hearing in two days time. The guards still encouraged people to come forward with information. But now it was all happening behind closed doors.

On the 23rd Jeremiah Cronin appeared before District Justice Gallagher and the case took a dramatic turn. Solicitor Ferguson spoke for his client saying how Jeremiah had been in a relationship with Ellen for some time and they had intended to marry.

Superintendent Gantley announced he was satisfied with the movements of Cronin on the 8th. Everything he had told them checked out and they no longer believe he was involved. He said Cronin was free to go and was beyond the shadow of suspicion or guilt. The judge noted the ordeal Cronin must have suffered over the last week.

Crowds gathered to hear the news, image courtesy of the National Library of Ireland and Independent Newspapers.

Shinnagh Cross in 1931, image courtesy of the National Library of Ireland and Independent Newspapers.

Jeremiah Cronin, 30, was from Clonbanin over seven miles on the Cork side of Rathmore. Cronin was obviously well heeled as he was unusual in the 1930's being the owner of a Ford motor car. On Sunday the 8th Cronin had indeed met Ellen in Rathmore after she had left her aunts. There was a dance in the village that evening but Ellen did not go to it. She had her bicycle so he agreed to walk home with her. He had arranged a friend of his Tim Kelliher to drive his car to Shinnagh Cross and meet them there.

When they arrived at Shinnagh Cross that night Kelliher had got there before them and was waiting. They had met a man on the road who Cronin did not know. Ellen did though; it was her neighbour David O'Shea. Cronin walked on further with her until a bend on the road when he turned back and let her go on the final short distance alone. Cronin thought it was about quarter past eight when he walked back to Shinnagh Cross. That was the last time he had seen Ellen alive.

What was not revealed in court that day was that the guards had arrested another man the night before. Now it was suggested the real killer had planted the body and bicycle to make it look like Cronin had killed her on their walk home.

It was impossible for the guards to keep rumours from spreading. Before long it was known who the new suspect was. It was David O'Shea a near neighbour of the O'Sullivan's who they had met on the road that night.

It was Thursday 5th of March 1931 when District Justice Gallagher began hearing evidence against O'Shea in a hall in Rathmore. The accused David O'Shea had arrived under a heavy escort by train the night before. He now stood charged that on the 8th of February at Knocknaloman he unlawfully and feloniously murdered Ellen O'Sullivan with malice aforethought.

Mr Brereton Barry prosecuted on behalf of the state, while Mr T O'Shea Killarney represented the accused. As one could imagine a huge crowd had gathered to catch a glimpse of O'Shea entering court. They watched as a bicycle was pushed into the makeshift courtroom by the guards.

Brereton Barry began by putting the state's case forward. He would prove Ellen's movements that night and also those of the accused. Medical evidence he said would show Ellen had died from a blow to her left temple.

John Murphy a farmer's son from Shinnagh was called for the state. He told how he and Patrick O'Donoghue had helped the guards in the search. On the 14th of February on the Kerry side of the river bank his attention was drawn to hair in the furze bushes. He immediately called the guards and did not disturb anything.

Sergeant Devoy from Rathmore gave evidence of being nearby when the body was found. He said he lifted out the body from the furze with Sergeant Reynolds. He recognised it as Ellen O Sullivan. The shoes were missing and all undergarments below the waist had been torn off. After a superficial examination the body was wrapped up and taken to Hassett's Hotel in Rathmore.

Medical evidence was given by Dr. Collins Rathmore. He described the injury on Ellen's left temple. He said it was a result of a blow by a heavy blunt object like a stone. This injury he concluded was enough to result in death.

He said there was no evidence of strangulation. The marks on her neck were caused by a man's left hand violently grabbing her, most likely while raping her. The doctor's opinion was that Ellen was struck on the head while the man raped her. In court though he didn't say it that directly but said "she had been violated and that violation had not completed before death" Other witnesses had told that Ellen was a pious respectable young woman, now with medical evidence the doctor described her as 'virgo intacta' up until then. He was of the opinion that she had died 7 or 8 days before the examination.

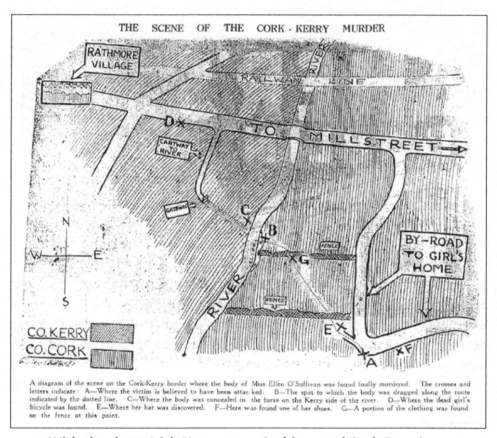

THE SCENE OF THE CORK - KERRY MURDER

A diagram of the scene on the Cork-Kerry border where the body of Miss Ellen O'Sullivan was found foully murdered. The crosses and letters indicate: A—Where the victim is believed to have been attacked. B—The spot to which the body was dragged along the route indicated by the dotted line. C—Where the body was concealed in the furze on the Kerry side of the river. D—Where the dead girl's bicycle was found. E—Where her hat was discovered. F—Here was found one of her shoes. G—A portion of the clothing was found on the fence at this point.

With thanks to Irish Newspaper Archives and Cork Examiner.

Co. Cork Tragedy.—A general view showing the spot (marked x) amongst the furze bushes where the dead body of Miss Ellie O'Sullivan was found. The river Annaskirtane in this picture separates Co. Cork and Co. Kerry, and the terrible crime was enacted on the right-hand side (Cork), and the hiding place was found on the Kerry side of the river.—Photo, MacMonagle.

X marks the spot she was found on the Kerry side of the river, with thanks to Irish Newspaper Archives and Cork Examiner.

Superintendent Gantley from Killarney also described the crime scene and finding the body. He discovered signs that the body had been dragged towards the river on the Cork side. Guard John Phillips from Millstreet described how on the 15th February he found a man's work legging downstream of the crime scene. It was produced in court, it was a left legging.

On the 16th February he went to David O'Shea's house and found women's clothes hidden in a fence, they were rolled up separately and concealed.

Timothy Collins a labourer in Knocknaloman told how he had often met the accused at his brother's house. They would sit around the fire by night talking. He said O'Shea wore work leggings, the same as the one produced.

Mr. Humphrey McAuliffe, a shoemaker from Rathmore took the stand. He had repaired leggings for O'Shea previously. He said the legging produced was similar to the one he had repaired the spring before for O'Shea.

Father of Ellen, Denis O Sullivan took the stand and described his daughter, at 4 or 4.30 on Sunday the 8th, was the last time he had seen her alive. David O'Shea lived just 2 fields away from his house for the last 4 years. When he was returning home on the 9th he met O'Shea on the road. What he didn't say was the reason O'Shea had moved into a house near his four years ago was that his parents separated. Before that the family had lived at Shinnagh, where his father and brother remained. He moved with his elderly mother and his sister Kate to Knocknaloman.

Barry didn't wish to call anymore witnesses until a later date. District Justice Gallagher said he would postpone his normal sittings and return to Rathmore on 19th March.

David O'Shea was taken back to Cork Gaol, his solicitor; also O'Shea had been granted permission to interview his client.

A few weeks later on Thursday the 19th David O'Shea was back before the judge. A huge crowd gathered outside before it began and remained there waiting for the doors to open despite a heavy downpour. The judge announced that there was to be no children allowed in the court that day, due probably to the graphic nature of some of the evidence.

The proceedings began that day by showing a large map of the area mounted on a sheet of plywood. All points of interest and where evidence had been found were marked at numbered points on the map. Several guards gave evidence about items found near the crime scene and items found near or in O'Shea's house. A sock found near the crime scene could not be proved to be matching one found in O'Shea's house.

Sergeant John Doyle described finding a ladies belt in a field near Creedon's house on the 15th of February. Doyle also told of escorting David O'Shea from Millstreet to Cork on the 26th of February. He began a sentence saying "when leaving Millstreet the accused said" but solicitor O'Shea objected saying the statement was not admissible as evidence. He then cross examined Doyle who revealed that three guards stayed in O'Shea's house from the 15th for several days until he was arrested.

Day and night they watched over him except for one day and one night. The judge ruled that the statement O'Shea had given was admissible as evidence. He said the caution Superintendent Gantly had given O'Shea was sufficient.

Members of the Civic Guard at the spot where it is presumed Ellie O'Sullivan was murdered. Her hat can be seen in the hands of the Guard kneeling, who found it under the stones. This spot is about a quarter of a mile from the place where the body was found.—Photo, MacMonagle.

With thanks to Irish Newspaper Archives and Cork Examiner.

Eventually Doyle was allowed tell what O'Shea had said leaving Millstreet. He had heard O'Shea say when facing a crowd of onlookers "I don't give a damn about them, they will have to prove me guilty for this".

The remainder of the day was taken with several more guards giving evidence of the search and where items had been found. Superintendent Gantly told how the guards had not been informed of her disappearance until the Thursday. The Friday was taken up with enquires to houses and relations in the area. Therefore the search did not start until Saturday the 14th, the day she was found.

Garda officials taking measurements at the point of the river where it is believed the body of Miss O'Sullivan was dragged across from the Cork to the Kerry side.

With thanks to Irish Newspaper Archives and Cork Examiner.

At the end of the day very little had been produced to directly link O'Shea to the crime scene, it was like he said it would have to be proved.

The following day they were back in court again early in the morning to get a full day of witnesses heard. The judge said he would sit until six that evening or later if needed. Again a large crowd attended on the Friday to hear details of the case.

The day began with Sergeant Skehan taking the stand. He described searching the land of Ellen's father on the 9th of March (a month after Ellen was murdered). Within sight of O'Shea's house he found a woman's underwear. At the same time detective Hannifin from Bandon found two other items of ladies underwear nearby. Several other guards took the stand giving evidence of where items had been found. A shoe was found near a gate in the vicinity of Creedon's house and a garter was found in the field opposite Creedon's.

Next to give evidence that day was twenty seven year old Nora O'Sullivan, Ellen's older sister. Nora stayed at home and helped on her father's farm acting as housekeeper since her mother had died. She could identify Ellen's clothes as they shared a bedroom and she did all the washing. Nora identified the blue knickers produced in court saying her sister had two pairs that colour. She also recognised all the other items of clothing that had been found, the skirt, coat and scarf. She had seen her sister wear all those clothes on the 8th when she last saw her alive.

Another witness Julia Murphy also from Knocknaloman explained how she had seen the accused at a funeral on the 8th of February. She recalled he wore an overcoat, black boots and black polished leggings or gaiters.

Jeremiah Cronin was called as he was the last person to see Ellen alive, except of course for the killer. He explained his movements that night as he had done before to the guards when he was arrested. Cronin said he had been to a dance that night in Rathmore with three friends, Tim and Dan Kelliher and Eugene Murphy.

He met Ellen arriving in the village sometime before seven with her cousin Kathleen Moynihan. While she went to Moynihan's to get the book he waited to walk her home as he had done many times before. Eugene Murphy had gone on ahead escorting girls from the dance. Dan Kelliher stayed in Rathmore, while Tim drove the car to Shinnagh cross to meet Cronin.

When the couple got to Shinnagh Cross that night they walked on to Inches Cross and turned down the byroad to Knocknaloman. Here Cronin said he met Eugene Murphy who was returning to the car at Shinnagh Cross. The couple then stopped on the road before Creedon's house and chatted for fifteen minutes. While talking a man passed by, Cronin said he did not know him then but now he did. Solicitor O'Shea objected not wanting the name to be revealed for obvious reasons, it was David O'Shea. The objection was overruled though.

Cronin said he turned back towards Shinnagh cross while Ellen went on alone.

He was back at the crossroad at quarter past eight, now both the Kelliher's and Eugene Murphy were waiting for him. He drove home and got there about nine. He admitted to not knowing the accused man and had never spoken to him.

Eugene Murphy, Dan Kelliher and Tim also gave evidence corroborating what Cronin had said. Now that the prosecution had proved Ellen's movements that night they now needed to prove O'Shea's movements.

Ellen Hickey also of Knocknaloman gave evidence. She lived on the Rathmore side of Creedon's house. On the 8th of February she told how she left home about half six heading towards Rathmore to meet her son Dan. On the way she met the accused and they walked along talking. She asked him was he going to Shinnagh meaning to his father's but he said he was going to Andy Murphy's shop in Rathmore. Bizarrely Ellen said the conversation turned to Hannah O'Sullivan, Ellen's sister. Hickey told him that the newlyweds had just returned from honeymoon the Friday before. Along the way that night they met Timothy Hickey, and when Ellen Hickey met her son she turned for home. She said that O'Shea headed on towards Rathmore.

At the end of the day in court Mr Barry proposed to produce no more evidence that day. The judge agreed to sit again to hear more evidence on April the 1st. The accused David O'Shea was remanded into custody again and transferred back to Cork Jail.

By now it was established that O'Shea was on the road that night and had in fact met Ellen and Jeremiah Cronin. The guards had yet to directly link him to the crime and he seemed to have a certain confidence that it would not be proved.

On the 1st April the crowds at the courthouse in Rathmore had very much dwindled due to the downpours of rain. The sordid details had still to be heard. Would O'Shea be found guilty and sent to Dublin for trial before a jury.

Superintendent Phillip O'Sullivan was sworn in to tell how he went to David O'Shea's house on the 15th of February. Mr Barry asked was he there that day, he was. Did you intend to arrest him that day? No. Solicitor O'Shea objected to the questions being asked but it was allowed. The superintendent told of a statement David had given that day without any encouragement. He revealed that the statement had been written down and O'Shea had signed it.

The defence solicitor again objected saying that how it was obtained meant it could not be allowed. The judge however referred him to the

Malahide Murder case saying it was only where a person incriminated themselves that a caution was required first. Solicitor O'Shea was not giving up and started a legal argument with the judge. He said his client had "after being eleven days for all intents and purposes been in custody, had not been a free agent making the statement". He suggested his client had been in terror for days and made several statements. Despite more objections the judge overruled and the statement was read out.

In it David O'Shea described himself as a labourer from Knocknaloman with three acres of land. He told all his movements on the 8th of February. First went to mass with his mother and sister. Afterwards he went home and stayed there all day doing some work around the yard. He stated that leaving home that evening before six he headed to Shinnagh. He admitted meeting Ellen Hickey and talking to her.

O'Sullivan's farmhouse in Knocknaloman, with thanks to Irish Newspaper Archives and Cork Examiner.

He also recalled meeting a tall man with two women; this would be Eugene Murphy walking the women home from the dance. O'Shea then admitted meeting a man and woman walking slowly. It would take him an hour he said to walk to Shinnagh cross from where he met the pair. In relation to how the girl was dressed he had said "I did not take much stock".

He then walked on to Shinnagh Cross getting there about seven and stayed walking about at Shinnagh Cross for quite a while. During that time he did not see a car stopped near Shinnagh Cross at all that night. He could have gone on to his father's house which was only five minutes away but didn't, saying he hung around for too long. He thought it was before eight when he headed back home, he didn't take the shortcut across the river. He had not since the summer before. On the walk home that night he met nobody on the road and got home around nine. His mother and sister were at home that night when he got there. The last time he had seen Ellen O'Sullivan was at three that afternoon when she returned home with her father.

He also gave reasons in the statement why he had not been involved in the search.

It was because he had not been asked and did not see men searching until the 15th. David was asked about the trousers but denied wearing them that day saying it had been too damp for digging that week. He finally revealed he knew that Humphrey O'Sullivan's dog and cow had been stabbed but denied that either he or his brother had been involved in it. Humphrey was Ellen's eldest brother who had stayed at home on the family farm.

Clearly O'Shea didn't give himself away in the statement but from what we know now he would have seen a car at Shinnagh Cross that night. He also would have met both Eugene Murphy and Jeremiah Cronin walking back towards the cross. Someone was not telling the truth. It had been rumoured that a dog belonging to O'Sullivan's had disappeared the same time as Ellen.

Many more witnesses were called that day. Timothy Hickey's testimony agreed with that of Ellen Hickey but he did not recognise David O'Shea with her that night despite knowing him for the last twenty years.

**Ellen O'Sullivan, with thanks to Irish Newspaper Archives
and Cork Examiner.**

Next called was Patrick Creedon whose house was nearest to the crime scene. He began by describing the 8th as a soft dark gloomy night and he left home at half seven or slightly afterwards. When asked by Barry "on the road did you hear or see anything", Creedon said "I heard voices". After passing the bend by his house he heard a woman's voice but thought he saw a man. The man said "goodnight"; Creedon returned the greeting and continued on his way. Returning home that night at eleven he met nobody on the road.

Chief Superintendent Galligan from Tralee told how he had led the investigation with Superintendent Gantly. He described the crime scene, especially the tracks left behind from Ellen's body being dragged. He had followed the tracks from near Creedon's house to a point on a cliff overlooking the river. On the other side of the river where the body was found he noted how the furze had been broken by hand and cut.

The prosecution then called detective Tormey who had been to O'Shea's house. Tormey said on the 18th he noticed scratches on O'Shea's hands and questioned him about it. Solicitor O'Shea again objected to any statement being read and was allowed first to cross examine Tormey about how the statement was obtained.

Tormey denied that O'Shea was threatened or frightened in any way to get a statement. He also denied questioning O'Shea until five in the morning or that the guards had drink taken. Solicitor O'Shea asked did one of the guards bang the table and say to the accused "Creedon is the man who will hang you". Tormey said no such words were said and O'Shea had no reason to be frightened when he gave the statement. Despite the objections of the defence the statement was then read out in court.

In the statement O'Shea accounted for the scratches on his hands from cutting furze on several days. He had given details of where and when. O'Shea had even demonstrated to the detective how he had cut the furze using a reaping hook and goulogue.

There was debate about the method he used and it was felt the injuries were not consistent with what he had said. The left hand would have been injured more and the right hand holding the reaper less so.

Several more statements from O'Shea were read out and his solicitor objected at each one but was overruled by the judge every time. One statement told his movements on the night of the 8th while another dealt with O'Shea going to mass on the 15th February. The statement about the 8th was extremely similar to the one heard before. It was now obvious that the guards had questioned O'Shea for several days before he was actually arrested.

Another statement he had given covered the 14th February the day Ellen had been found.

David O'Shea being led away, image courtesy of the National Library of Ireland and Independent Newspapers.

This time O'Shea said he had taken his mother to a meeting in Millstreet that day. On the way home he met a man who said "she is found". Arriving home his sister Kate said "Ellen has been found down the land". She advised him to untackle to pony quickly and go over to O'Sullivan's and offer assistance. David O'Shea admitted going over to his neighbours and met Lizzie O'Sullivan saying to her "sorry for your trouble". O'Shea said the rest of the family had gone to Rathmore but he recalled in his statement the visitors at the house that night.

Yet another account of David O'Shea's movements on the 8th while being questioned by Chief Superintendent Galligan was read out. The next witness was strategically to show that O'Shea's statement was false.

Daniel O'Keeffe a farmer from Shinnagh was called to the stand. He had left home on the 8th at seven in the evening, passing Shinnagh cross he passed a car stopped with its lights on. He passed back sometime after and the car was still there. He left home again to play cards at John O'Shea's house; John he explained was the father of the accused. Again passing Shinnagh Cross the car was still there with the lights on. He played cards till late at John O'Shea's house but never encountered David O'Shea that night at all.

Now the prosecution were beginning at last to build a circumstantial case but more was needed. Mr Barry hoped the case would be concluded at the next sitting which was set for the 8th of April. It had been due to sit the following day but defence solicitor O'Shea could not attend or was buying time.

When it sat again on the 8th of April in Rathmore it was the fifth time David O'Shea came before District Justice Gallagher. It was felt though that it would be concluded today and the judge would make a decision to send it to trial of not. It left a lot of evidence to be heard that day which could implicate the accused.

Dr Arthur Moore professor of Pathology at UCC gave evidence of the post mortem which had not been heard at the inquest. He said the wound over the left ear had caused a large haemorrhage but the skull was not fractured. Her left eye was black and swollen and the body had bruises all over. The groin and thighs were also scratched. He felt death was as a result of shock due to the severity of the blow on her head. Obviously the pathologist withheld much of the more intimate details of his report. The coroner had read it and been profoundly shocked, in 1930's Ireland it was felt not everyone needed to know such things.

A young boy of fifteen Jeremiah O'Leary told how on the night of the 8th of February he was out looking for his cousin Denis. At about twenty past eight he met Jeremiah Cronin heading towards Rathmore at Inches Bridge. He found his cousin and they went to Dan Hickeys. When leaving Hickey's at quarter past ten he heard a bicycle pass quickly towards Rathmore. The bicycle had a distinctive rattle and he knew it was Ellen O'Sullivan's. He often heard her pass him on her way home from work. Young Jeremiah said he could not tell if the bike was ridden by a man or woman that night despite trying to run after it, as it was very dark.

Several witnesses gave evidence of passing Shinnagh Cross on the night of 8th of February. Some passed by several times and saw the car stopped with lights on. Two even spoke to Tim Kelliher and Eugene Murphy who were waiting in the car. None of them however had seen David O'Shea at the cross that night. Now eight to ten people had seen the car and each other that night, O'Shea's story stood out as a fabrication.

The prosecution had been keeping the best evidence for last to make an impression on the judge on the day a decision would be make. Garda Keane was called and said he took part in a search of David O'Shea's house on the 15th of February. When the search party left Keane said he remained in the house under a bed off the kitchen. He revealed hearing a conversation between David and his sister Kate. After leaving the house that day he went straight to the barracks and wrote down the conversation which he now produced in court. The defence objected but again the judge ruled a conversation between the accused and a third party was admissible as evidence. The statement was then read out

Sister: My god where is the legging did they take it

David: see is it behind the box, look quick is it here

Sister: rush quick take it away burn it

He then heard David rush out to the yard and return minutes later

David: It is all right now.

Sister: Was it not the luck of God they did not take it away, we were ruined.

David: They are looking for clothes, I wonder did they take my trousers, they were looking at it but I told them I got wet digging drains and they went looking at the drains.

Sister: Didn't I tell you to brush your clothes when you came in and the state you came home to me that night, wasn't it well we washed the pants. Go and brush your pants, didn't I tell you not to leave a trace of clay on them that's what they are looking for.

David: What did you do with the sock?

Sister: I was looking for it all day and could not find it; my God I must burn it if I find it.

They were looking at the hammer and hatchet. They must have some suspicion on you. I suspect it was Timothy Hickey that told them he saw you. Do you think they will come for you tonight? They might come in the middle of the night for you.

David: Let them they will have to prove it, sure I gave a good account of myself in the statement I gave. I said I was at Shinnagh Cross at 8pm. sure I saw Ellen with Jeremiah Cronin that night but I would not tell them.

Sister: If they call again, don't tell another word, don't leave the house, and don't go to the wake either.

Keane said he remained under the bed until the rest of the search party returned and he left with them. While all this was read out in court David O'Shea didn't seem to be the slightest bit interested or concerned how it looked for him.

Solicitor for the defence couldn't object enough and said it was the most remarkable evidence he had ever heard. Barry announced that this finished the evidence of the prosecution leaving the defence the opportunity to present their case.

O'Shea for the defence argued that his client had not been connected to the crime. He could have called witnesses but who would have come forward for him. His sister who now seemed to have some knowledge of guilt, she would not have been believed anyway. The elderly mother but what could she say to help her son. David O'Shea had said he went straight to bed when he came home on the 8th, now they knew this was lies based on what the sister had said.

Was there no respectable person from the area willing to come forward and give a character reference for the accused? Maybe there was and it would not have helped him but implicated him further.

District Justice Gallagher had no option but to find that a prima face case existed but noted how circumstantial the evidence was. He returned the case for trial before a jury at the next Criminal Court in Dublin. He asked O'Shea "have you anything to say"; he replied "I am not guilty sir".

The crowds outside that day were much greater than before, they knew the case was coming to an end and a decision would be made. As he left the court room the crowd hissed and booed at him while he was taken away in a car. There was never even a suggestion of bail in a case of such violence and he went back to jail.

After sitting for several days in a makeshift courtroom in Rathmore and weeks in jail David O'Shea still didn't seem to realise the consequences of what he could face. He had been described as a labourer of limited intelligence who at thirty three lived with his elderly mother and sister. His prospects in life where limited but he seemed oblivious to this. Just as oblivious as he was to his fate which now rested in the hands of a jury in Dublin.

Now for the first time we get an insight through the voice of O'Shea and his sister who seems complicit in it. Not only that she seems to be directing him but would it be enough proof before a jury to convict him.

On Tuesday the 9th of June at the Central Criminal Court in Green Street Courthouse Dublin, David O'Shea came before Justice Hanna. For the state Mr Barry was now assisted by Vincent Rice and Mr Lavery. O'Shea from Killarney was now assisted by Thomas O'Donnell for the defence. It was expected that the case would take at least a week in court to hear all the evidence. That day in the courtroom a wooden model of O'Shea's small cottage was produced in court. Engineers were called to prove the accuracy of the maps produced.

Mr Rice opened the case for the prosecution and went back over all the details that would be discussed. He argued O'Shea had plenty opportunity to know Ellen O'Sullivan's movements as Cronin often walked her home on Sunday nights parting at the same spot. The murder and rape he said took place after quarter past eight. He also claimed it was O'Shea who passed on the bike after ten having killed her and thrown the body into the river. He then took the bike to the main road and left it there. Evidence would show that her sky blue knickers were found hidden near O'Shea's house. He also claimed the sock found in the river could be proved to be a match for the one found hidden in O'Shea's cottage.

Over the next few days all the evidence was gone over again, in even more detail than before. The same witnesses told the same story and David O'Shea's account of the 8th did not fit in anywhere. Solicitor

O'Donnell asked witnesses far more questions but it changed little how it looked for O'Shea.

On the final day the 12th of June crowds gathered outside more so than usual, hundreds waited on the streets despite knowing a verdict would be hours away. The first witness called for the defence was Kate O'Shea, sister to the accused man. It was a dangerous game to play for what little she could add to the defence, under cross examination she could make a serious slip. From the conversation overheard with David though she seemed to be more calculated that he was.

Great interest was shown in the closing stages of the Cork murder trial at the Central Criminal Court yesterday evening.—Large crowds awaiting the jury's verdict.—*Irish Independent* Photo.

With thanks to Irish Newspaper Archives and Independent Newspapers.

She told the defence solicitor that she went to bed at half eight with her mother on the night of 8th February. Half an hour later she heard her brother's footsteps. She denied ever having a conversation with her brother that was overheard by Garda Keane under the bed. She identified a pair of leggings or gaiters belonging to him but denied he had a third one. She also denied knowing about the sock found in a milk tankard in their house and could not identify any socks produced in court.

Mr Lavery cross examined and asked did she discuss Ellen's death with her brother at all. She said they never talked about it and claimed she was not curious. Judge Hanna intervened asking if you thought he was innocent why did you not talk about it. She just said she didn't ask questions and again was not a curious person. She then denied that Humphrey McAuliffe had ever repaired leggings or gaiters for her brother. Mr Lavery said "he said he did, is it untrue" but Kate made no reply. He asked did she read the notice in Rathmore and Shinnagh Cross requiring all men living East of Shinnagh to report to the Guards. Kate said she had read the notice but had not informed her brother of it. David O'Shea never reported to the barracks as the notices had requested men in the area to do.

Justice Hanna asked her when she discovered a guard had hidden under the bed. She said it was not until the 8th of April at court in Rathmore. He asked her again did she have a conversation with her brother that day when the guards had left. Kate said she spoke to her brother that day about clearing the table. In reply to the judge she said when her brother wore gaiters on Sundays they were brown.

As the defence only called one witness, several of the prosecution witnesses were recalled by jurors to answer further questions.

O'Donnell then made his address to the jury to save the life of his client. He began "I ask you to come to the conclusion that the state have not made out a case against the accused man". The solicitor then went on about how inconceivable it was that David O'Shea would have done it, never did he mention the lies about going to Shinnagh Cross. He then made the mistake of saying how difficult the whole thing was to do saying "the thing was impossible".

But possible it was as someone had done it and it could be O'Shea because he could not account for himself that night since meeting Ellen and Jeremiah on the road. O'Donnell went on to the statement of what Garda Keane had heard under the bed. He claimed it was the most extraordinary way to get evidence he had ever heard of. He asked why then did the guards not arrest O'Shea immediately on the strength of this evidence, where he had not been arrested for several days. He had instead been kept at home under house arrest.

O'Donnell then moved on to motive saying his client had none. He was (even according to Ellen's father) on good terms with them. He occasionally did some work for them. The solicitor questioned why O'Shea would suddenly commit this terrible crime without spite or passion between them. He did mention that while they were friendly there could never be a relationship between Ellen a farmer's daughter and O'Shea with a paltry three acres. He finished by saying again "the state have no case against this man".

After lunch Mr Lavery got the opportunity he had been waiting for several days. He put forward that the murder was committed, the body hidden and then the bicycle taken to near Shinnagh Cross. The murderer then most likely returned across the river and had the remainder of the night to take the body to the Kerry side of the river. He said because of this and the way items such as the book and knickers were hidden the murderer was done by a local man who knew the area well. Lavery suggested that Garda Keane was an honest and accurate witness. He claimed if the defence was to be believed on this point the Guards were guilty of conspiracy against an honest man.

Justice Hanna began summing up the case before four in the afternoon. He commended the jury for their attention listening to the sixty five witnesses over several days. Hanna spoke about criminology and the study of crime to the jury. He said this crime was known to those that study such things as a "lust murder". That is why he explained it lacked motive for the crime itself was the motive. He compared the crime to those of Jack the Ripper and explained what necrophilia was for the jury. For most people in 1930's Ireland this was not only shocking but totally unheard of.

The judge went back over the evidence for the jury in every detail, did he make it to Shinnagh Cross that night, why did he turn back, the black leggings, the knickers, the sock.

He said either Garda Keane was telling the truth or he should be writing plays for the Abbey Theatre. Either Keane was telling the truth or he should be in the dock.

He then mentioned the notices put up and how Kate never told her brother. The judge said if O'Shea was innocent would he not have reported to the barracks and not wait for the guards to turn up.

The jury retired at quarter past five but were recalled by O'Donnell to clear up some points about the notices. It was shown that the notice was not read until the 15th and the guards had turned up at his house that afternoon. Therefore he didn't have reasonable time to report to the barracks. The jury then requested a full written account of Keane's statement before retiring again.

At half seven that evening the jury returned with another question. "Was there any definite reason why no evidence of the accused's character was given by his parish priest or other responsible person?" The judge explained how this could have been done but had no reason why it was not.

It was quarter past eight when the jury returned again with the verdict. The judge announced guilty but with the following rider: that the murder was not premeditated and committed during a period of mental abnormality. They recommended these facts to be considered during the sentencing. O'Shea was asked had he anything to say but gave his usual reply in a quiet voice "I am not guilty sir".

Justice Hanna then sentenced O'Shea to death on the 8th of July at Mountjoy. Hearing that his life would end in less than a month David O'Shea didn't seem to react in anyway. The judge also revealed that he agreed with the verdict before O'Shea was removed from the courtroom.

O'Donnell applied for the right to appeal on the grounds that inadmissible and irrelevant evidence had been submitted and that the verdict was against the weight of evidence. Justice Hanna dismissed the application and the court concluded.

Outside there was thought to be up to 3000 people congregated on the street for an hour before the verdict was heard. Did they expect to see O'Shea emerge as a free man? Instead they heard the verdict and quickly dispersed with nothing to see.

If it was the 1700's or early 1800's O'Shea would have met justice on the following or by Monday at the latest. It wasn't though it was 1931. It would be another thirty three years before the death sentence was abolished for murder.

The fight now became one to save a so called simple minded labourer's life from the hangman and there were only weeks for his legal team to do it. Within days O'Donnell lodged an appeal on behalf of David O'Shea. A date was set for the 22nd for the application to be heard before the Court of Criminal Appeal in Dublin.

On that day in the court of appeal three justices sat to hear the application. First they applied for legal aid and a free transcript of evidence which had been submitted during the trial.

Now assisted by a barrister Michael Comyn they appealed the verdict on twelve separate grounds. Basically O'Shea's legal team claimed Justice Hanna had misdirected the jury and allowed inadmissible evidence. Another reason for appeal was the judge had compared it to Jack the Ripper.

David O'Shea in custody, image courtesy of the National Library of Ireland and Independent Newspapers.

Chief Justice Kennedy noted that there were grounds for appeal and the discussion changed to legal aid. It was argued that the state should not pay for more than the legal counsel the defence had at the trial. However Mr Comyn, who had not attended the jury trial, was doing all the talking that day. The Chief Justice did not want the state to cover his fees. After much debate Michael Comyn said he was willing to proceed with the appeal without fees as did Mr O'Donnell. The date of execution now had to be postponed to allow time for the appeal.

The appeal consisted of several days of legal argument. The trouble was the statement the jury had given after finding O'Shea guilty, stating that the crime had been committed in a state of mental abnormality. Several more paragraphs could be written on the appeal alone but it discusses evidence already heard.

When Chief Justice Kennedy made his decision on the 20th July he said "on the grounds raised, the application for leave to appeal. In the opinion of the court it fails and it must be dismissed". In fact it failed on all grounds and he argued that the verdict and the rider must be separated. The verdict was guilty of murder and rider he said did not change this. Mental abnormality he said was not a legal term and did not mean O'Shea was insane; no mention had been made to manslaughter.

Mr Comyn then said "I beg to ask your lordship for a certificate of leave to appeal to the Supreme Court under Section 29 of the Courts of Justice Act 1924", the Chief Justice refused.

The date of execution was then set for Tuesday the 4th of August.

One hope for David O'Shea was that the Executive Council could still grant a reprieve. His legal team went directly to the Attorney General applying again for the chance to appeal before the Supreme Court.

When the Executive Council sat in late July they found no grounds to interfere with the due process of the law. By the end of the week the Attorney General had also made it clear there would be no appeal before the Supreme Court.

By August the execution was only days away and there would be no eleventh hour reprieve. Throughout July he had held out hopes that the sentence would be commuted but now even O'Shea with his limited understanding was resigned to the reality. In Mountjoy arrangements had been made and an executioner from England was due to arrive. The executioner was to be Thomas Pierrepoint brother of Henry and uncle of the famous Albert, all were executioners.

On the morning of the 4th O'Shea had to be woken by the warder at six thirty having slept soundly. David O'Shea displayed the same indifference from the day he was arrested. He then attended mass and afterwards the executioners came to his cell to pinion him in preparation for the scaffold.

Meanwhile outside the gate of Mountjoy hundreds had gathered out of curiosity as they would see nothing. Public execution had ceased over sixty years before.

Just before eight O'Shea was lead from his cell to the scaffold. All executions in Ireland at that time were carried out at eight in the morning. Had everyone expected O'Shea would make a confession on the scaffold but it does not seem to happen? O'Shea stood on the trapdoor and the executioner pulled the lever to release it. Pierrepoint with over 25 years experience made no mistake and in moments it was over, death was instantaneous. In accordance with the strict procedures the body was hung for an hour, just to be sure.

After eight no bell was rung at the prison only a warder emerged from the gate and placed a notice on it. It read that the sentence of death had been carried out. The crowd pushed forward read it and once people knew they dispersed. No relatives of the sentenced man had attended that morning.

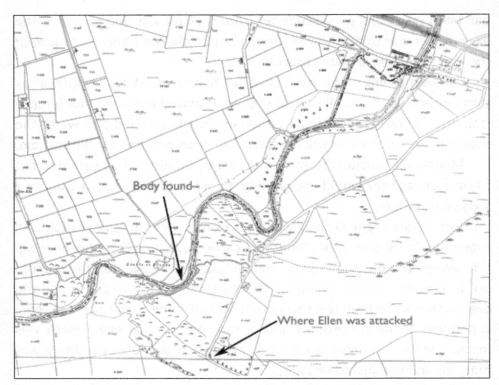

Map showing the road Ellen walked home that night.

I shot him!
Bowen's Court, Farahy, Kildorrery 1912

All that is left of Bowen's Court now is the entrance and lodge. The track leads up to where the grand house once stood but little trace of it remains. Over a hundred years ago Bowen's Court would have resembled a scene from Downton Abbey.

Many people from the area would have been employed in the house and on the large estate. The Bowen family mostly only visited in the summer months and many more employees were needed when they were in residence.

In 1912 the Bowen's were living in Kent as Henry Charles Cole Bowen had taken ill some years before. His daughter Elizabeth who would become a famous novelist was then only thirteen years old. Back in Farahy the estate continued to be run by an agent and a team of workmen some of whom lived on houses on the estate.

On Saturday the 21st of December 1912 David Barry a farm labourer was on his way home when he heard a gunshot nearby. It was half eight and unusual to hear a gunshot at this hour. He walked on towards the source of the gunshot which was near his own house. There he found a man he knew well thrown on the roadside in a dying state. The man was a worker on the estate, James Kelly, who had lived locally all his life. Now Kelly was lying there helplessly with a gunshot wound to his left eye.

David Barry lived in an estate cottage and his brother Patrick lived close by. Another two nearby cottages were also occupied by brothers. Recently married James Kelly was in one and Michael the other. Carpenter James Hanlon was another neighbour.

When David Barry first saw the man lying on the road he must have known of an argument that had occurred that night. James Kelly and James Hanlon had an altercation over the trespass of goats about an hour and a half before. James Kelly had left his house with his brothers young children, outside he ran into James Hanlon. Earlier Hanlon had turned out the goats belonging to Michael Kelly, and now James Kelly asked why. Their argument was enough to frighten the children who started crying.

Michael's wife Nora emerged and took one of the children. James Kelly then brought the other child inside out of harm's way. Hanlon left heading towards Farahy and James Kelly headed after him. It was fifteen minutes later the gun shot was heard.

Barry ran for his brother and they did all they could for James Kelly. Dr Cornelius Buckley from Kildorrery was called but Kelly died before he had arrived at almost eleven that night. Michael Kelly was the one who went off and informed the police in Kildorrery. He must have told them what he knew about the earlier argument. Sergeant Plover proceeded to the scene of the crime; he had also informed his superior District Inspector Lewis from Mitchelstown.

That night the police searched for Hanlon as he was surely the killer. There was no sign of him in his house or around the estate which made him seem guilty.

The following day District Inspector Lewis found Hanlon at his brother John's house in Ballyenahan at the other side of Kildorrery. He admitted his part in it but claimed it was in self defence he shot James Kelly. He made no attempt to conceal it and told them where to find an American six chamber pistol the murder weapon. Leaving Hanlon was heard to remark to his eleven year old niece Katie "I'm going where I will be breaking stones all my life, if I don't get the rope".

James Kelly and Hanlon had known each other for most of their lives and had been friendly. Those close to them knew it was more than just a row about goats that had ended in this, there was more to it. Hanlon's family originally came from Blarney but his father moved about forty years before to become the carpenter at Bowenscourt. James Hanlon himself had been away for several years. He was a policeman in Brisbane for five years. He went to England and America for some years before returning home to what was his father's job. Since returning from abroad people found that Hanlon was not his usual self and his mood was very low.

Kelly on the other hand remained at home as the gardener on the Bowenscourt estate and had married Nora Kelly from Castletownroche the September before. She was several years younger than him and they most likely met when she was in service at Shanballymore near Farahy.

The entrance to Bowenscourt, Kelly lived across the road.

So how does all this lead to James Kelly lying at the side of the road dying? In the middle of October, a few weeks after getting married, Kelly went to the funeral of Mary O'Connor in Kildorrery. He returned home from the funeral drunk with none other than James Hanlon. Kelly seemed to be in far worse a state than Hanlon that night and most likely slept it off.

The next morning Nora Kelly (Michael's wife) claimed to have seen Hanlon in a compromising position with Nora Kelly (James's wife) the night before. Nora went straight to Hanlon and told him straight what she saw but he denies it. So she told her brother-in-law James.

James Kelly accused his wife of having an affair with Hanlon, she also denied it but it causes a divide between the couple. Hanlon pleaded his innocence on several occasions and even informed the priest of the rumours about him. The priest it seems did not want to get too involved and does not investigate any further. To further prove his innocence Hanlon informed the police but what could they do. From then on Kelly and Hanlon obviously don't get on but they seem to keep away from one another and avoid conflict. Without resolution the hatred does not go away it just intensifies. Not only does James Kelly believe his wife was up to no good with the carpenter but he also has Michael's wife next door telling him. So now none of the other Kelly's were talking to Nora and they only live right next door. So bad was the row between the couple that Nora moved out for a few weeks.

On the road to Farahy where Kelly was shot.

Hanlon also left his place and lived with his brother at the other side of Kildorrery. He travelled about getting work as a carpenter and only returned to Bowenscourt a few times.

It was said to be the intervention of Mrs Young a shopkeeper in Farahy that brought James and Nora back together. Nora returned to her husband and he seems to believe her but it's not the same and their newly married happiness is ruined. It was now though something which could no longer be hidden and people in the area talked. This was the situation that intensified over the next few weeks and came to a head just before Christmas.

The inquest was held on Monday the 23rd by Coroner Byrne and a local jury of twelve men, with Thomas Carroll acting as foreman.

James Kelly's sister in law, wife of Michael, Nora Kelly was called. She told of the altercation between the men that night. She saw Hanlon leave and then tried to get her brother in law to stay as she was worried another argument would break out. Later while walking to Farahy she heard that Kelly had been shot.

David Barry who found Kelly that night said he returned home with a bucket of water from the well and James Hanlon was there. He left again to go to his brother's house nearby where he only stayed a few minutes. As he left his brother's house he heard a gunshot, heading towards the source of it he came on Kelly lying on the road.

Dr Cornelius Buckley told how he was requested in Farahy that Saturday at just before ten but did not arrive on the scene until an hour later. He carried out the post mortem the following Monday assisted by Dr Walsh. They found the brain had been torn badly by the bullet which entered the skull. Death he said was a result of this injury and haemorrhaging of blood.

The coroner addressed the jury expressing his regret, especially with the terrible tragedy so close to Christmas. He stated that there was no doubt that an altercation had taken place between Hanlon and the deceased man that night. As an inquest though he stated their duty was just to find the cause of death. The jury did just that, their verdict merely agreed with the medical evidence. That James Kelly died as a result of a shot fired by a person or persons unknown.

The same afternoon James Hanlon was charged before a special sitting of the court in Kildorrery. Only evidence of arrest was given by the District Inspector and Hanlon was remanded to appear again in the next eight days. There was no real need for a big investigation as Hanlon was admitting what he had done and they also had the murder weapon.

Normally crowds gather outside courthouses to catch a glimpse of the killer being rushed inside. On the 30th of December they need not have bothered trying too hard. James Hanlon was escorted up the street of Kildorrery to the courthouse and he appeared completely calm and collected. He strolled along with the police and smoked his pipe. Hanlon instead of hiding himself saluted those he knew with his normal familiarity.

Inside the court house he was again charged with murder before Resident Magistrate Dickson. District Inspector Lewis represented the prosecution while Hanlon was defended by Roger Fox.

Nora Kelly, wife of the dead man, admitted that her husband had accused her of having "immoral relations" with Hanlon in their house. She said since that day she never had a happy day with her husband as he was always on to her about it. Nora told how both she and Hanlon denied the allegations but from that day on the men never spoke again. It was so bad that Hanlon did not occupy his house after Kelly made the allegations. His house was joined to Kelly's.

Doctors Edmund Walsh and Cornelius Buckley gave medical evidence from the post mortem. The bullet was produced in court that they found lodged inside Kelly's skull. Both doctors agreed that the shot was fired from a distance of only three or four feet.

Fox at first declined to cross examine the doctors but Buckley was recalled and concurred with Dr Walsh. Then Mr Fox chose to ask him did he attend to the accused man the April before. Buckley admitted he had seen Hanlon medically who he said was suffering from a severe attack of nervous depression. The defence was trying to build a case for a reduction of the charge to manslaughter.

Several more witnesses were called that day, Michael Kelly and his wife Nora who testified to the argument between the men. Patrick Barry and his wife Margaret could place Hanlon close to the scene of the crime within minutes of the shot being fired.

David Barry told how he was terrified when he came across Kelly that night. He said he never spoke at all but was alive and groaned when he first came on him. David got his brother and then ran to tell Michael Kelly. He never saw Hanlon fire the shot nor did he see him afterwards.

Sergeant Plover gave evidence of the arrest on Sunday the 22nd. After being charged and cautioned that day Hanlon made a statement to him while going to Kildorrery in a side car. The sergeant then read out the statement.

"I was never arrested before but when I am going at all I am going for a decent thing. It won't be the capital charge, manslaughter I suppose the next highest on the calendar. I am sorry the poor devil is dead but he deserved it all. It was the other man's wife was the cause of the whole of it, his brother's wife you know. I am a misfortunate man I suppose I will swing but no the charge will be reduced".

Sergeant Clune was called; he told how he arrived on the scene that night at five minutes past nine. He found James Kelly a few yards past the wicket gate to Pat Barry's house. The left eye he said resembled a large blood clot. At that time Kelly was lying on his back with hay around him, he was unconscious. Clune said he was the one who sent for the doctor and remained there until Kelly died about half ten.

Sergeant Clune told how he was present when Hanlon was arrested the following day. He took charge of Hanlon while the superintendent searched the house. Hanlon said to him "I could not help it Sergeant, he followed me with stones, I told him I would shoot him and I shot him inside the wicket".

At this point in the proceedings the superintendent applied for a remand as all the evidence could not be produced that day.

It took another day in court in the middle of January before the judge made a decision.

More witnesses placed Hanlon near the scene that night and he was seen in Lyon's pub in Kildorrery that night.

John Hanlon told the court how his brother arrived at his house at half nine on that Saturday night. After two in the morning he said Jim called him saying "the police will be here any minute". John asked why and enquired what his brother had done. James told him "I shot Jim Kelly last night". James told him how Kelly followed him into Barry's house. When he came out Kelly still pursued him. Hanlon told his brother he warned Kelly not to follow him inside the wicket gate to Pat Barry's house. But when Kelly did he shot him.

He then asked his brother to go to Kildorrery the following morning and find out if Kelly was dead or not.

It was clear the principal evidence against Hanlon was his own statements. Had he kept his mouth shut and covered his tracks he might just have gotten away with it. Hanlon claimed it was not premeditated but why was he walking around the countryside a few days before Christmas with a loaded pistol in his pocket.

Another policeman read another statement from the accused. "It was an unlucky day for me that Kelly got a wife but she was not long until she was a widow. I shot Kelly in behind Barry's gate. There were some goats outside and I chased them away and Kelly came out and said leave them goats alone. I will be hung for you yet. Kelly blamed me for being with his wife but I never had anything to do with her."

Finally District Inspector Lewis gave evidence of arrest on the 22nd. He said he was about to search John Hanlon's house that day when John said to his brother "give up what you did with it and don't have the house turned upside down". James was willing to and replied "I will, I will show where it is, it is in a ditch in the field outside". Lewis told how when Hanlon was led out of the house he showed them where the gun was hidden under a stone.

After two days in court the judge had heard enough, he returned the case for trial before a jury. This would most likely be the Spring Assizes held in Cork. Meanwhile James Hanlon went back to Cork jail to wait for that day when it would be decided if he would escape the hangman or not. Hanlon had already stated he was prepared for a life in jail but could not face the death sentence.

Two months later at the Cork Spring Assizes James Hanlon pleaded not guilty to murder before Justice Kenny. At the last minute a Sergeant arrived with the news Nora Kelly, Michael's wife had taken ill during the night and would not be able to attend. The prosecution had their case prepared but felt Mrs Kelly was a key witness. The judge sent Dr Buckley and Dr Walsh who were in court to ascertain her condition.

Buckley returned with the information that it would be unwise for Mrs Kelly to come to court. She was eight months pregnant and her condition may have been brought on by the pressure of the court appearance. It was decided to adjourn until the next Assizes in the Summer.

By July Nora Kelly had given birth to a baby boy John at home in Farahy. The other Nora Kelly, that is the dead James Kelly's wife, had also given birth to a baby boy, James on the 14th of July. She was now living at home with her mother in Skenakilla near Castletownroche. A baby born in July would have been conceived in October the very time when Kelly accused Hanlon of being with his wife.

Again the court case was adjourned as widow Nora Kelly was unable to attend due to having a newborn baby. So Hanlon now had a much longer wait in jail, it would now be almost a year in jail before the trial. Nowadays this is normal or even short but back then justice was much swifter. Back then having committed a murder in January one could be hung by early April.

By the end of the year both Nora Kelly's babies were several months old and they were able to come to court. Nora Kelly the widow most likely remained at home with her mother in Castletownroche; it is hard to see her going back to Farahy after what happened. The other Nora Kelly, Michael's wife, the one Hanlon blamed for it all, had four young children in as many years of marriage.

So it was December 1913 when James Hanlon finally faced Justice Moloney and a jury of twelve men. On that date the crown prosecution came well armed with the Attorney General and several other including Anthony Carroll. While the defence was represented by Mr McElligott and his own solicitor Roger Fox.

The Attorney General opened the case saying there was no doubt at all about it for they had it from Hanlon himself he shot James Kelly. The defence though he said would try to claim self defence and justify the shooting.

The prosecution painted the picture of Hanlon as a powerful man over six feet tall, experienced in firearms with five years in the police. Whereas James Kelly was a slim man of only five foot seven and no match for Hanlon. Would Hanlon really need a gun to defend himself from Kelly? Would Kelly really pursue Hanlon knowing he was no match for him?

The Attorney General put it that Hanlon came to Bowenscourt that Saturday to cause trouble. He turned out the two goats to start with and was armed with a revolver he had only bought weeks before. He claimed Kelly had gone looking for a donkey that night. He met people on the road and they had not seen the donkey so he returned with them. Hanlon meanwhile was in Mrs Barry's house where he made no complaint of being chased by Kelly. Hanlon left to go to Pat Barry's and that was when they met but there was no evidence of the stone throwing the Attorney General claimed. The statement that Hanlon made that he was chased from one of the Barry's houses to the other he said was false and would be proved. He ended by saying the only conclusion for the jury after hearing the evidence was to find Hanlon guilty of murder.

The first witness called was Nora Kelly the widow. She said on the night of the 16th of October her husband returned from the funeral with Hanlon at seven. He went to bed a few minutes later but Hanlon stayed for about an hour and then left. As for the shooting itself Nora said she knew nothing of what occurred that night. In reply to McElligott, Nora admitted that it was she that went to the parish priest about her husband's allegations.

Then the other Nora Kelly was called and told a very different story altogether. It certainly made it clear the Nora's were not friends or at least not anymore. This Nora told how on the 16th of October 1912 she saw the other Nora in a position with Hanlon that made her suspicious. Nothing new was revealed until she was cross examined. Then under question she admitted that James gave her money until he had got married. She said she was not against him getting married but was not at the wedding.

Nora admitted to leaving twenty minutes after James Kelly had that Saturday night. She heard the shot when near the Rectory. This was past Pat Barry's house. She had not met James Kelly when passing by either of Barry's houses that night.

Mrs Young a shopkeeper from Farahy related how Hanlon was in her kitchen in the November before Kelly was shot. Hanlon told her he was afraid of the Kelly's. He pulled out of his coat a gun and said "if the Kelly's come into my house I will give them that".

The shopkeeper tried to calm him telling him Nora was back with James again and it was all sorted. She had told James that the woman seen with Hanlon might not have been his wife at all. Mrs Young said a woman was about begging at that time and she may have been the woman with Hanlon. She said though that Hanlon did seem genuinely afraid of the Kelly's and she felt he might do something to protect himself. Under cross examination Mrs Young said it was James Kelly who did not want to live with his wife until she intervened. She said he was in a jealous rage over the whole thing.

Mrs Catherine Barry said that when Hanlon was in her house that night he seemed normal. He did not complain that Kelly was after him. It was only minutes after leaving she heard the shot fired. Many more of the Barry family were called as witnesses as all had been near to the scene of the crime.

John Hanlon gave evidence like he had before of when his brother was arrested in his house. When questioned by the defence he admitted his brother's health had been bad for some time and he was seeing two doctors. John said his brother had a good house from Mr Bowen and a good job but was not happy. John said his brother wanted to move but he told him not to give up his house.

Several policemen were produced and related the statements Hanlon had made admitting the shooting. At the end of the day in court the jury were held like prisoners in the Imperial Hotel till court the next morning.

On Thursday morning the Assizes sat again to conclude the case that day. The foreman of the jury made a remark about being locked up in the Imperial Hotel for the night.

The prosecution had completed their case and now McElligott got his chance to paint a different picture to the Attorney General. The defence started by telling about the Kelly family and how James had supported his brother Michael until getting married. They claimed it was Michael's wife who poisoned her brother-in-laws mind about his wife and Hanlon. They had only been married just over a month, it was Michael Kelly and his wife that claimed they were not happy with the marriage.

McElligott also claimed James Kelly had planned to leave the area but had sworn to get revenge against his wife and Hanlon before leaving. He admitted his client was a powerful man of six feet but said he was a nervous wreck with sometime. Hanlon he said was the one who went out of his way to avoid the Kelly's and seldom went to Bowen's Court after the allegations were made.

He described James Kelly as the man with the jealous rage, while his client he said was living in terror. McElligott clung to the story that Hanlon was in fear of his life that night and only shot in self defence. James Kelly he said had threatened his life by throwing stones at him.

He described Kelly as a howling madman who had literally pushed Hanlon into a corner that night. Firing a shot in the air would not have frightened away Kelly he claimed.

Ellen Kelly was called for the defence; she told how on the 20th of December she visited James Kelly and his wife. This was the day before Kelly was shot. James told her he was the happiest man until the day he heard the rumours about his wife. She also learned that day the couple were still not talking despite being back under the same roof. James told her that day he intended to leave his wife and go to Canada but more than once said he would kill Hanlon before leaving. She described Kelly as being in "a woeful temper" that day.

Ellen admitted to once seeing Hanlon in his workshop at the back of Kelly's house. That day when Hanlon saw Kelly he ran from the workshop from him.

The Attorney General then questioned her saying "tell me was he (Kelly) a decent respectable fellow". Ellen replied that Kelly was a "bould rogue".

It was strange that Peter Young was now called for the defence as his wife had been called for the prosecution the day before. Mr Young said he went to the scene of the crime that night having heard the shot; he noticed marks on a nearby wall that was like stones had been thrown. He returned there the next day and was sure stones had hit the wall and also found stones near the wall which were about 2lb.

Young also recalled a conversation he had with James Kelly the November before. Young admitted being friends with Kelly and advising him to ignore the rumours. Kelly said to him "it was Hanlon did the whole thing, and went to the priest and shamed me".

Doctors were produced that told how Hanlon was suffering from a nervous condition. The prosecution claimed it was alcohol related but the doctors described Hanlon as a nervous timid man who at times had no control over himself.

Henry Cole Bowen's agent Major John Creagh took the stand, he told that Hanlon came to see him in Mallow on the 18th of October 1912. This was just the day after Mrs Kelly had made the allegations. Creagh said Hanlon had always been a good worker but also described him as a nervous, timid man. The agent said he agreed with Hanlon that day to relocate him to the village of Farahy away from the Kelly's.

This ended the evidence of the prosecution and they had made a good case. Often in murder cases the defence had no witnesses at all to call. At that time the accused could not give evidence in court, so Hanlon could not defend himself. James Kelly was dead so he too could also not defend his actions that night.

The defence then made their address to the jury. Their claim was that James Kelly laid in wait to attack Hanlon that night. Hanlon they said had no motive to kill him and evidence showed he was trying his best to avoid him.

The judge then made his address to the jury and remarked how well both sides of the case had been put across in court. He was very fair in his assessment of the case and presented both sides for the jury. He also outlined other conclusions they could make and explained provocation.

The jury returned after forty minutes and foreman was adamant that they could not agree a verdict. McElligott was satisfied with this result but it was the Attorney General who encouraged them to give it another thirty minutes.

After another forty minutes the jury returned with the verdict of not guilty of murder but guilty of manslaughter. Hanlon was asked had he anything to say but just said "No my lord".

The judge then addressed Hanlon directly and said he agreed with the lenient view the jury had taken. It remained a very serious crime and he told Hanlon how he was still responsible for taking away a man's life. Finally the judge said "I sentence you to twelve years penal servitude". Hanlon then asked "may I see my brother my lord" and the judge agreed he could.

He was then removed from court to begin his sentence.

Nora Kelly the widow left court that day to go home to her nearly five month old baby also called James Kelly. Had the other Nora not thought she saw something suspicious that night, the couple would most likely have been happily married with their new baby. Kelly despite his shortcomings had been very fond of his brother's children. Yet his life was cut short and he never got to see his own child.

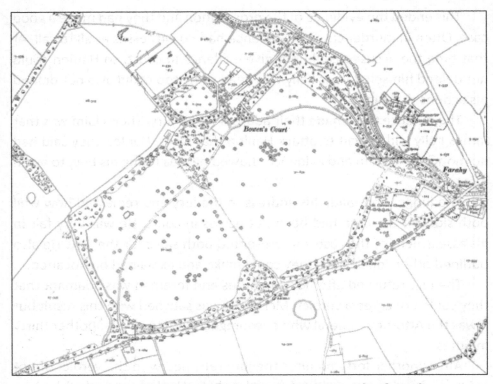

Map showing Bowen's Court and the stretch of road where the shooting took place.

A Sudden Disappearance
Castletownroche, 1877

This story begins as far away from North Cork as one could imagine, New Zealand.

Detective Walker with the Auckland police was given the job of tracking down an Irish man, William Sheehan. He made his enquires and found that William Sheehan had come to Auckland eighteen months before, with his wife and two children on a ship called the Doric.

Further inquiries led him to believe Sheehan was living in Pakaraka near Bay of Islands.

At first though Walker was unsure if it was him, was there another family of Sheehan's? Then word was received that Sheehan was coming to town. Detective Walker waited at where the steamers docked and once he saw him he knew he had the right man. Instead of swooping in and arresting him then, he stood back and let him on.

For the next few weeks, unbeknownst to Sheehan, his every move was watched. At first he went to Gleeson's Hotel in John Street Auckland and stayed for a week. Then Sheehan went back to what he knew best and bought a twenty acre farm in Waikomiti. That arrangement did not last long as his wife did not like the isolation. After only a few days she persuaded her husband to move back to town which they did on 21st of December.

Now after weeks of surveillance the police knew that their cover could be blown at any moment and he could flee. So on the 22nd of December Detective Walker went to Waikomiti with backup and a warrant to arrest Sheehan. Near Waikomiti Station they met Sheehan driving a horse and cart heading to town, he was on his way to sell them. When stopped they read the warrant to him but he denied the charge. He did admit to being William Sheehan from Castletownroche.

He said his mother, brother and sister emigrated to America seven years before and he had not heard from them since. None the less the police arrested him and took him back to Auckland. Sheehan was adamant he had not read any of the reports in the newspaper about what he was alleged to have done.

The following day, crowds of onlookers gathered outside the courthouse hoping to catch a glimpse of William Sheehan as he was taken inside, just like they would in Ireland. That day in court William Sheehan was charged that about October 1877 he killed his mother Catherine, brother Thomas and sister Hannah. All William had to do that day was answer to his name when called.

A superintendent read out the statement he had taken from Sheehan at the time of arrest. He described how back in October 1877 his mother, sister and brother headed to Fermoy six miles away. William said they had talked about going to America but never told him they were leaving that morning. He at first thought they were only going for two weeks but they never returned. William also told how he still had two brothers living in Ireland John James and Edward. He also had a sister Kate married to a merchant from Cork called Michael Spillane

William told how he had worked the 60 acre farm after they left but the landlord was tough. Otherwise he said he would still be there. He admitted receiving a letter from home some months before and learned there was still no tenant on what had been his land.

Whatever Sheehan said wasn't going to change a thing now. The police in New Zealand had received information from Ireland. This man was wanted for a triple murder back home which it was alleged to have occurred seven years before.

He made several more appearances in court over the course of the next few weeks but there was nothing the police could do. They were only waiting for an officer to arrive from Ireland with an arrest warrant and Sheehan would then be taken back to Ireland to be tried.

It was March 1885 before Sergeant Dunny from Kildorrery arrived with the original warrant for his arrest. His legal representation had refused to accept the copies of the warrant. By now the warrant was nearly six months old having been issued in October the year before. Now it was also learned that a onetime servant of Sheehan's, David Duane had now become a witness for the crown. He implicated William Sheehan and his brother-in-law David Brown as an accomplice.

Arrangements were made for Sheehan to travel back to Ireland. Sheehan himself had said the government were going to great expense to transport him back to Ireland but was adamant of his innocence. He was heard to say once he was proven innocent the government would have to pay his fare back to New Zealand again.

Tuesday the 7th of April he left Wellington on the steamship Raupeha under the escort of Sergeant Dunny and Detective Walker. Thirty six days later which was considered fast back then they landed in Plymouth. One evening in late May he stepped off the train in Cork still under the same small escort. He didn't stand out one bit in Cork and nobody would have guessed he had travelled over twelve thousand mile to answer charges for events that had taken place almost eight years before.

Sheehan was taken to the barracks where press began to gather. He was heard telling the press he was an innocent man and they should be careful what was said about him as he would take proceedings against them. It was strange that Sheehan had travelled alone. His wife Mary Anne and their children had remained down under. Mary Anne's brother was also rumoured to be involved, and her father James, who was said to have recently attempted suicide.

So why had William Sheehan been brought all the way from New Zealand? It led back to a discovery made near Castletownroche months before in a townland Lisnagourneen. A farmer called Broderick had a well on his land that had been dry for as long as he had the land. It fulfilled the image most of us have of a well, a circular shaft with a bucket on a windlass suspended over the top of it. That was many years before when the tenants of the nearby farms used it. The landlord George Bond Lowe had dug it for his tenants. It had since been used as a dumping ground of sorts. Broderick had covered it with a whitethorn bush fearing that cattle might get stuck in the shaft.

The summer of 1883 must have been dry because Broderick resigned himself to getting the well operational again. In August of that year men were employed to clear it out which was no easy task. They lowered themselves down and cleared the well bucket by bucket of stones and rubble that had fallen in over the years.

They were not long at it when at about seventy feet down they came on a large stone too big for buckets or for men to haul up. It took some work to break up the stone with a hammer and chisel. Soon all work ground to a sudden halt when a man called Fitzgerald discovered three human skulls on a Saturday evening.

Early on the Sunday morning Sergeant Dunny from Kildorrey arrived and another man went down the well. By Monday three complete human skeletons had been brought to the surface. There were all sorts of wild rumours spreading about the countryside. Between the police and doctors they began to discover some clues to how they had come to being there. The bones were there with several years Dr Quinlan from Castletownroche claimed and still had some flesh clinging to them. He also verified that the skeletons were two women and a man.

People quickly suspected that the Sheehan family had left in mysterious circumstances back in October of 1877.

It was well known in the area that William Sheehan had been evicted about two years before and had gone to New Zealand. Another brother John was still living in the area and also people who had been servants to the Sheehan family. It did not take long for those people to identify shreds of clothes found in the well as being clothes similar to what the Sheehan family had worn seven years before.

The county coroner James Byrne from nearby Wallstown Castle was sent for and the inquest took place on the 2nd of September. A jury of twelve local men with foreman Thomas Furlong had the grim task of looking over the remains before the proceedings.

William Fitzgerald was the first witness that day. He told how on Saturday the 30th of August he discovered human remains in a well. Fitzgerald recalled also finding clothes and two pairs of boots in the well. He also said he had been back down the well several times since and was now working twelve feet below where the bodies had been found.

Key to the case was a woman called Mary Reilly who had worked for the Sheehan's in 1877. She began by saying back then she had been in service with the Sheehan's for about a year. Mary recalled the day before the Sheehan's had disappeared stations were heard in the house and the entire family was there. The next morning Hannah Sheehan went to stations held in her brother John's house. She said that morning William and Thomas had breakfast together and then went out together, this was the last time she saw Thomas. William returned alone and told her to fetch the horse from a field a bit away. Mary said when she left for the horse Mrs Sheehan and Hannah were in the house. When she came back with the horse William emerged from the house in a bit of a state. He told her the horse was not needed and to bring the cattle from the lime kiln field for water.

Mary said when she returned from the cows about one, Mrs Sheehan, Thomas and Hannah were gone and she never saw them again. Despite the seven years that had passed Mary could still describe the clothes the Sheehan's once wore. That evening the Sheehan's brother-in-law Michael Spillane arrived from Cork and stayed the night. She recalled mentioning it to her parents at the time but they told her not to mention it again.

John Sheehan whose mother, brother, and sister's bodies were found in the well was called to give evidence. His recollection was that on the day they went missing stations were held in his house. Only his sister Hannah attended and that was the last time he saw her.

Later that day he went to the house as he knew his brother-in-law was arriving from Cork. He asked William where his mother was and William said they had left in hired car that day. William told him he had arranged to meet them at Ballyhooly train station the following Tuesday. But he had added that if they were not there, they would not write for 2-3 months.

John said the farm had been in his mother's name and she was opposed to the match between William and Mary Anne Browne. William married Mary Anne within two weeks of the mother leaving he said. John revealed his brother received money after marrying Mary Anne but John got £100 of the sum which was due to him. John was not at all sure about what had happened to his family.

James Browne recalled the negotiations he had with Mrs Sheehan at shrove time the year before she had disappeared. Shrove was a busy time for weddings as back then no weddings were allowed during Lent. So every year there was a rush to get married before lent and many got married on Shrove Tuesday.

Brown said he could go as far as paying £170 to Mrs Sheehan to marry Mary Anne but Mrs Sheehan wanted £300. In October 1877 William came to him and said his mother had agreed to the £170 before she left. The couple were married not long after on 6th of November in Glanworth.

Was the inquest ever going to reveal anything of what had become of the Sheehan's and who had been found in the well? Surely if anyone had known anything material in the case they would have come forward before now.

Another ex-servant of the Sheehan's was called and he told a different story altogether.

John Duane was living with his wife near the Sheehan's in 1877. He clearly recalled the day they left and said he saw them drive off about ten that morning. About two days later William Sheehan gave him a pair of boots which had belonged to Thomas.

Dr Quinlan told how it was on the 1st of September when he had examined the three bodies. In his medical opinion the remains were six to seven years old and still had flesh on the bones in places. The only other thing the doctor could tell was the remains were that of two women and a man, one of the women appeared to be much older than the other two.

After hearing the evidence the jury retired for only fifteen minutes and returned with their verdict "We are of the opinion the remains we have seen this day are those of Catherine Sheehan, Thomas Sheehan and Hannah Sheehan of Carrigdownane and that the bodies have been thrown into the well at Lisnagourneen, parish of Castletownroche by some person or persons unknown about seven years ago".

The police continued their investigation sure that someone in the area must know more. John Duane made a grave error at the inquest and this must have drawn attention to him. Within days he was arrested and sent to the county Gaol. Mary Reilly was taken in as crown witness and was moved out of the area by the police. She was the one who could identify the fragments of clothes down the well. For the police it was very difficult as it had happened so long ago. They were not sure of the motive and were yet to find the murder scene. Any traces of the murder scene would have disappeared over the years. The distance between the well and Sheehan's farm led the police to believe more than one person was involved. They also thought that the murders had not occurred in Sheehan's house.

One day after the petty sessions in Castletownroche a private inquiry was held by the police and a local magistrate. It was assumed to have gone back over the evidence heard at the inquest. It does seem however that Duane's story began to change over time and this caused the police to think he may have been involved. Duane could not deny that he was present and working on the farm when the Sheehan's disappeared. He now introduced the notion that he saw another man come to the house about noon and gave a name. The police were not willing to release that name at the time.

Duane also now said it was William who gave him boots belonging to Thomas. His wife had also received clothes belonging to Mrs Sheehan but Duane added that William asked him not to say where he had got them from.

Slowly the police were ruling out all possible eventualities of where the Sheehan's could have gone. William had implied to John they had gone to Mrs Sheehan's sister. Now the police contacted that sister, Mrs Magner, who confirmed neither Mrs Sheehan, Thomas nor Hannah, had come to her after October 1877.

Soon the police knew that they could go no further in the investigation until they had spoke to William Sheehan. All they knew was he had gone to either Australia or New Zealand about 1883.

This is where Sergeant Dunny and Detective Walker come into it. Dunny knew William for several years and dealt with him before. So it was Dunny who headed down under with the warrant as he could identify him. At the same time telegrams were sent ahead to New Zealand with information.

By late October 1884 papers in New Zealand began to publish details of the case and were aware the suspect was living there. In November the story had become widespread and every newspaper carried some account of the gruesome discovery and the motive.

William Sheehan lived near Auckland and seemed to have no idea of the discovery back home. If he had any inkling at all one imagines he would have made attempts to conceal himself or leave the country. It just goes to show he had not spent the last number of years looking over his shoulder expecting to be found.

So what could have driven William Sheehan to kill his family and why would anyone cover for him, even now when the deed was known? Like most murders in Ireland at that time the motive was either land, money or a woman or in this case, all three. Back in the 1800's a farmer's son wanting to get married couldn't just go out and propose to a woman, it was more complicated than that. If one son was to get married arrangement would need to be made for the other siblings and where the parents would live.

Such negotiations began in 1877 between the Sheehan's and local farmers the Browne's about the match between William and Mary Anne. Catherine Sheehan's husband David had died some years ago so it seems she was leading the discussions. Catherine insisted on settling for no less than £300 but James Browne, Mary Anne's father could only come up to £170.

Don't think that Catherine was being greedy and wanting more money for herself. This was the way it was back then between anyone with land. Whichever side of the family was marrying into the land had to provide money in the arrangement. Catherine would then have used the sum to settle a marriage for her daughter Hannah or maybe provide for her other son Thomas.

For her accepting a lower amount meant her other children would have to also settle for less. John Sheehan had already been married and setup as a publican in Rockmills. It was William that could not see it from his mother's point of view and just wanted to get married. Up to the point where it all goes wrong it sounds like a story from Eamon Kelly without any element of comedy. Kelly in his stories explains how "in my father's time" a marriage settlement would pass on though many families resulting in many matches.

This it was believed was the source of it all, William living at home with his mother and siblings had a farm coming to him but could not make any decisions for himself. His mother still had the farm in her own name and had the final say. For William to run away and marry Mary Anne Browne he would have disinherited himself of the farm. Many waited for their parents to die before getting married and then left it too late to have children. William it seems had no mind to wait and this led to months of bickering between them.

So now it had taken months but William Sheehan was back in Cork and would be questioned by the police. Then he would face a judicial inquiry and a trial before a jury. William was confident no evidence would be found against him but about the same time his brother-in-law David Browne was also arrested at his house and taken to the county gaol. It must have been Duane who was now providing information implicating Browne as an accomplice.

Within days a magisterial investigation was opened in Cork by resident magistrate Eaton.

Now both William Sheehan and David Browne stood charged with the triple murder. That first day in court many witnesses were called repeating what had been heard already.

John Sheehan did explain better why he didn't take any action when his mother disappeared. He told how she had often said once William was married she would leave the place and setup in business on her own. He described his mother as a capable, independent woman, so he believed William's story and of course also received £100. There were still doubts though and he told the court how he searched in several towns for them. He said William never gave him a clear indication of where they had gone.

The next day Sergeant William Dunny gave evidence starting with how he knew William Sheehan for several years. Sheehan he said was evicted in November 1882 but remained in the area until July 1883. Dunny had arrested Sheehan for wrecking the house of a man involved in his eviction. The sergeant went over the discovery in the well and how he came to be in Auckland. He said he arrested William Sheehan again on the 13th of March that year in Auckland. He said Sheehan protested "It was no I that did it, you came to the wrong man and you will have to return without me". Later that day William and Mary Anne asked had David Browne been arrested, but he had not when Dunny had left Ireland.

The third day in court, Detective Walker from Auckland gave evidence of arresting William Sheehan the December before. At first he said Sheehan would not admit who he was or where he came from but soon relented. He then said "all right I never killed my mother", Walker noted that at this point he had never told Sheehan the charges against him.

Catherine Duane was called as she had often worked for the Sheehan's, her husband was John Duane. At one time she said when Hannah Sheehan was away she often worked for Mrs Sheehan. Catherine explained in detail the clothes worn by Mrs Sheehan and how she received some from

William. She identified fragments of clothes which had been found in the well. She was sure that pair of boots found in the well was Mrs Sheehan's saying how she had cleaned them on several occasions. She said the night after they disappeared two of the Browne sisters visited William Sheehan and they played music in the parlour. The following Sunday she cooked a roast goose at Sheehan's and James Browne was invited to dine there. The roast goose dinner was a tradition in Ireland once the match had been made. This clearly showed that William Sheehan wasted no time at all but it was yet to be proved he was a killer.

The one man who it was believed could prove William a murderer was called next, John Duane. Over time John had changed his story but because of him David Browne was now in custody. John told how he worked in Sheehan's yard that day. He saw Mary Reilly going for the cows. Afterwards he said David Browne arrived at the house and a little later Mary Browne also went into the house. Then William Sheehan said to him "John did you see the side car going off the road". John who had been working in the yard all day said he saw no one leaving and William insisted he had saying "you did". John claimed he disagreed again and all William replied was "they are gone".

In the afternoon Duane said he was sent a few miles away with a pig by William and was away for several hours. Over the next few days he said William tried to persuade him again he had seen them leave. William even told him to tell people who asked that he had seen them leave.

That day David Duane a son of the last two witnesses was brought to court. He had come from Mountjoy prison because he had been caught stealing £160 from a Mrs Magner in Fermoy the year before. Could it be the same Mrs Magner that was related to the Sheehan's? The fact he was a convicted criminal made him an unreliable witness in the eyes of a magistrate or jury.

David Duane recalled living with his parents which was two fields away from Sheehan's. The night after the Sheehan's left; he heard concertina music coming from the house. David told how he went outside and listened to the music for nearly two hours. When the music ended it was late and the lights in Sheehan's went out.

He then saw William bring the horse and cart to the yard. David Browne was there at the time with another man that Duane did not know. He said they brought out three bodies and loaded them onto the cart. Young Duane then said he followed some distance behind them towards Broderick's farm. He remained behind the ditch so as not to be seen by the three men. Duane claimed he saw William Sheehan remove the wood that covered the well and he even heard the noise as each body was dropped into the well. It was David Brown and Sheehan who dragged the bodies. He didn't see the other man do anything. Young Duane said he followed them back to Sheehan's and saw William washing the cart. Young Duane never went home that night. Instead he slept in a nearby outhouse to avoid his father who often beat him. The next day he told how he got a terrible fright the night before but never elaborated. Duane was then questioned in detail by both side but was able to answer all questions despite how farfetched his evidence sounded. The defence obviously brought into it the fact he was a criminal himself to doubt what he had said.

At the end of the day the judge was ready to return the men for trial but it was agreed to adjourn for another week.

A week later in court a Dr Curtis gave detailed medical evidence and tried to prove the cause of death. He had examined the remains in Rockmills churchyard. On the male skeleton he had found a puncture wound to the skull. That wound would have been as a result of a blow from a sharp cutting instrument like a chisel he said. On the other side of the head he found another fracture which was the result of a fall or from falling down the well. The first wound though he said was enough to knock a person unconscious and result in death.

The second skeleton was that of a female between 20-30 years old. He could find no signs of violence. The third was similar but the doctor could tell it was the skeleton of an older woman. There was much questioning Dr Curtis about how the wounds were inflicted, but the doctor remained adamant. The wound on the left side was of the man's skull was caused by a blow of a sharp iron object.

After several more witnesses were heard the judge then returned the case for trial before a jury at the next Assizes in Cork.

There were strong suspicions that David Duane was not fully telling the truth, it was thought he knew the third man. That third man was believed to be his father and young David was reluctant to reveal it. He didn't need to tell the truth though because John Duane finally relented. John admitted to being the third man that night and had not realised he was seen by his own son. He even went further admitting to being present when Thomas Sheehan was killed.

The game was up now for William Sheehan and David Browne. William would never return to New Zealand again as he thought he would. He may not ever see his wife or children again. His wife must have had some indication of what had occurred; maybe that was why she stayed well away.

John Duane's statement was public knowledge no matter how hard the police tried to keep it quiet. In his statement he made it clear he was there against his own will. Duane began saying that William Sheehan said the morning before they disappeared "Johnny you won't tell what I'm going to do today". John said this was an hour before anything occurred but William had not told him what was going to happen.

He saw Thomas going to the stable that morning, David Browne was inside and William followed him in. William then struck Thomas on the head twice with a graffaun. David and William then went to the house, while John Duane waited outside at the door. Both Mrs Sheehan and Hannah were in a small room off the kitchen. William went in and struck his mother with the graffaun, then threw it down and choked her to death. Meanwhile Browne had taken up the graffaun and gave Hannah a crack of it as she was screeching. Browne then choked her.

Duane said they asked him for help and he did take the bodies to the stables and William locked the door. The following day he arrived for work as usual. William Sheehan told him he would need him to come back later that night and tackle the horse and cart.

He did this and while waiting outside heard the concertina music as his son also had. He was aware that the Browne sisters were in the house. Later on William and David Browne emerged and loaded the bodies onto the cart. William said "here Johnny, here's a pair of boots belonging to my brother Tom, if they don't match you, you can put a rag in them if they are too big". John then led the horse on a shortcut across the fields and turned on to the boreen leading to the well. It was between eleven and twelve when they arrived at the well.

After throwing the bodies into the well they all returned together. The Browne sisters were still playing the concertina in the house. Duane untackled the horse and William washed out the blood out of the cart. William told him not to tell anyone and he must have kept his word for some time. John Duane said he just went to work the following morning as usual.

After taking this statement the police returned to the farm which had since been unoccupied and found the murder weapon. Now they had a strong case against David Browne and William Sheehan.

By late July the Cork Summer Assizes were imminent but John Duane back tracked on his statement again. The accused were called before the Assizes and pleaded not guilty. A trial date was set for the following week. By the time the trial started the counsel for the accused applied for an adjournment. They claimed that the leaking of John Duane's statement was prejudicial to the case. They said no jury could look on the case with an unbiased view now. Their application was upheld and the trial would now be delayed another six months until December. All they had achieved for their clients was merely to buy some time and hope John Duane would change his statement.

On Monday the 14th of December William Sheehan was charged with murder before Justice O'Brien. On Wednesday afternoon, after three days in court the judge began a lengthy speech. The court room though had to be cleared for a while as cayenne pepper had been spread around and made people cough to such an extent the judge could not be heard. So it took the judge four hours before he left the jury go. It was ten that night and the jury still could not agree. Justice O'Brien was willing to wait until midnight but after eleven the jury abandoned all hope of reaching a verdict. They had been very close - eleven were for guilty but one was for acquittal.

The following morning saw William Sheehan back in court and a new jury were to be sworn in and do it all over again. He now looked far more agitated than in the previous three days.

Another three days of the same evidence again before another jury brought it to Saturday the 19th. That day in court it was noted that one witness was not able to attend. Mary Reilly had attempted to commit suicide that morning in the Bridewell, Cork. The months of being away from home and under police protection had obviously taken its toll on her.

It only took the jury an hour this time to come to their verdict of guilty. When William Sheehan heard this he had to be assisted before he fell over. But despite this when asked had he something to say he began a speech as long as a senior legal counsel.

Sheehan used the opportunity to plead his and Browne's innocence. He said the Duane's were telling lies and would never been able to keep such a secret for so long. He also said he would not be so stupid to allow Duane to witness such a thing. He went on for some time but offered no other logical conclusion of how his family disappeared or ended up in a well. He just over and over stated that the verdict was wrong and that they were innocent.

When the judge got his chance he told Sheehan he would have been found guilty with far less evidence and proceeded to sentence him. Justice O'Brien said "It is not I who condemn you, it is not the jury who condemn you, it is not even the law condemns you, it is your own crime condemns you". The judge then made it clear there was to be no mercy for him and that his time was limited.

He put on the black cap and announced that he was to be executed by hanging on the 20th of January. William Sheehan was then led out of court and as he was leaving said "Browne is innocent". Within days William Sheehan became resigned to his fate but now tried to save his brother-in-law. David Browne was to appear before the Assizes after Christmas charged with the murder of Hannah.

Since the death of William Marwood the year before James Berry had applied to be the replacement executioner. In his memoirs My experiences as an Executioner, Berry describes how on hearing of a death sentence in Ireland he sent a business card. This was to secure the contract as he was only paid per execution plus expenses.

James Berry's business card.

The executioner James Berry.

Meanwhile Sheehan indicated that he would make a statement before Browne's trial and did so. "I here publicly state that Brown and his family are quite innocent of the murder of my mother, brother and sister. What John Duane swore and his son and wife is all false. It was I committed the deed myself about eleven o'clock am and I kept the bodies in the haggard and covered them with stray. I put them into the car about 6:30 pm in the evening. My brother came into the yard and after he had left I took the dead bodies immediately to the well about 6 40 pm and I afterwards went straight for Spillane."

"My reason for committing this deed was that my mother would not give her consent to marry the girl. We were engaged in ripping up the threshing machine when I murdered my brother about ten o'clock am. When my sister came from the stations she brought a letter to have me go with herself and her mother to Fermoy. I went for the purpose of getting ready and asked would they let the girl go for the horse. While the girl was for the horse, I took the sister into the haggard to fill a bag of straw for the purpose of sitting on and killed her there. The girl was coming close to the house when I told her to go and bring the cows to water. Then she went for them. I returned to the haggard and my mother wondering at the delay came into the haggard and caught me covering the bodies of my brother and sister in straw and then I murdered her and covered her dead body with straw. I then followed the girl and told her leave the cows there as she was carrying them to the kiln and told her they were gone to Fermoy".

On the 31st of December David Browne pleaded not guilty to murder before a jury.

The Attorney General admitted that this case hung even more on the evidence of the Duane's old and young.

Again Duane told his story and said the same as he had before, that Browne was there and killed Hannah. No evidence was called for the defence, James Browne was likely not capable of coming to court but his sisters could have.

On the second day of the trial the jury acquitted David Browne, on the murder charge. They must have felt his motive to kill was far less than that of Sheehan. When the verdict was read out there was applause in court.

All that was left now was for Sheehan to receive his punishment. By the middle of January the arrival of executioner James Berry from Bradford was expected. He was the man who had further refined Marwood's long drop technique scientifically.

About that time Mary Anne Sheehan came to see her husband in jail and their parting made for a most upsetting spectacle. His sister Kate asked to see him but her request was refused.

The condemned man being watched in his cell for his final night.

The final preparations were being made at the jail. With some time the scaffold had been a permanent structure, where the prisoner did not need to climb any steps. The last time it had been used was in 1883 for Timothy O'Keeffe Kingwilliamstown who also features on these pages.

On the morning of the 20th of January 1886 William was up early and spent several hours in prayer. A few minutes before eight that morning the guards came to the door and led Sheehan out to the execution chamber. The executioner Berry placed the noose over his neck and the white cap over his face.

In his last few seconds Sheehan begged God for mercy for what he had done. At exactly eight the executioner pulled the bolt which released the trapdoor. Berry had calculated a drop of six feet which resulted in an instant death. The black flag was then hoisted over the jail, to let the crowd outside know that justice had been served. His body was left hanging for an hour and then taken down for the inquest which was merely a formality.

Things didn't always go so well for James Berry, the year before he had two serious incidents. On one occasion he decapitated a man by over estimating the drop. On another occasion he failed to carry out the execution, when several times the trapdoor did not open.

So at the end of it all William Sheehan killed his family in order to marry the woman he loved. He wanted to marry her and keep his worldly possessions and yet within five years he was evicted and left the country. He could have eloped with Mary Anne Browne five years before and saved all the trouble but then he would have had less money. Despite being evicted and having to pay his passage to New Zealand, William had bought a farm just before being arrested.

He must have inherited money; by killing Thomas and Hannah he saved paying their marriage settlements. William Sheehan killed his family to get what he wanted and maintain his standing in the world. Being evicted must have been a relief to him and an excuse to get away from the reminders of his terrible deeds. He never thought for one second that he would have been found out and pursued to the ends of the earth. He may very well have gotten away if not for the skills and perseverance of Detective Walker and Sergeant Dunny.

Murdered for money
Curraghmore, Mitchelstown 1874

Leaving Mitchelstown heading towards Ballyporeen one passes through the townland of Curraghmore just on the Tipperary border. Back in the 1870's an elderly couple lived down a tiny boreen off the main road. Griffith's valuation tells us that the Fleming's held no land or outhouses. The plot they were renting was just big enough for the cottage. The little plot was rented from local farmer Jeremiah Moher, who in turn rented from landlord the Earl of Kingston.

Francis and Alice Fleming had reared their family in the tiny mud cottage so common in the countryside back then. Francis was seventy years of age and his wife five years younger. Their children were all grown up and had left home travelling to different parts of the world. All had one time lived there in the tiny cottage fifteen by ten feet which would be a small room nowadays. The couple now had the single room cottage to themselves. They had worked hard all their lives to keep the roof over their heads.

They were well liked and respected by their neighbours and never caused any trouble or drew any attention on themselves.

Francis now made a living by going around with a donkey and cart dealing eggs. He bought eggs from farmers and sold it at market towns in the area. Carrying cash and travelling the countryside was asking for trouble. It would have been well known to carry out his little business he had to have money at home.

People in the area also knew one of their daughters living in Wales wrote regularly to her parents. She sent small sums of money to them to supplement their income. The Flemings were now in a position to save a few pounds. They had also recently sold a few pigs but put the money in the bank before going home. In fact they had £20 in total deposited in the Munster Bank in Mitchelstown.

Several times intruders demanded money from them and they gave in as they didn't really have a choice. Francis's health had begun to fail him and he attended a local doctor.

On the morning of Wednesday 23rd July 1874 Jeremiah Moher's son passed by Flemings cottage. He noticed the donkey cart positioned across the only door to the cabin. The door itself was lying on the ground in pieces and the young lad was curious what had happened. He looked through the cart into the cabin but saw something he was not prepared for. Inside was what looked like Mrs Fleming lying on the ground. The young boy ran off to get help. The first adult he met was a man called Kelly who in turn went for the police in Kilbeheny the nearest village two and a half miles away.

First on the scene were a police party from Kilbeheny led by Constable Devine. Police also arrived from Ballyporeen. They removed the donkey cart from the doorway to reveal the full extent of the horrendous scene. Mrs Fleming's body lay on its back with her head at the door. There was no doubt that she had come to a very violent end. Her skull was fractured in several places and the brains could clearly be seen. Fragments of bone and brains were all over the tiny cottage. A shovel which was most likely the murder weapon lay close by spattered with blood.

The cottage had no window just the front door but looking in the police could see another foot resting on Mrs Flemings wrist. It was the boot of her husband Francis who also lay on the floor inside. Without even stepping inside the door, marks could clearly be seen on the low rafters above. This was from when the murderer lifted the shovel over their head and swung with full force.

The police had to light a candle to peer further inside the darkness. Inside Francis Fleming was also beaten in the same way his wife was, his face severely disfigured and skull fractured. It was obvious to the police a great struggle had taken place and the old couple had fought for their lives.

Their thoughts were that he was attacked first and struck on the head with the shovel while she tried to get the murderer from behind. Then he turned on her and finished her off by the door.

Every cupboard and item in the cottage was ransacked and thrown about. The attacker was looking for money or valuables and broken everything in their desperate attempt to find it.

Even their old cockerel got it. The headless body was found near Mrs Fleming. The head had been twisted off to quieten the bird.

Near Curraghmore today where the Fleming's were murdered.

Dr Edward McCraith from Mitchelstown arrived shortly after the police but knew immediately there was nothing he could do. News spread quickly of the terrible crime and the police were under pressure to catch who ever had done it. Inspector Creagh was quick on the scene and the County Inspector also arrived from Cork.

Two suspicious men from the area were quickly arrested and taken to Mitchelstown. John McCarthy and Thomas Browne were living rough and had no jobs. They were both found to have blood stained clothes though they claimed to have killed a horse.

The Flemings son-in-law Michael McNamara was also arrested. He was arrested in his own house near Ballyporeen. He had blood stains on his shirt and waistcoat that could not account for. In fact the police thought he was expecting them as the shirt had been washed and was folded under a bed.

An inquest could not be arranged for the following day as the coroner's position for the area was vacant. A resident magistrate Mr Eaton had to travel from Dublin to carry out the inquest.

On Friday the inquest was held. Jeremiah Moher told how the night before he had heard a woman's scream about eleven. He thought it was just some drunken people passing on the main road; he did not leave his house to investigate and paid no more attention to it.

Doctor Edward McCraith gave evidence after carrying out the post mortem with Dr William O'Neill. His evidence showed how grim the task was, so disfigured were their faces that identification was based on their clothes. The doctor described one wound which stretched across Alice Flemings face. The doctor concluded it had been carried out by the spade produced. He said the spade had been shoved into her mouth and cut her from ear to ear. Her index finger on one hand had also been almost severed off also done by the spade.

The wounds on Francis Fleming had also been carried out by the spade. Not only was his head fractured badly he also had several wounds on his chest. The doctor concluded that both had died instantly from their head injuries.

Right from the start the verdict was obvious, wilful murder by some person or persons unknown.

After the inquest the mutilated bodies were given to the family to hold a funeral.

The funeral was attended by a huge amount of people from all over the area. People were fearful in their own homes and kept their doors locked especially at night. During the day women gathered together in groups waiting for the men to return from the fields.

The following Saturday a fourth man was arrested Michael Roller in Doneraile; he was a discharged soldier from the 21st regiment. Despite the arrests people in the locality grew more worried when there were reports of more murders in the area. On the 31st of July an old woman was killed near Tallow and the scene was almost identical. A blood spattered shovel was found near the body. She even dealt in eggs as the Flemings had; a daughter of hers sent home money from America. The little house she lived in was also ransacked in the search for money and her strong box broken opened, the contents missing.

The police must have been worried they had the wrong men and there was in fact a serial killer in the area. Then on the 1st of August a woman was attacked and killed in broad daylight in her own home near Rathcormac. A man however was later tracked down for this killing, see 'Murder Most Local, Historic Murders of East Cork'.

Back in Mitchelstown the police struggled with the evidence against the arrested men. Back in the 1870's there was no way of analysing the blood stained clothes and finding the source. They could not even tell if the blood was human or not. There was no doubt at all though whoever was found guilty would most certainly hang for this dreadful crime.

Later in August a magisterial inquiry was held in Mitchelstown behind closed doors. They must have tried to conceal the fact there was little or no evidence against the arrested men. The men were remanded more that once but by late August the story disappears into obscurity.

At the same time there was a massive rise in crime in the North Cork area. All with the clear motive of robbery by someone with no conscience as to how they came by it. There seems to be no record of anyone being tried for one of the most brutal murders of two innocent elderly people. It would be a long time later before people in this normally quiet part of the world felt safe in their homes again.

A family affair
Kingwilliamstown 1882

Almost on the Cork and Kerry border near the source of the river Blackwater lies the village of Ballydesmond. It was started as a model village in the 1830's and was named after the King at the time William IV so it became Kingwilliamstown. Before that the townland was known as Tooreenkeogh.

It was not until 1951 that it changed to Ballydesmond so for the purpose of this story dealing with events in the 1880's we shall call it Kingwilliamstown. In this area in the 1880's one would think it was safe to assume it was a peaceful quite part of the country. It was however quite the opposite.

Tenants were unable at the time to pay the high rents forced on them by mostly absentee landlords. The Land League had been founded to bring about change in a non violent way but in places such as this people took the law in their own hands.

So many tenant farmers fell into arrears in the area and were dealt with harshly by their landlords. We all can picture the scene where hundreds of police turn up and turn out a family before tearing down the house.

One such small farmer Denis Donoghue, with ten in family was evicted. Despite hundreds of sympathisers being present it happened without trouble. The rent on the farm was unreasonable being £26 while being valued at £8 5s. Donoghue had offered to pay £12 but it was refused by the agent. Within a day however hundreds more came back organized by the land league and rebuilt the house. Donoghue was intending to remain on the land without paying with assistance from the Land League. Others in the area were also under threat of eviction for refusing to pay huge rents for poor mountain land.

A lot of activity however took place under the cover of darkness and the countryside went back to the way it was decades before. Gangs roamed the roads at night behaving like the Whiteboys had before. There were case of farmers who paid their rents were searched at night by masked men. If the rent book showed they had in fact being paying the rent, the books were burned and violent scenes often broke out. Some farmers tried to hide and there were cases of shootings or money being demanded of them.

Several farms were boycotted by the land league or taken over from the landlord. The landlords fought back by hiring men to stop the work of the land league. Men who worked on the league controlled farms were threatened at night at gunpoint.

But in one family in the area it was not the landlord or the system that they fought but amongst themselves. Brothers Denis and John O'Keeffe had grown up on a farm together close to Kingwilliamstown in the townland of Carriganes. When the first of the brothers came to getting married decisions had to be made about the farm. They were though in a privileged position compared to most. Their father had farmed about 180 acres which could be divided between them. It would still give each of them a reasonably good living compared to the majority who struggled at that time.

John Keeffe got 80 acres and a house with it, while his brother Denis received the larger portion of 100 acres that also included a farmhouse. Their rent was said to have been little trouble to them compared to others in the area. John paid £14 yearly for his 80 acres, while Denis paid only £8 for his 100 acres. The difference in rent however was that John's land must have been better than his brothers.

Over the years John farmed his land well and prospered with his 80 acres. His first wife died after only five years and he remarried again. He ended up with a big family of five daughters and three sons.

Denis O'Keeffe on the other hand did not prosper like his brother. He had married and had a family of several sons but financially he had debts. His brother John with a big family was not inclined to assist so something was going to happen. People were however surprised of Denis's predicament. He owed money to a Mr Casey from Kiskeam and Casey was pushing to recover the debt. His situation was so much different to most with high rents; his at £8 was described as a mere trifle.

It came to a head in 1879 when Denis O'Keeffe's interest in the 100 acres was put up for sale by the Sherriff. John had the means to do something about it but he also had a large family of his own. He didn't want to see his brother thrown out or the family land end up owned by anyone. So John attended the auction sale and paid £80 for the interest in the 100 acres.

An arrangement was then made between the brothers, Denis would reoccupy the lands but had four years to repay. He was to repay four yearly instalments of £20 otherwise he was to leave the land without any trouble.

It soon became clear though that Denis either couldn't or wouldn't repay his brother nor would he keep any part of the arrangement they had agreed to. John obviously felt he was not in a position to just let his brother have it, having paid £80.

Denis after all had got himself into trouble where he had managed to do just fine.

So John not getting repayments from Denis began proceedings against him sometime in 1880. Over the next two years the family would become a regular sight at the Knocknagree petty sessions.

Denis and his family were to be evicted on 10th of May 1880 but John relented seeing the pitiful situation his relations were in. The sheriff and John O'Keeffe agreed to allow Denis to stay on for a while longer as care taker. It was agreed to a period of four more months to allow Denis to repay the money or leave the farm.

However bad relations were between the family it was only to get worse. It was brothers against brothers, cousins against cousins, nephews against uncles. None of the members of each family were on speaking terms.

Early on the morning of 17th of August John O'Keeffe was out on his land when he came across Denis O'Keeffe junior his nephew. He enquired of the young lad what he was doing on his lands and the young fella pulled a gun on him.

Denis took aim and fired but John quickly threw himself to the ground. Denis ran off and John picked himself up off the ground uninjured. John reported the occurrence to the police but Denis went into hiding and was not to be found.

About a month later the sheriff came to evict Denis and his family for a second time. John would not relent this time considering what his nephew had done to him.

The weather that year in September was said to be bad and quite stormy about the time of eviction. None the less the sheriff proceeded to Denis O'Keeffe's house armed with a team of police from Kanturk. The house was located in a very out of the way place but still they went to evict the family.

There was no resistance to the proceedings and their worldly processions were taken out of the house. Then the house was knocked so they could not reoccupy. Seems strange nowadays to pull down the house, but the money the land it could generate was where the value was. Denis O'Keeffe and his family were then without a home and forced off the land. That night at least they were said to have squatted at the roadside in a makeshift shelter.

Denis O'Keeffe junior though was by now well used to rough sleeping. He had been on the run with over a month now since threatening his uncle with a gun. He was said to be hiding out in the hills around the area. Then he was spotted at the railway station in Rathmore and the police duly arrested him. Most likely he was trying to get away from the area where he would not be recognised.

It was weeks later before Denis appeared before a magistrate at Knocknagree petty sessions. He was charged with intent to murder his uncle John O'Keeffe. Solicitor Henry Barry from Kanturk prosecuted and O'Keeffe had no one to represent him.

Barry argued that the area was lawless and O'Keeffe should be made an example to all. He called for something to be done in the area to prevent the active resistance to the law. This case he said stood out in the seriousness of it as John O'Keeffe could have been killed.

The magistrate agreed with Barry and returned Denis O'Keeffe for trial at the next Assizes in Cork. The court however went on until late into the night dealing with numerous cases of rioting, stone throwing and police assaults in the area. Denis O'Keeffe was sent to prison to await his trial where most likely he would get a jail sentence.

Having spent almost three months in jail Denis O'Keeffe was called before Justice Fitzgerald at the Cork Winter Assizes.

Uncle of the accused John O'Keeffe took the stand and gave evidence against his nephew. He told how the young lad appeared out of nowhere and he asked what he wanted. When he did a gun was pulled on him and fired at him. John then revealed much to the amusement of the courtroom that he had not actually seen the gun just something "yellow" in his nephew's hand. John told how he went on his hands and knees before hearing the shot. He saw no smoke from the gun nor did he smell the powder. Before he got a chance to get up Denis was gone.

The judge intervened and said the gun may have in fact been a "pop gun". He ordered the case to be dismissed and Denis O'Keeffe acquitted. The jury seem to agree as the foreman was surprised the case had been sent to the Assizes at all. Foreman Daniel Murphy asked why a magistrate could not have dealt with this at the petty sessions.

Back in Kingwilliamstown Denis O'Keeffe senior it seems took procession again of some part of what he considered his. Another makeshift house was erected and the feud between the families rumbled on.

By April 1882 they would appear in court eighteen times in total. They were charged with trespass, threatening the life of John O'Keeffe and taking forcible procession of a house. John sought to get his brother off the land and begin to recover the money he had invested in it.

At Knocknagree Petty Sessions for one last time an order was passed to evict Denis O'Keeffe from the house he had made. At the suggestion of the magistrate John again gave his brother a chance. One month was agreed by which time Denis O'Keeffe would leave the land where he grew up. The date was fixed Thursday the 4th of May was to be their last.

On Sunday 30th April 1882 John O'Keeffe travelled with his family the mile or so to mass at Kingwilliamstown village. It was just four more days before his brother would finally leave and this must have bore heavily on his mind. While the troubles would be over, he would gain complete possession of the lands. Dealing with family though he cannot have thought of himself as victor it was merely something that had to be done.

After mass however his wife and daughters travelled home and John remained in the village. Most likely he spent a few hours in a pub in the village that day. It's easy to imagine him in a pub drinking to try and forget about the bitter feud and upsetting scenes that were to follow.

At about five he was seen leaving the village heading towards the Newmarket road. His family waiting at home grew worried when the evening grew dark after seven. They could not understand why John had stayed out so late especially as it was getting dark.

Some of the daughters then went out looking for him and went as far as the village but could not find sight of him. Several villagers knew something was wrong when the saw they young women searching frantically and crying as they did. For John's daughters intuition with all that was going on must have told them something bad had happened. Maybe he had been waylaid or assaulted by one of the feuding family.

Nothing would however prepare them for the reality of what had happened. Sometime between eight and nine John's body was found under a furze bush not a few hundred yards from his own front door. It was obvious from the moment he was found that he had been beaten to death. Then the body was dragged off the boreen out of sight to buy some time to get well away.

Nobody had seen it being done but everyone knew who the chief suspects were going to be. Close by a pike was found under a bush and the handle had been broken in two.

Denis O'Keeffe senior and one of his sons were found at the wretched hovel they still called home. They were quickly arrested by the police and taken to the local barracks. The other two brothers Timothy and John were found at farms where they worked as labourers. The police searched Denis's house and the entire locality but failed to find the murder weapon there. Nor could they find any other evidence against the family such as blood on their clothes. They did find at Denis O'Keeffe's an unsent letter indicating their intention to take action and recover the land.

No matter how shocked people in the area were about the murder not many came forward to give evidence albeit circumstantial. The police tried to investigate the events leading up to the murder that evening by asking the villagers produced little. The priest Fr McMahon gave a speech at mass asking for anyone that had information to come forward and tell the truth.

An inquest was held in the days following but the result was no surprise. They found that John O'Keeffe had died as a result of head injuries inflicted by a person or persons unknown to the jury. Timothy O'Keeffe was sent to jail in May as was his brother Denis and father.

At the Munster Winter Assizes in January 1883 before Justice Barry three members of Denis O'Keeffe's family were charged with murder of John O'Keeffe. The crown entered a nolle prosequi against Denis junior and senior meaning they were no longer proceeding with the case against them. Denis's other son John would also have been charged but he was working in Limerick at the time of the murder.

Twenty one year old Timothy O'Keeffe was now alone charged with wilful murder of his uncle John O'Keeffe. Timothy pleaded not guilty. If he was found guilty he would face the scaffold on his own. Now that they had gotten off, Timothy may have thought differently about the whole thing. If he didn't do it then he knew who did but most likely wouldn't say. It was not his life and his life alone that was at stake. It was clearly a crime of revenge about land that was material. Timothy should have had a long life ahead but because of revenge it was in jeopardy.

Sixty fiver jurors were present to form a panel for the cases. A further twenty had been called but failed to show up, these were now fined £50 each, a huge amount.

The jury was then reduced down to twelve by both the prosecution and the defence.

One juror Maurice Hickey was left off because he lived near Kingwilliamstown.

James Murphy Queens council opened the case for the prosecution. He gave the background to the case and how the two families were at war with each other. Denis O'Keeffe senior he said was careless with money and got into debt. His cattle had been seized and the land sold from under him. John however was a different man and was able to do the right thing and purchase the land. Murphy said from that day till now relations were extremely bad between them.

Murphy claimed everything in the case of murder pointed to the guilt of Timothy.

He had been seen watching his uncle that day and he would call witnesses to prove the case against him. They had found a letter during a search of Denis O'Keeffe's house, now Murphy claimed it had been written by Timothy for his father as Denis Senior could not write. It was addressed to John O'Keeffe Denis's eldest son who was in service in Limerick. The letter was then read out in court and allowed as evidence.

It read: Immediately to Timothy O'Keeffe answer, Sorey John I am very much in grieve to say that you are not sending answer to us about sevilians and place or what your doing or are you life if there is any possible chance I would enjoy it. You are a extraordinary boy. If I were in your place I would not forget you in so long a terrim. Let me know what you are getting. I don't know your master at all who he is or what is his name? Let me know how long you are agreed, and what's the wages. We are all very well if we had one thing alone and I hope that wont fale us to come by that too. We are on the brink of a quagmire of having it. Now there is not many minutes more when you will have 100 acres of land in the place of not having none at all. Do your business as well as you can and that's the best of business. I am your affectionate father.

Denis O'Keeffe to John Keeffe, signed by Timothy O'Keeffe.

Murphy said this was clear evidence that Denis O'Keeffe and his family intended to do something. How else were they going to recover the 100 acres without doing something drastic?

The principal evidence against him was circumstantial as no witnesses had seen him actually do the crime. The footprints at the scene match closely the boots Timothy had on when arrested. He had also been seen lurking around the area up to the time the crime was committed. Not forgetting motive, well the motive was obvious to all in the locality.

Several witnesses were then called who had seen Timothy leave Kingwilliamstown heading towards his uncles house that evening.

A local Patrick McAuliffe told how he had seen Timothy hiding in a bush a week before the murder. He said that was not the only time, that week he had seen him hiding several times without any business there. On one occasion Timothy asked him to put up some money for his father's bail. McAuliffe refused saying John O'Keeffe would be after him of he did. Timothy remarked though "it might not come to that at all".

A police constable Robert Frizelle took the stand and recalled seeing John O'Keeffe leave the village that evening. He also saw Timothy leave in the same direction shortly afterwards.

A man called James Bradley took the stand and told the court how he had seen Timothy and his father Denis on the evening of the murder. It was in the yard at the back of Herlihy's, he recalled Denis had dark clothes but Timothy wore light coloured trousers. Bradley was close enough to hear Denis tell his son the police were on the street. Afterwards he saw Timothy carrying an iron bar under his coat big enough he said for making horse shoes.

A servant boy called John Connell who worked for Timothy Murphy recalled seeing Timothy running across a field on the evening of the 30th April. He then crossed a road and headed towards the place where the murder took place. The man he saw wore white corduroy trousers and darker coat with a soft hat. Connell was sure it was Timothy he had seen that evening saying he knew him well as he was in school with him.

A farmer called Ellen Sullivan was called to give evidence as she was Timothy's employer up to when he was arrested at least. She told the court of hiring him on 1st of February that year. It was a live in job and he slept in her house. On the 23rd of April he left without a word to her. Normally he would leave on Saturday night to go home until Sunday night. This time though he didn't turn up for a week.

On the night of the murder he arrived back as it was getting dark. He was asked why he was gone for the week but said he had to leave. She recalled Timothy being wet that night and drying himself by the fireside.

Another local farmer Owen McAuliffe father of Patrick explained how he had rented land from John O'Keeffe. While out attending to his cattle one day Timothy O'Keeffe approached him. Timothy told him to take the cattle off the land as his father was in dispute about it. McAuliffe did take the cattle away as he was afraid.

The arresting sergeant Michael McArdle was called to take the stand. He told of the night he found Timothy in bed in Ellen Sullivan's house. He pulled the bed clothes off him and Timothy said "is that you sergeant". McArdle said that Timothy's demeanour changed when he read the charge against him, he then began to sweat and seemed worried. He cried and claimed he was innocent before being taken away. As they left the house Timothy asked the constable was it true his uncle was dead.

The court then adjourned for the day and the jury went to the Imperial Hotel to spend the night under watch of police constables.

Constable Drohan told the court how he was at Knocknagree Petty sessions in April of 1881. He overheard Timothy threaten his uncle John saying settle the case against his father or he would be sorry.

Doctor Verling from Newmarket gave medical evidence having examined the body. He told how the head injuries were numerous and caused by a large heavy blunt object at least two inches wide. Marks in the groin suggested John had been kicked several times also. Several of the head injuries were to the right hand side and the ear had been badly split.

A police constable then told the court about finding what he believed was the murder weapon 45 yards from where the body was found. A pike was also found in the same field.

Doctor Verling was then asked by a juror could this be the murder weapon. The doctor agreed that it was likely that the wood produced in court could cause the injuries.

The last prosecution witness was a shop assistant Julia Connell who worked for her father in Kingwilliamstown. Julia said she sold Timothy a pair of boots about seven or eight that Sunday night.

Sullivan cross examined her and she recalled talking to Timothy that night about his uncle. He then left wearing the new boots having left the old ones in the shop. She told how country people will not buy boots on Saturday to wear on Sunday. They often bought boots Sunday evening as the shop stayed open till late.

Sullivan revealed that Julia had earlier made a statement that Timothy bought the boots Saturday night. She now denied this and denied giving any information at all. Julia when asked even admitted to withholding information from the police.

Constable McArdle was then recalled to clear up the confusion about Julia's testimony. He confirmed that he called on Julia several times and questioned her. Once she told him that she did not sell the boots on Sunday night. On another occasion she could not recall whether it was Saturday or Sunday. Finally she told him that it must have been her sister who sold the boots. The jury could now only disregard everything Julia had said.

After the witnesses, Sullivan for the defence gave a long speech for his client. He said as far as evidence was concerned anyone in the village could have been charged with the murder. He called Bradley's statement about the iron bar "absurd" saying he only came forward in December. Sullivan questioned the motive asking would Denis O'Keeffe be restored his lands by the death of John. He claimed Timothy O'Keeffe would not gain by his uncle's death saying they always wanted to settle with John. The speech took almost two hours and when he finished there was applause in court. Did the crowd in court think Timothy was innocent and agreed with his solicitor or were they just happy it was over?

O'Brien then gave a speech for the crown case.

After this the judge went over the evidence again for the jury which took almost two hours. It was six in the evening when the jury left to decide the fate of Timothy O'Keeffe.

At half seven a message from the jury stated they would be at least another two hours deciding.

The court then adjourned until ten to allow for some refreshments after the long day. Just after ten the judge sent for the jury. The foreman Mr Varian entered court and said "there is no chance of our agreeing my lord". The judge offered any help in explaining the evidence but knew it was no use. He then discharged the jury saying he was sure they had considered the case thoroughly.

After deliberating for over four hours, eleven of the jury were to convict Timothy O'Keeffe while one decided that he should be acquitted. Most likely this juror believed there was a clear lack of evidence against him.

Timothy O'Keeffe was taken from court and returned to jail. He had come so close to his own end. There was only one person's opinion between leaving the court and facing the scaffold in a week or so. Now though his fate was unknown but he got a reprieve from the sentence of death.

He soon realised however that he was to be tried again at the Cork Spring Assizes sometime in March.

When it was called again to court it appeared to be a rerun of before with all the same people saying pretty much the same thing. Despite this everyone expected a different result having heard the same evidence before Lord Justice Fitzgibbon.

Patrick McAuliffe though now could not even recall what he said at the last trial. He recalled seeing Timothy a week before the murder but otherwise was of no use to the prosecution. Before he had said he saw Timothy hiding in bushes several times that week.

On the other hand Patrick's father now told how he was herding cattle near Denis O'Keeffe's house on the night of the murder. He had seen Timothy heading towards where John's body was found quite quickly. He never said this at the last trial only that Timothy had threatened him for taking land from John O'Keeffe.

The second day of the trial 30th March was to be the last day. After hearing some clarification from a witness the defence had another chance to put doubt into the juries mind. Sullivan solicitor for the defence again made his pitch for his client.

Julia Connell was now called for the defence. Despite being caught out at the last trial she now gave detail of the boots she sold Timothy the night of the murder. She was able to recognise the boots produced saying there was a peculiar groove on the heel. She now said after closing the shop she was home by eight that night having only sold the one pair of boots that day. She did admit that another man Dan Herlihy was present when she sold the boots to Timothy.

Again under cross examination Julia's evidence was questioned but this time differently. Murphy asked her did the constable know that she was secretary to the Ladies Land League. She denied lying about it preferring instead to claim she avoided answering. Further questioning however and she did admit to in the past lying to the police and in court.

A respectable shopkeeper from Kingwilliamstown Dan Herlihy was called to corroborate what Julia had said as it was difficult to believe her. Herlihy said he was in the shop between seven and eight that evening. Timothy he recalled buying the boots between seven and half past.

When questioned by the prosecution Herlihy denied being related to Timothy and also said they were not friends. He had not met him for a week up to that night. They talked in the shop about how John O'Keeffe had offered to pay his fare to America with his brother the year before. Herlihy recalled how Timothy regretted now not accepting the offer.

After further questions Herlihy admitted to once saying the boots were sold on Saturday night. This he said was to avoid being called as a witness.

Constable McArdle was again called and gave evidence of having got very different statements from Julia Connell and Dan Herlihy on several occasions.

Solicitors for both sides then gave long speeches ending with the prosecution.

O Solicitor O'Brien for the prosecution questioned why Denis O'Keeffe senior or junior had not been called by the defence.

The judge then went over the case and remarked how the evidence was indeed circumstantial. He then spoke about reasonable doubt to the jury saying the prisoner should have the benefit of it. He did ask the jury to be sure of their verdict saying a young man's life depended on it. He finished saying to the jury "do your duty with extreme case but at the same time with just courage".

It was ten past four when the jury left the courtroom to do their duty and decide on a man's future or not. At quarter to six the foreman returned saying they were unable to agree. The judge was dismissive and asked they try again to consider the matter further.

The foreman though said "there is not the slightest hope of reaching a verdict". Justice Fitzgibbon insisted however that the jury must try again. Before returning the foreman asked for further clarification about the purchase of the boots which was in so much doubt. Had Timothy bought boots in the village between seven and half past he could not have killed his uncle at the same time.

The judge went over the evidence again at some length and the jury left at just before six. At seven the judge sent for the jury and again there was some talk of the boots before retiring again.

Finally at quarter to eight the foreman returned with a verdict the jury had agreed on. He read out the verdict of guilty, but with it came the recommendation of mercy. This they said was on account of Timothy's young age and the fact it was a family feud that went on for some time.

The clerk of the court then asked Timothy why the sentence of death should not be applied to him. Timothy however was crying and could not be understood, he was however asking for his life to be saved.

The judge then addressed Timothy directly saying he could not get mercy as the jury recommended. His age he said was only a small part of it the fact now was he had committed the crime. He had forfeited his life on being found guilty. The judge said there was nothing to do now but pass sentence and he would receive his punishment.

He then put on the black cap which was customary in such circumstances. He then told Timothy that he would be hung from the neck until dead at Cork Gaol on the 30th of April. This would be exactly one year to the day since the crime took place. Timothy was then removed from the court and knowing he had only one month to live.

By early April a petition was being prepared to be sent to the Lord Lieutenant to ask for mercy for Timothy. The signatories believed that the jury recommended mercy and he was entitled to it. They also said that Timothy was likely influenced heavily by family members and at his young age was impressionable. Several notable people had signed the petition including bishops, clergymen, magistrates and even the mayor.

Public opinion they claimed was on their side, the murder had been brutal but penal servitude for life was a fitting punishment.

By late April Timothy's fate was determined for sure by a letter received from Dublin Castle dated 25th April 1883 "Sir, with regard to your letter, on behalf of Timothy Keeffe, a prisoner under sentence of death in Cork Male Prison. I am directed by the Lord Lieutenant to inform you that after a careful consideration of all the circumstances of the case, his Excellency regrets that he has felt it to be his painful duty to decide that the law must takes its course. I am your obedient servant W.W Kaye."

A week before the date of execution Timothy was visited in jail by his two brothers. It was a painful scene the two knew there was nothing in the world they could now do for him. The whole affair had gone too far.

Timothy himself gave in to the fact that soon he was to die and prayed in his cell every day. He never however made any admission of guilt.

Then there was doubt an executioner could be got as the famous William Marwood was double booked. Rumours spread quickly Marwood was seen arriving in Dublin on his way to Cork.

William Marwood was the hangman for the British Government who had developed the long drop method of execution. The long drop method ensured that the person would die instantly having their neck broken at the bottom of the drop. They then died of suffocation while unconscious. Previously with a shorter drop the prisoner died a slow death by strangulation which was much more difficult to watch.

On the 29th of April he went to bed in prison at the normal time, but spent the night restlessly without sleep. The following morning he was up out of bed dressing himself when the guards came for him just after six.

He went to mass at seven and was in the chapel for nearly an hour. Just before eight he walked the fifty or so yards to the scaffold. Executioner Marwood was there ready and waiting for him. Timothy without hesitation surrendered himself to Marwood who tied his hands or pinioned as they called it. The noose was placed over his head and Marwood had already calculated the drop of nine feet for O'Keeffe's body weight.

In his final moments young Timothy O'Keeffe made no admission of guilt but neither did he claim to be innocent.

On the stroke of eight Marwood pulled the bolt and almost instantly Timothy's body hung lifelessly from the rope. Marwood had done his job right and there was not complications as often occurred with inexperienced executioners.

Just two hours later the coroner J Horgan held an inquest with a jury of thirteen men at the Laurels Mardyke. The jury wanted the rope produced saying it was the instrument of death.

Marwood however refused to attend the inquest and also would not hand over the rope saying it was his own private property. The governor of the gaol also declined the request to attend the inquest. Eventually the doctor's evidence was heard and a quite obvious verdict agreed upon.

Marwood who was anything but popular left Cork under an escort of twelve policemen but he would be back again to take more lives.

Twenty years later there was but one O'Keeffe living in the townland of Carriganes. It was a twenty year old John O'Keeffe who worked as a servant. He would have been just a baby when his namesake was killed.

Village of Ballydesmond today or Kingwilliamstown as it was known back then.

A brutal end for all
Paal Kanturk 1780

Somewhere near Kanturk in October of 1780 James Geran went to bed and never woke up again. During the night he was brutally beaten and stabbed in his sleep.

The following morning the body was found and reported to the police. Suspicions fell on the wife of the dead man, Julianna Geran, but it was felt she must have had an accomplice. The Geran's had two servants Catherine Donoghue and John Daly. Both ended up implicated in the case, as how could it have been committed without their knowing.

Early on Tuesday 24th of October a military party of Blackwater volunteers set out to Paal near Kanturk to capture Julianna and her suspected accomplices. The men were led by local officers Colonel Richard Aldworth from Anne's Grove, Lieutenant Colonel Stannard of Stannard's Grove and Captain Philpott of Bloomfield. With might on their side the men successfully arrested the three and transported them to Cork gaol to await a trial.

On Good Friday 1781 Julianna Geran was tried in Cork for the murder of her husband James. Also on trial for their lives were her two servants John Daly and Catherine Donoghue.

Once found guilty justice was to be swift and final. Under the Murder Act 1751 those found guilty had to be executed within two days unless the second day was a Sunday. The three were not just guilty of murder but also petty treason. Society at that time was all about keeping everyone in their place in the order that the upper classes felt appropriate. So when one kills a person above their station it was considered petty treason. Daly and Donoghue were guilty of killing their master and Julianna her husband, also her master. At the time if a man killed his wife it was murder, but for a woman to kill her husband it was petty treason as he was seen as her superior.

Julianna and Catherine received the sentence, "to be taken to place of execution and burned till dead". While John Daly punishment was to be hanged and quartered.

At Gallows Green in Cork on Easter Monday 16th of April 1781 the brutal punishment was to be carried out. The three were taken to the spot and allowed to pray for a while before meeting their destiny.

In the final moments Lord Tracton arrived with some further information concerning Catherine Donoghue. What she had not known was that morning he had been to court on her behalf armed with new evidence. Now he made it to Gallows Green just in the nick of time. It was enough to save her it seems but she was sent back to prison.

Julianna in her last words claimed she had encouraged her servants to kill her husband. She had strangled him but only after Daly had given him a few blows while sleeping. There was however nothing that could save her now and she was most likely telling the truth, or was she?

Catherine Donoghue had earlier made a statement. Even before she got a reprieve she never admitted any guilt. She claimed to not seeing the body until the morning after. His chest was stabbed with a needle and his arms had been broken. It was normal back then if guilty to admit it before meeting their maker. Anyone who didn't admit it on the scaffold was always afterwards considered innocent by the public but died anyway.

As the crime was not just murder but petty treason the punishment was even worse. Julianna Geran was publicly burned before a huge crowd. People normally flocked for hangings but a case like this would attract more attention because not many women were burned. This is believed to be the last burning of a woman in Ireland.

Often to ease their suffering the executioner would first strangle the woman so she would be unconscious at least before the fire got going.

Daly was hanged; he was likely to be alive but unconscious when his head severed from his body. The body was then quartered by hacking it up before the crowd.

Take That
Bluepool Kanturk 1898

Jeremiah Barrett married Hanora Buckley in Kanturk on the 20th of November 1870. It was remembered for years as being a great wedding. Jeremiah had returned from America where he was in the Army. He had enlisted the year after the American Civil War and was discharged three years later in April 1870. Now aged twenty six his employment status was a humble labourer. Hanora was the daughter of a Kanturk merchant, Sylvester Buckley. Jeremiah was paid a dowry. Kanturk was a thriving market town. Hanora, 19, was a dressmaker and maybe Jeremiah promised to take her away to America.

When folk married back then outside of what was called their class, it sometimes led to trouble, although in this case it would be decades later.

After getting married the couple travelled to Australia where he became a miner. Here they lived for some years and did well, until Jeremiah's health began to fail. They travelled to America, where their third child John was born in New York in 1887. Jeremiah re-joined the army.

A few years later a sister of Barrett's died suddenly and left him a considerable sum of money. The sum of money was entrusted to eldest son William to take care of. Jeremiah suspected that the money had been taken from him and blamed his wife Hanora. America was, as it is now a very litigious country and there was a lawsuit. This would never have happened in Ireland. Jeremiah ends up winning the case but never got his money back. The family do not live together anymore; Jeremiah leaves his job and disappears.

By now the eldest son William was about twenty and settled in America. Hanora decides to leave America and heads for home with their youngest child John now aged eight.

Arriving in Queenstown around June 1895 Hanora stood out from the Irish. She stood out so much that shortly after coming off the boat she was robbed of £200. Later though the thief was caught and the money recovered. She then headed for her elderly mother's house in Kanturk. Her father Sylvester had only died the year before at the grand age of eighty five. She stayed with her mother Mary in their house in Bluepool, Kanturk, and her brother Sylvester who continued his father's business dealing in clothes.

Not long after she arrived in Kanturk her husband Jeremiah turned up. He most likely got lodgings with his own people while she continued to stay with hers. The couple must have met at some point otherwise it would have been a wasted journey for him. After all he was there looking for the money or to get custody of his son John.

Either way without any incident Jeremiah Barrett left Kanturk again about ten days later and headed back to America. Nothing more was heard from him for some time.

On the 19th of February 1898 at eight of a Saturday morning Hanora was about to light the fire when in walked her husband into the kitchen. While she kneeled at the fireside he sat down and said "I'm here for my sister's money". She quickly replied that it was gone and that it had been sorted out legally in New York.

As she went to get up after lighting the fire he picked his moment. Sitting there like a scene from a Tarantino movie he calmly said "take that" and opened fire with a revolver. Two shots were fired and she fell to the floor. Her brother tried to intervene and Jeremiah turned the gun on him. As he made for the door Sylvester was shot in the back before the gun was turned on Hanora again. He fired another two shots at her while she lay on the ground to make sure he had done what he came for.

Now he headed for the bedroom, while Sylvester must have gone for help. Poor Mrs Buckley in all her eighty something years had surely never witnessed anything like it before. Worse still her daughter and son had been shot and she could be next, but young John was also in the house. Would this gunman shoot his own son?

Jeremiah found his youngest son aged only eleven. He now pointed the gun at him close range and pulled the trigger in another moment of madness. When he did all that was heard was a click. The gun only had five bullets and he had shot his wife four times and Sylvester once.

He then fled the house. Mrs Buckley had her wits about her and locked the door fearing he may return.

Meanwhile Sylvester had managed to get out of the house and raise the alarm despite being seriously injured. Sylvester had gone to the house of Sergeant Hutchinson who lived nearby.

By the time Jeremiah left the house the Sergeant was closing in on him fast. When Hutchinson saw the pistol he stopped for a second, he was unarmed and knew well what could happen. Instead of calling his bluff Hutchinson clearly said he was unarmed and asked him not to shoot. The sergeant then took a chance and rushed forward the twenty yards that was between them. In an instant he had disarmed Jeremiah and was taking him to the barracks. This wasn't going to be a case that needed much investigation.

Bluepool Kanturk near the scene of the shooting.

Half an hour later Jeremiah Barrett had been searched at the Barracks and cautioned by District Inspector Cosgrove. On him he had nine more bullets, a knife and £17 in notes and silver. The gun was an American Bulldog revolver which held only five bullets. Had he a colt with six bullets John would also have been shot. Cosgrove managed to get a statement from Jeremiah. Sylvester was well enough to also go to the barracks and make his own statement.

Back in Buckley's house Hanora was slumped on a chair in the kitchen in a bad way when Dr O'Leary arrived. Local priest Fr Brew also attended the scene as did the Head Constable Talbot. Sylvester however despite being only shot once was now found in bed in a far worse state than his sister.

Little could be done for their injuries there and then. Both were examined by the doctor. Hanora had five wounds caused by four bullets. She had been shot in the leg, chest, shoulder blade and twice in the arms. One of the bullets had exited and was found in her clothing but there was no hope of extracting the other three until her condition improved.

Sylvester had been shot only once in the back but the doctor found the left lung had been hit. Dr O'Leary thought there was little hope for Sylvester as infection would set in and he thought the area would become inflamed. Dr Walter Verling who was also a surgeon from Newmarket assisted Dr O'Leary.

On Sunday morning Sylvester's condition got worse and another doctor Dr Richard Leader from Millstreet was sent for. Despite their condition the victims gave statements before justice of the peace Mr Lysaght. To make matters worse Jeremiah was also present when they gave their statements.

When he laid eyes of Sylvester, Jeremiah said "I'm sorry I did not scalp you". He turned to his wife and said "Ah I know you, I'm sorry I did not scalp you, Believe me Willie will lose that money yet whatever part of the States he is in".

It was obvious now that Jeremiah had lost his mind and become obsessed by recovering his sister's money. He had earlier admitted to the police he had bought the revolver in America to kill his son William the year before.

Later that Sunday Jeremiah was brought before magistrate Major Hutchinson and charged with grievously wounding and attempting to kill his wife and brother-in-law. The statements taken from the victims were read out in court. Evidence was given by District inspector Cosgrove and Sergeant Francis Hutchinson told of the brave arrest.

Barrett was remanded into custody for eight days and was to be transferred to Cork Gaol. Hearing this, the prisoner said "your honour this court is only a farce".

By Monday the doctors had managed to extract one of the bullets from Hanora, her condition was improving and she was described as strong. There were still two further bullets to find but the doctors were confident that none of the vital organs had been hit. They planned to extract the other two and were confident she would recover if there were no further complications.

Her brother on the other hand was quite different, he was much weaker than her and the doctors had no idea where the bullet was. With every hour his condition got worse and they believed there was little hope for his recovery. Their last hope was that Dr Horace Townsend from Cork could find the bullet using X-Rays.

The first medical X-Ray had only occurred just over two years before. To the average man on the street back then if the bullet could be found by this new technology it would be nothing short of a miracle.

On Tuesday Hanora underwent surgery again and the last two bullets were successfully extracted. She was said to be making good progress. In Sylvester's case everyone suspected the worst but Townsend managed to complete an X-Ray. It revealed that the bullet was lodged close to his ribs. On entering the body the bullet took an unexpected course and its location would never have been found otherwise.

Now that they knew where it lay it would minimise the amount of surgery and for the first time they thought he might make a recovery.

Hanora's condition improved so much in the few days following that the doctors allowed her to go home where she could be nursed back to health. Her brother's recovery was much slower and his condition made no improvement so he stayed in hospital.

Within days Hanora's condition took a turn when infection set in. She was taken back to Hospital but there was little doctors could do without antibiotics to fight the infection. Her condition grew steadily worse as the days went on, her brother remained stable. Dr O'Leary and Dr Barry at the hospital did what they could for her but an abscess on one of her wounds was causing the infection. By early March her condition was very grave and now it was Hanora who had a slim chance of recovery.

On the 5th March Jeremiah was again brought before magistrates at the Cork Police Office. The district inspector again applied for a remand, saying the health of the victims was in such danger that the case could change. The application was granted.

In Kanturk on Saturday morning Hanora's condition was such that the priest was called to give her the last rites. At 11:30 she passed away at the hospital.

An inquest was organised for the following Monday and the Coroner notified.

This changed things dramatically for her husband; his frame of mind was such that he didn't grasp the consequences of his actions. He would now be charged with a capital crime for which the penalty was death.

The inquest was held on Monday in Kanturk by coroner James Byrne.

One of the witnesses was young John Barrett, who had suffered the terrible ordeal and now his mother was dead. Sylvester also gave a statement but did so from his bed at home. The police were represented by District Inspector Cosgrove and Sergeant Hutchinson.

Dr O'Leary and Dr Barry gave medical evidence describing the wounds and condition Hanora had suffered. The doctors said death was caused by exhaustion and syncope, loss of consciousness caused by her wounds. The verdict was obvious from the start - death was a result of bullet wounds caused by her husband.

A week later on St Patrick's Day Jeremiah was again before a magistrate and now charged with the wilful murder of his wife. Bizarrely he entered a plea of not guilty.

He was represented by Solicitor Barry from Kanturk who spoke for him. His solicitor was trying to show how his client was insane and ideally get the charge reduced to manslaughter. He applied to have the case postponed requesting it not be read till the next Assizes in the summer. The reasons he gave was that Sylvester was still not well enough to attend as witness. He also said Barrett spent time in America and had left paperwork there which pointed to the motive. The solicitor revealed that his client had previously been imprisoned in the states. This was related to the family dispute and the litigation between them. The solicitor mentioned his client's mental state saying the paperwork could prove it.

The prosecution pushed for the case to be heard at the Spring Assizes. The judge however said with capital charges they needed every light to be thrown on the case.

He agreed to postpone until the Assizes in the summer.

It was on the 18th of July that the case was heard at the Cork Summer Assizes. Several individuals were sentenced for lesser crimes and the case against Jeremiah Barrett was called. The charge was as before, the capital crime of wilful murder of his wife before Mr Justice Andrews. Two solicitors called Wright represented the crown prosecution case.

One of the prosecution solicitors began and outlined the facts of the case. He said there was no question of how Hanora had met her death and the prosecution would give evidence to prove it. There was also no denying it was premeditated, he had after all travelled thousands of miles with the sole objective of killing his wife. Jeremiah had even admitted to leaving Dublin to find a secluded location. There he hung a sheet of paper and practiced his shooting, just to make sure.

Wright said one question needed to be answered "whether the prisoner was legally responsible for his own act". The defence he said were going to argue that he was insane, yet the prosecution would prove otherwise.

Justice of the peace Mr Lysaght gave evidence that he had taken a statement from the deceased Hanora Barrett. The statement was then read out to the court. In it she told how he shot her four times. She actually saw her husband go and point the gun at their son. Hanora had admitted she thought that there was another bullet left but thankfully heard the click.

The eleven year old John was then called to give evidence against his own father. By doing this he would be ensuring that both his parents would soon be dead. John recalled the morning his father entered the kitchen and shook hands with him before he started on his mother. John said he actually saw his mother and uncle being shot and tried to flee after the first shots were fired.

Slyvester Buckley was now well enough to come to court and take the stand.

He told how when Jeremiah walked into the kitchen that morning he was in his bedroom off the kitchen saying his morning prayers. His brother-in-law said good morning to him and while the couple talked he went outside to get turf. While there he heard two shots being fired and ran in to the kitchen to help his sister. After being shot himself he ran outside to get help. Before the shots were fired he said his elderly mother was in bed.

During his time in jail Barrett had been very talkative and the police had several statements against him. Sergeant Leonard was in the barracks on the morning Barrett was arrested. The first question the accused asked him was "is she dead?"

While he took him to court later he started again saying "it's all over money, I'd have scalped her, I'd have satisfaction. I'm sorry I did not shoot the young lad in the legs. I'm sorry I did not do enough damage". Later that day Barrett told him he timed the murder knowing the Assizes was coming up soon. He told the policeman he had slept in Banteer the night before and got up at seven that morning to get to Kanturk early.

The head constable Mr Talbot had taken a statement from Barrett on the 9th of March after the inquest had been held. He read it out in court and it was allowed in evidence. In it he mentioned reading the newspapers in jail and following the case.

He said "I didn't mean to kill her right off just disable her and leave her no use"

Barrett also mentioned his disappointment when he wasn't heard at the Spring Assizes saying he didn't want to spend too much time in jail saying "I would get the thing over me".

It was a case where the prosecution didn't need to do much to prove Barrett had done it. Now they wanted to prove that he was sane and responsible for his actions.

Dr Thomas Moriarty from Cork male prison where Barrett had been held for the last four months was called to the stand. The doctor said during that time he had observed the accused and was now well able o form an opinion on his mental state.

The doctor was clear he believed Barrett was in fact quite sane. The only thing Moriarty noted was that Barrett "was a little fanciful" but showed no actual signs of insanity. After being admitted he had suffered not being able to sleep but was given medication to help.

One of the Barry's representing the accused decided to cross examine the doctor. The only thing the defence could do for their client was plead insanity and avoid the death penalty. Barrett himself was not helping his own case in this with his statements.

Barry asked several questions to the doctor about what conditions Barrett was suffering from. Moriarty described facial paralysis on his left side but was eating and sleeping well in prison. The doctor believed the paralysis was caused by a disease in the brain.

The prosecution called another doctor from the Cork District Lunatic Asylum.

Dr Oscar Woods had visited Barrett in the prison two or three times a week for the last few weeks. In his opinion Barrett's mental state was the same now as it was when he shot his wife. He believed that Barrett was sane. The doctor mentioned that he suffered from softening of the brain on one patch. This was the result of what the doctor called apoplexy or what we call today a stroke.

Barry again cross examined asking questions of the doctor to cast doubt on Barrett's mental state. He managed to get the doctor to concede to the fact that Barrett had a flawed logic. Barry asked "would you say he feels acutely or that he is capable of feeling about the death of his wife? I don't think it troubles him very much, nor his own position either.

The defence asked another question but the answer didn't help their case. "Nor the fact that he is on his trial here?" "He says there is too much bother about it altogether, that he would sooner have it over and be hanged."

Jurors then posed questions to the doctor; the first was about Barrett's brain.

Woods replied any man suffering from softening of the brain could not be totally sane but he knew what he was doing. He went on to say many suffered from similar conditions and led normal lives.

The prosecution then closed their case satisfied they had provided enough evidence to secure his conviction for murder.

Barry then addressed the jury making the case for his client. He admitted Barrett had reason to hate his wife but said "no man in his senses would turn upon his own innocent child and then boast to the police he was sorry he did not give the boy a bullet".

The defence solicitor despite not being a doctor disagreed with the medical evidence. He even described some of his client's statements as "rambling vapours of a lunatic that were not to be taken as admissions of guilt". Barry argued that the fact Barrett didn't care about being hanged proved he was not sane, nor conscious of his actions. The man was on trial for his life and he asked the jury to consider was he responsible for his actions on that day.

A juror then asked about Barrett's military career in American. His records from the Army were then read out for the court. He had enlisted in November 1866 and was discharged three years later. During his time in the army he served as a private in the 14th regiment.

No matter what Barry had said for his client the prosecution now got the last word to influence the jury. He merely asked that they not go with the argument of the defence. He claimed Barrett was indeed responsible and aware of his actions. Moriarty asked they find him guilty and hold him responsible before the law.

The judge went back over the case again before letting the jury decide the fate of Barrett's life. Justice Andrews remarked how there was no getting away from the fact Jeremiah Barrett did shoot his wife. Often in cases he said there was doubt but not in this one.

He also remarked how the law looked on everyone as being sane until proven otherwise. A long speech about the man's mental state and how it could affect the jury's decision was then given. The judge then went back over of all the evidence for the jury and clarified that it was their decision.

When they did leave the court, it didn't take them long to reach their verdict. About fifteen minutes later the foreman returned with the verdict of guilty.

After reading the verdict Barrett was asked had he anything to say but he didn't grasp what was happening. It was repeated to him and he started "oh yes a few words, my Lord. I believe since the creation of the world there never was such a case as mine. This money there is no mistake I gave it to the son. I got locked up for the son. She sued me and took advantage of me while I was in the Tombs in New York. I went to no jury. I sued the son and it went to the jury. I beat the son on the jury and my wife sends a letter over to the New York court saying I never had any call to the money any time and I got three weeks gaol in New York. She believed I was crazy. I am not crazy. I have no fault to find with you (referring to the judge). I got hard knocks from son, wife and brother-in-law. He is another drunkard. Now I don't care what this court does to me. I am ready to take the consequences because I believe I'll get a fair show on the other side".

The judge asked "is that all you have to say?" That is all my lord was the reply.

The judge addressed the now guilty man "you have had a very patient trial. I don't intend to make your position more painful than it must be at the present time and prolong an extremely painful scene, but I have a duty to discharge and the consequences that are to follow are not in my hands".

Now that he was found guilty the judge seemed to have some sympathy for his predicament. Barrett knew what was coming next. The judge put on the black cap which meant only one thing. The judge then began the usual speech. One life had been taken already now Jeremiah Barrett's life was forfeited as a result of his own actions. The judge sentenced him to be hanged at the Cork Gaol on 18th August 1898.

Barrett didn't cry out or make a scene like many in a similar situation. Instead he turned and was heard to thank the judge before being taken down.

It was not to end there however Barry applied to the Lord Lieutenant in Dublin to have the sentence commuted on grounds of Barrett's mental state. This was despite the fact that Barrett himself had said he was not crazy nor was he afraid of being hung.

Normally in such circumstances as we know the Lord Lieutenant would reply back that he had no intention of interfering with the course of the law. However in this case he did intervene in August and decided to change the sentence. Barrett was saved from the hangman's noose and now he would have to serve penal servitude for the remainder of his natural life. Barrett had already said he didn't wish to spend long in jail.

Despite what the doctors had said in court the general feeling was that Barrett was indeed suffering from some kind of madness. After the change in sentence he was removed from Cork County Gaol and transferred to Mountjoy.

Back in Kanturk young John remained living with his uncle Sylvester at the Buckley family house in Kathleen's Lane. Sylvester continued the family business dealing in clothes. Did Willie Barrett ever return from the states and learn of the dreadful consequences of what happened when his father could not find him?

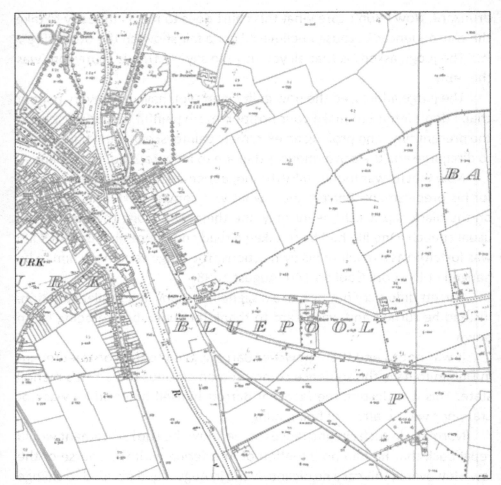

Map of Kanturk town and Bluepool.

A fatal shot
Cullen 1902

On Sunday night the 19th of January William Riordan from Dromiscane was shot in Cullen village close to the Kerry border. Several other men were present at the time but people struggled to come to terms with a motive. Most put it down to a pure accident. Why would anyone have shot him in plain sight of others? Surely such a person would wait until he was alone.

During the day twenty five year old William Riordan, a farm labourer, had been to a local football match and afterwards went to the village for a drink with friends. When the shot was fired several people were around the village but many fled immediately. Local Sergeant Patrick O'Sullivan and Constable Daniel O'Halloran came on a body at the side of the road. By now though there was nobody to be seen. Most likely the pair had heard the shot in the distance and hastened their approach. Riordan was lying in a pool of blood on the street but the body was still warm. It was obvious to them despite not being doctors that Riordan had no hope, blood had spurted from his jugular and formed a stream in the gutter. Messages were sent for a priest and doctor to attend.

William Riordan was well known locally; he had worked in England for a few years and had only returned a few months before. He had been living with his brother Michael, mother Margaret and stepfather Thomas Murphy who was better known as Tom the doctor. Thomas, a farmer, had married their mother 16 years before but earned his nickname working as a cattle doctor. It was common knowledge that William did not get on with his stepfather as was so often the case where a farm was involved.

Rumours spread that the crime was agrarian and the result of an eviction from a farm. Locals however knew that there were no foundations to these at all.

Despite having happened in the middle of a village nobody knew for sure what had happened. There were houses on both sides of the road and still nobody from them had seen anything or were they not willing to talk? It was no coincidence, however that the gun was also nowhere to be seen.

The following morning the village was swarming with police, District inspector Waters from Kanturk, County Inspector Gamble and many more. It was obvious to the police that more was known about the case but there was a reluctance to talk. The police notified the coroner and an inquest was organised for the following day.

On Tuesday the 21st the inquest was held at Maria Hickey's public house in the village of Cullen. A jury of twelve locals were sworn in to decide the reasons why Riordan died. The police county inspector and district inspectors from the county were present.

The first witness was Constable Daniel O'Halloran who arrived on the scene shortly after Riordan was shot. The constable explained how he was on patrol duty that night at eight with the sergeant when he heard the shot. They saw a man lying on the road near Andy Cronin's house and there were two men standing nearby. A pool of blood had gathered in the street, the body was still warm. The Sergeant he said found no signs of life from Riordan. A juror asked the constable had the body been moved at all. He replied that it had been moved to make room for a passing car.

The next witness was Denis Hickey, a thirty three year old farmer from Gortnacreha. He was better known as Denis Thade Hickey as another younger Denis Hickey lived in the village. Before he got the chance to say anything District Inspector Waters cautioned him about what he was about to say.

Hickey told how he was on his way home Sunday night and passed through Cullen. Near Andy Cronin's house he passed several men, the dead man had been one of them. The other two were John Connors and Richard Fitzgerald from Two Gneeves close by. There was another group on the street but Hickey said he didn't take any notice of them. Not a few paces after passing them he heard a shot. Looking around he saw Riordan on the street and the other two running away. He too fled the scene saying he was excited and scared.

Several questions were put to him by the jury and the coroner. One juror asked were the men arguing as he passed, but Hickey said it was quite the opposite they were laughing and joking.

Another witness from the village was called forward. Patrick Murphy, 77, was in his house that evening when he heard a noise which he at first thought was glass breaking. Looking out though he realised nobody had flung a stone through his windows. Outside he saw a body on the road and two or three men nearby who cleared across the fields. He had heard voices "Bill what ails you", "what happened to you" and "can't you get up".

Andrew Cronin was called whose house was nearest to the scene and right across from Patrick Murphy's. He had heard the shot but kept his door closed and did not go out that night according to himself.

Following this District Inspector Waters said the crown would call no further witnesses. He felt that enough evidence had been given for the jury to come to a verdict.

The only other witness called was Dr Thomas Ryan from Cullen. It was half eight that night before he examined the body and at that stage he thought Riordan was dead thirty minutes. That night he saw what he believed was a gunshot wound to the neck and the clothes were soaked in blood.

The following morning he performed a post-mortem with Dr Leader from Millstreet. They found a round bullet wound on the left side under the jaw line. He had found signs of powder near the wound on the skin. The bullet had hit the jugular vein and then passed through the spinal cord. It was found lodged in the base of the skull what the doctor described as the occipital bone. He concluded that cause of death was the severing of the spinal cord but no other injuries had been found on the body.

Several questions were put to the doctor regarding how far away had the shot been fired. Leader replied to the jury that he thought the shot had been fired at close range about three or four feet. He also revealed that the incident could indeed have been accidental. It didn't take the jury long to come to the verdict that "William Riordan of Dromiscane found dead at Cullen on the 19th of January 1902. We believe the cause of death was a gunshot wound inflicted on that date and that the occurrence was due to an accident".

Following their verdict the foreman offered their deepest sympathy to the mother and family of William Riordan.

Even before the inquest began that morning, developments had been unfolding in the case. The senior police who were present must have been aware but said nothing. The only explanation was they wanted to get the inquest out of the way and reveal as little evidence as possible.

It would now make sense why Sergeant O'Sullivan was not present at the inquest. He was otherwise engaged and up early that morning. At half four that morning the sergeant led a party of police to arrest Richard Fitzgerald from Gortnacreha. He was not hard to track down as he lived so close by and worked at the local Cullen creamery as a stoker.

Fitzgerald was taken to Killarney barracks where he was charged with the murder of William Riordan before resident magistrate McDermott. The magistrate remanded him into custody for eight days and later that day he was transported to Cork jail.

Once this was widely known the rumours in the area took another turn. Some still claimed it was an accident as there was no apparent motive. Riordan was known to own a pistol and there were reports he had it that night. After being drinking all evening it was easy to see him fooling around with a gun. Could it be by coincidence that he shot himself so fatally and the others fled in terror? Many felt something more sinister was at play and this was no ordinary shooting.

The police soon learned the men playing football that Sunday evening. They were John Riordan, Denis Hickey, Cornelius Lenihan, Maurice Connors, John Connors and obviously enough William Riordan. Afterwards the six went to Goulding's pub and had several drinks. Sometime after seven they left the pub and walked up the street when the shot was fired. The three that left the pub first were Denis Hickey, John Riordan and Maurice Connors. Following behind that night was the remaining three.

The local lads in Cullen village knew Riordan as a troublesome man who was not afraid of a fight. He was well built and at twenty five in his prime. He had fallen out with several from the village of Cullen. A few weeks before at a football match there was a row and Riordan had come out the worst of it. He sustained injuries sufficient enough to be laid up for several days and needing a doctor.

Afterwards Riordan issued threats of vengeance against his enemies. People that knew him felt he would be determined and single minded about it. Worse still it was rumoured he possessed a revolver and would use it. There was some foundation to this as two years before the Kanturk police searched his house and found one there. This was a result of his history in being involved in fights after drink had been taken. Riordan however never saw himself as being under threat at all saying he wasn't afraid of the boys from Cullen.

As the police pieced the case together the motive seemed to make more sense. They still took time to find evidence against Fitzgerald. He was called to court many times in January and February and charged only to be remanded back to custody again.

It was well into March before a magisterial investigation into the case got under way in Millstreet and started to hear witness evidence. Henry T Wright crown solicitor prosecuted with district inspector Waters. While Edward Beytagh solicitor Kanturk defended.

The first day the only significant witness called was Cornelius Lenihan and he now had plenty to say. He was in the village with Riordan that night. He recalled being there when Fitzgerald approached. He heard the accused say many in the village wanted to beat him for helping Riordan to the doctor in the past. Riordan laughed it off saying "there is no fear of that". The witness then saw Fitzgerald raise his arm and point towards Riordan. He did not see the revolver in the dark but saw the barrel of it as it was pointed at Riordan's ear. The single shot was then fired by Fitzgerald and the man dropped on the street. The shooter now grabbed his enemy by the collar and held him up in a sitting position. But then he left the body fall and stepped away and thrown the gun over a ditch. Lenihan then backtracked a little saying he had actually left the scene before the shooter.

When questioned by the defence Beytagh he was not as clear. Lenihan recalled how Fitzgerald had helped Riordan in a previous fight and afterwards took him to a doctor. He said Fitzgerald appeared sorry or shocked that night and had gently laid him in the road saying "my god". Nobody else went to his assistance that night except the man who shot him he said.

Weeks later on Saturday the 10th May the case was called in Millstreet Court and would hear the remaining evidence.

Dr Richard Radley Leader the eminent general practitioner from Millstreet was called. He gave evidence as he had done at the inquest, the cause of death was clear enough.

The next witness was Timothy Mahony who was the Cullen Creamery manager.

He said he was returning home that night to Cullen in a side car when he came on a gang of people on the road. He discovered then a body was on the road and was held up until it was cleared to the side. At work in the creamery the next day Fitzgerald never mentioned the night before. Under cross examination by Beytagh it emerged that many more were present that night. He revealed that it was Fitzgerald who stepped forward as Mahony's horse approached and said there is a body on the road. Then Fitzgerald went back to the body held the head and said "my god he is dead". Then several others helped him clear the road and Mahony passed by.

Sergeant Sullivan gave evidence of having come on the body that night. He said approaching the village he encountered people leaving in two's and three's but nobody reported to him what had occurred. The body was lying on his back on the road, with blood flowing down the gutter. Sergeant Sullivan reached down and put his hand on his chest and it still felt a little warm. There was no one around to help. The body was moved to Mrs Hickey's house in the village. The following day he searched the area. He found only a penknife and a halfpenny.

Sullivan then told of the arrest saying Fitzgerald had verbally given a statement.

He proceeded to recall the statement but Beytagh objected. The Sergeant said he himself had written down what the accused said half an hour after. It was clarified that these notes were only to aide his memory and could not be used as actual evidence.

In the statement Fitzgerald had asked who was giving evidence against him after he was arrested. Later he said "what a queer thing I would do to a man whom I took on my back to the doctor not long ago".

Sergeant Leonard from Kanturk took the stand and said he searched Fitzgerald's house. In it he found three pin fired revolver bullets in a press. Upstairs in a bedroom another revolver bullet was found but of a more conventional type.

District Inspector Waters gave evidence of the investigation he had led. He told how exhaustive searches had been made for the gun but it was never found. This was despite the evidence that it had been thrown over a ditch near the scene.

Mr Beytagh's argument was there was no evidence against his client to prove it was a premeditated crime. He said it was Fitzgerald who shot the gun but held that it was purely accidental.

The judge decided that a case existed against Fitzgerald and he would be tried before a jury on the capital charge. Mr Wright objected to him getting bail and he was sent back to prison till the next Assizes which were held in the summer.

During the Cork Summer Assizes in late July Richard Fitzgerald was called before Lord Chief Justice. He pleaded not guilty on the charge of wilful murder of William Riordan.

The crown prosecution brought all the big guns to try the case. The Solicitor General Mr James Campbell, Redmond Barry and a Mr Moriarty. For the defence was a solicitor Mr O'Sullivan and Edward Beytagh from Kanturk.

The jury was selected from a large panel, several were objected to by the defence and more by the prosecution were asked to stand down. During the proceeding one name was called Richard Baker. Baker was a Quaker and objected to being on a jury where capital punishment was involved. The judge gave in and excused Baker from the case.

A much quieter scene in Cullen Village.

Robert Peard a boot maker from Ballintemple also objected saying he would not want to be responsible for hanging a man. This time though the Lord Chief Justice tried to shrug off the objector telling him he would find a verdict. Peard however was insistent he would not come to a guilty verdict of murder and would always choose manslaughter to save a life. The judge was not going to be swayed saying how he would not excuse him.

The solicitor general opened the case giving a long speech of the circumstances surrounding the case. He asked the jury to search their own conscience but seemed to favour a severe penalty. He claimed there was some kind of bond between the men on the street that night. He also felt not all the witnesses were telling as much as they could.

The first witness was Denis Thade Hickey and gave testimony as he had before.

John Riordan when called told the court he was a cousin of the deceased man. That night he was in the first group of three men to leave. Fitzgerald approached them and held a gun across his chest. They walked on though leaving the village and Fitzgerald went towards the village. Later he heard a shot but was afraid to go back and see what had occurred.

Cornelius Lenihan again gave evidence of being there when Riordan was killed.

When they encountered Fitzgerald that night he shook hands with Riordan, asked Connors did he have a penknife and said goodnight to Lenihan. After giving similar evidence as he had previously he answered questions. The witness replied to the judge saying it could not have been accidental. He said Fitzgerald raised the gun and held it within an inch and a half of the man's ear. This was clearly not a man fumbling with a gun that went off in error. John Connors, the other man who was there that night, gave similar evidence to Lenihan.

Finally for the prosecution Dr Leader gave the medical evidence and produced the bullet he had found in the head.

The defence then called witnesses who they claimed would prove that the deceased and the accused were in fact friends.

A man who came on it that night was Jeremiah Goulding. He heard William Riordan tell Fitzgerald "there is no fear of that". He said Fitzgerald replied pulling the gun "there is no fear while I have this" and pointed it directly at him. The witness admitted to the Solicitor General to telling lies in the past about what he saw. Before he didn't want to get involved and claimed to have seen nothing. When asked was he in a secret society of some sort the witness denied it. Campbell then asked did the Parish Priest denounce from the altar a secret society in Cullen but again Goulding denied any knowledge of it.

Timothy Fitzgerald recalled the 22nd of December last when there was a fight on the street outside his house. That night William Riordan dared any man in Cullen to fight him for a pound. That night he got a beating and needed a doctor afterwards. Fitzgerald was also in Cullen on the night Riordan was shot. When he passed he saw Richard Fitzgerald with a revolver in his hand. He was laughing with Riordan. Moments later he heard a shot fired.

Several more witnesses were called not just friends of the dead man. These included Denis Thade Hickey and Timothy Mahony the Creamery Manager.

After hearing the witness statements it was O'Sullivan who spoke for the defence.

There was no denying his client had fired the gun. The solicitor stated that it was because of his behaviour afterwards that proved he was not guilty. He directly asked the jury to return a verdict of not guilty against Richard Fitzgerald.

The judge summed up all the evidence again for the jury and at ten past five they left the courtroom. Before six the foreman returned with a verdict of guilty of manslaughter.

The lord chief justice then started the sentencing saying had he been found guilty of murder he would have lost his life. He said that the jury had taken a lenient and merciful view of the case, "you owe your life to the jury who tried you".

Fitzgerald thanked the jury for their verdict. The judge went on "in deference to the verdict of manslaughter, I sentence you to what I consider under all circumstances to the very lenient sentence of ten years". The crowd in court were shocked at the sentence and quickly Fitzgerald was removed.

Was the verdict always going to be manslaughter? Could the whole proceedings be argued a mistrial? The judge should have dismissed the juror Peard when he was morally against committing a man to die. Maybe this one juror convinced the others and they came to the decision of manslaughter. The judge believed the sentence was lenient but he had no one to blame but himself. The crowd in court were equally surprised but now nothing could be done.

Maybe it was Robert Peard that Fitzgerald should have thanked for his life. Now instead of facing the scaffold he would be released from prison in 1912 aged about forty.

Some of the Solicitor General's questions to one witness touched a raw nerve. The parish priest having heard he was mentioned wrote to the solicitor general and turned up at the trial to find it over.

Within a week it had led to questions being asked of the Attorney General in the House of Commons. The parish priest Fr O'Sullivan made several statements denying any existence of a secret society in the village. His claim was he could not denounce a society he did not believe existed in the first place. The parish priest was worried the area would have its name blackened by these insinuations.

No matter what the priest said there is something not quite right about a shooting in front of others. How did Richard Fitzgerald think he could possibly get away with it in a village with so many around? This was how the theory of a secret society began, his comrades would be sworn to not give evidence against him. However the two that where there that night did give evidence otherwise he might have got off.

A long standing dispute
Ballyshonock Kildorrery 1923

On Sunday the 16th of September 1923 Michael Walsh left the village of Kildorrery heading home to his farm in Ballyshonock. He had been to the last mass having left home at eleven that morning in a pony and trap. After mass many were travelling in lorries to go to a hurling match in Buttevant. Walsh didn't go to the match he turned for home before two in the afternoon for his dinner.

The country had just months before emerged from one of the bloodiest periods of history - the Civil War. People could now go about their normal lives in peace. But that was not the case for Michael Walsh on that Sunday afternoon.

As he turned into the boreen leading to his farm house a shot rang out.

A servant in Walsh's farmhouse ran out into the yard knowing the shot was close by. The pony and trap came galloping into the yard with Michael Wash thrown facedown inside.

When the pony was caught and settled down Mary unshackled the pony and then dragged her employer out of the trap. She found blood on his coat and inside the trap, Michael was dead.

She ran to neighbours to get help but nothing could be done. Another neighbour and cousin of the dead man went to Kildorrery to fetch the priest and inform the guards.

Mary probably knew the moment she heard the shot what it was all about. It was a murder of revenge and not political but rather agrarian. She had worked for her employer for seven years, in the last two years there was some trouble about land.

Michael Walsh had lived and farmed in Ballyshonock all his life. He was 53 year old unmarried man living with his sister and farm workers. In 1902 he had taken another farm of seventy acres in nearby Tankardstown for grazing. The tenants of the farm had been evicted and not many wanted to get involved. The agent John Therry encouraged Walsh to take on the land with favourable rent. The Land League was active back in 1902 and many denounced Therry calling him a grabber.

More recently though a man had returned from America and reclaimed this farm. Threats were issued to Walsh on many occasions and he was dispossessed of the farm against his wishes. Many in the area had turned against Walsh or were forced to. At one time leading to the village the words "boycott the grabber Walsh" were tarred to a wall.

Now with Michael Walsh lying dead on the flat of his back in his own yard the people of the area were shocked. Many however could guess who was behind it and soon the guards would know too.

The local curate from Kildorrery Fr Barrett arrived on his bicycle and read him his last rites. It was almost five before the guards arrived to begin their investigation.

On Tuesday the 18th an inquest was held at Thornhill's Hotel Kildorrery on the body of Michael Walsh. Coroner Richard Rice presided over the inquest with a jury of twelve local men. The state solicitor Mr Daniel Casey represented the authorities while a Mr O'Brien was for the next of kin of the deceased. Sergeant Higgins from Mitchelstown was also present as he was investigating the case.

Medical evidence was given by Dr David Barry from Kilworth who had carried out the post mortem. He told the jury about finding three gunshot wounds in Michael Walsh's back. One gunshot entered about six inches from the spine and went right through the body hitting the liver. Another wound penetrated the kidney and also exited the body. The third wound was lower down and remained lodged in the body. The doctor concluded he had been shot from behind to his left and it was at close range.

Michael Linnane revealed to the inquest he had got a lift home from mass with Michael Walsh that day. When Walsh had turned into his own boreen Linnane got down and walked away. A few steps later he heard a shot and a loud scream. Turning around Linnane said he saw two men with guns running away inside a field at the other side of the fence. He went on to say they wore raincoats and caps but Linnane failed to recognise them.

When questioned by solicitor Casey, Michael Linnane told how his daughter was Mary Linnane who worked for Michael Walsh. Not two weeks before Michael Linnane was woken from his bed early one morning. A man outside threatened him to prevent his daughter working for Walsh and to keep away from the farm himself. Michael Linnane told the jury he was aware Michael Walsh had some trouble over another farm.

Mary Linnane gave evidence having been at Walsh's and also heard the shot that day. She ran out of the farmhouse to see the pony and trap enter the yard. Her employer was slumped over on his hands and face. After a few minutes she raised the alarm, she knew he was dead.

It did not take the jury long to come to their verdict "that the deceased died from shock and haemorrhage following gunshot wounds inflicted by some person or persons unknown, and that such person persons were guilty of wilful murder".

On the same day as the inquest, Michael Walsh's funeral took place as was the custom in the countryside then. He was buried at the family plot at St Mologga's graveyard to the east of Kildorrery.

The road in Ballyshonock close to where Walsh was shot.

The guards under Sergeant Higgins scoured the countryside in pursuit of the perpetrators. In early October there were four arrests made so swiftly on a Saturday night that people in the country hardly knew who they were. The four were taken to Fermoy barracks under the watch of inspector Sean Sutton. Another was arrested on Sunday and also brought to Fermoy Barracks. All five were to appear before the district court at its next sitting on the following Wednesday.

On Monday the 8th of October the Fermoy District court was in session and Solicitor Carroll for the five arrested men questioned their arrest. He applied to Judge O'Farrell for a copy of the charges against his clients but got nothing. O'Farrell said he knew nothing of the matter as it was in Mitchelstown area. Carroll continued and said the barracks where the men were held had been condemned on medical grounds. Then Carroll admitted he was told the case would come before Fermoy District court today. The judge insisted he had no knowledge of it all and could do nothing that day.

By the time it did come before Mitchelstown District court everyone had a good idea of who was arrested. On that day people congregated outside to see the men being taken into court. They were Thomas Fitzgerald, John Hannan and John Bermingham all from Meadstown near Kildorrery. The other two were Patrick Hannan, Tankardstown and John Shinnick from Old Castletown. The guards were still investigating the case so the five ended up being continually remanded in custody until mid-November.

On the 13th of November at Mitchelstown District court justice Farrell began hearing evidence relating to the case. Mr D Casey state solicitor was for the prosecution, while Anthony Carroll still represented the five accused. Despite the amount of time that had passed the courtroom was packed with the general public eager to hear some details of the shooting.

Inspector Sutton began by submitting a statement accused Thomas Fitzgerald had previously given.

"My father was evicted on the 30th May 1879 and was let in as caretaker on the same day at one penny per week. We were a family of nine children and needless to say in a bad way. This went on until 1883 when Patrick Mahony Kildorrery for a debt of £30 or thereabouts due by my father, got an injunction in the Queen's Bench Dublin and bailiffs and police were sent on two occasions. Mahony fell into difficulties and mortgaged this place and others to the Bank of Ireland and being unable to pay the farm subsequently became the property of the bank. This was in or about 1900. The bank put the place up for sale by private treaty but no buyer came forward. After several attempts to dispose of the property the bank surrendered their title to it and Mahony again held it up to

1903 when it was taken possession of by the deceased Michael Walsh of Ballyshonock Kildorrery. Possession was given to him by John Therry the agent of Springvale Kildorrery and one year's rent was remitted as an inducement. He was declared a grabber by the Land League at Kildorrery at the time. Michael Walsh held the place up to the 11th March 1922 when I took possession and held it until the 7th June 1923 when the Free State troops arrested me."

Carroll immediately objected to the statement being allowed as evidence against his client. It turned out the statement had been made to the Evicted Tenants Association and Carroll knew nothing about it until it was read out.

Sergeant Higgins then took the stand and explained how he was involved in the investigation of the case. On the 19th of September he took a statement from Patrick Hannan. At that stage Hannan was not yet a suspect but was interviewed as he lived locally. In his statement Hannan had detailed his movements from the Friday before the shooting till the Monday after. He had gone to the first mass the day of the shooting and returned home after ten. He had breakfast before attending to a sick cow. Hannan then went hunting with a man called Willie Clohane before returning home at two. Hannan claimed to have his dinner at about half past two before again feeding his sick cow. He then went through a few fields to get a few loads of soil and returned home again at half three when he met Fr Barrett and they talked for a few minutes. He stayed at home for the remainder of the afternoon and milked the cows about six. Later that evening he called to his sister Catherine Shinnick, she was the wife of John Shinnick who was also accused.

Patrick Hannan told how he knew Michael Walsh and about the trouble over the farmland. He admitted that both he and his brother in law John Shinnick had rented some of the disputed land from Thomas Fitzgerald. Most of the land was in grass and hay had been cut on what he called Fitzgerald's farm. They also kept cattle there until when Walsh was reinstated and their cattle driven off by the military. Later he said Walsh kept his cattle there but they were also driven from the land as the dispute rumbled on. Hannan said he was not friendly with Walsh before but afterwards Walsh refused to talk to him. He also revealed that the Farahy Creamery refused to take milk from Michael Walsh.

After hearing this statement the Judge, Casey and Carroll discussed the best way to proceed with the case. Mr Carroll objected to the way the case was being heard over many days causing hardship to his clients who were in custody all this time. They were constantly being brought from jail to court house and back. He wanted to see the case heard at a special sitting at either Fermoy or Cork and being dealt with sooner rather than later. Justice Farrell agreed to arrange a special sitting but remanded the five back into custody again until the next sitting of the court.

Village of Kildorrery around the time of the murder.

The following week Farrell kept his word and a special sitting of Fermoy District court was held on Monday the 19th to hear more evidence. Now more time could be given to the case so it would be dealt with faster and the prisoners either released or returned for trial.

The first witness was guard P Doherty who had taken a voluntary statement from John Shinnick. In the statement Shinnick told how he left home on the 15th of September and went to Lisdoonvarna for his holidays until the 23rd. During his time on holidays the guards arrived and asked when he had left home. They also asked about the whereabouts of his gun. He was not sure where the gun was. He told them it was either at home or at his brother in law Pat Hannan's house. They asked him several questions about the gun how many cartridges he had and where they were bought. The cartridges he had were Murray No5; he had bought fifty, several weeks before and had given twenty five to Pat Hannan.

John Shinnick's statement is at first confusing. He refers to two Pat Hannan's - his brother in law and his cousin. Further research reveals that he is referring to the same person. Simply put John Shinnick was married to his first cousin Catherine Hannan. Their mothers Julia Fox and Mary Fox were sisters. Thomas Fitzgerald was also connected as his sister Ellen was married to John Hannan.

To Doherty, Shinnick had admitted to loaning the shotgun to his brother in law Patrick Hannan three weeks before.

In court Doherty recalled how he had taken a statement from Thomas Fitzgerald on the 25th of September. The statement was read over at the time and Fitzgerald had signed it. Solicitor Carroll objected when Casey asked for the statement to be read out in court. The statement was however read out and admitted as evidence.

In it Fitzgerald detailed his movements from the Friday night before to the Sunday night of the killing. According to the statement Fitzgerald got out of bed at nine that morning. He went to the last mass at eleven thirty (as did Michael Walsh) in Kildorrery. Afterwards he went to Roche's in Carhue to see about going to the match in Buttevant but found they had already left. He then went for a drink or two with Pat Coughlan in O'Dwyer's pub. Afterwards he got a lift home in Coughlan's trap. No dinner was ready as his sister was sick in bed. At quarter to two he left by bike for Buttevant and recalled meeting a man called Farrell at Shanballymore at about two. He reached Buttevant at three having missed the first half of the match. After the matches Fitzgerald cycled back to Kildorrery where he had two drinks in David Collins pub before heading home.

At the end of the statement the guard had written below Fitzgerald's signature, "I noticed Thomas Fitzgerald was in a very shaky condition". This led to a long debate in court that this note could not be used in evidence against Fitzgerald. After several objections by Anthony Carroll the prosecution relented and allowed the note on the statement to be disregarded. Casey however said that note was there and could later be used as evidence when the time was correct.

Doherty continued giving evidence and moved on to a statement he had taken from John Bermingham on the 23rd of September. Again Anthony Carroll as pointless as it was, objected to the statement being read but they carried on regardless. Doherty explained how the statement had been given voluntarily and he had asked no questions.

Bermingham was a teacher and younger than the others, at first it's not obvious his connection to the others. His mother was Julia Hannan so he was related to them and often in their company.

The statement like the others detailed his movements that Sunday in September. Bermingham said he was up early and took milk to the creamery before going to the first mass at eight. He then returned home for breakfast and stayed home all day until three in the afternoon. During that time John and Nellie Baker called before two. He then went out for a walk with them after three. Later that evening he met up with John Hannan.

After reading the statement Carroll asked the witness Guard Doherty several questions. There was some controversy about how many times he had met Bermingham and what questions he asked. Doherty however denied telling Bermingham he had received further information. It was suggested he had told Bermingham a witness had seen him in a field where his statement says he was at home until three.

The guard then moved on to a statement he had taken from John Hannan and of course Anthony Carroll objected again but the statement was allowed.

It started with "I John Hannan do hereby state I was up between six thirty and seven on Sunday the 16th". He then went to first mass at Kildorrery and arrived home about ten, where he stayed until one in the afternoon. He left at one to go hunting near Burn's Rock and pursued a fox towards Bowenscourt. At about two Hannan estimated he was a mile from Farahy and didn't hear a shot from that direction. He stayed hunting until six that evening.

His statement then reveals that Thomas Fitzgerald lived in his house. On that day he did not see Fitzgerald between leaving for mass until he returned from the match about eight. Hannan at first declined to mention about the trouble his friend Fitzgerald had with the farm. But he admitted to have had cattle grazing on the disputed farm before Walsh reclaimed it. Hannan continued telling how he was not friendly with Walsh saying he was a cross man. Hannan said he was shocked when he heard Walsh had been shot and had never thought it would have gone this far.

Anthony Carroll declined to question the guard who had taken so many statements from the accused. The five men were then remanded back into custody until another hearing. Even John Shinnick who claimed to be on holidays in Clare when the shooting took place was remanded. Surely it could have been proven where he was and he could be released or charged with a lesser crime or none at all.

It was obvious that the prosecution was struggling to come up with evidence against the five men. The five ended up being held in custody until the next evidence was heard on the 3rd of December. By now the five men had spent over two months in custody without any evidence being produced. At this point the only thing the prosecution had against them was motive.

When the court sat again in early December the prosecution had arranged several witnesses. Daniel Dwane a thirty one year old labourer was called to the stand. He told how on the 21st of September he worked at Patrick Hannan's farm. That day the ricks or wynds as they called them of hay were being brought into the haggard. He said the hay had been settling in the field for several weeks so they could be brought in on a float complete. In the haggard they piked the hay into bigger ricks to be stored for the winter. While the men were hard at work a coat and hat were discovered hidden among the hay. One of the workmen gave it to Patrick Hannan; he checked the pockets and found a mask inside. It was suggested to him to report it to the guards as an investigation was going on. When asked by Carroll, Dwane said Patrick Hannan made no attempt to hide the coat nor was he reluctant to report it.

Another witness was produced who worked at Patrick Hannan's, a young labourer called Daniel Hannan. Daniel recalled the 16th of September and being at Patrick Hannan's that day. He had returned from mass about half twelve to Hannan's where he worked. Having had his dinner he left to go to Farahy about two. While walking on Hannan's boreen towards the public road he heard a shot. Walsh was shot about five hundred yards away and he heard a scream after the shot. The distance between Walsh's yard and Patrick Hannan's he estimated at 800 yards. Daniel then went on to talk about the 21st September when the coat was found. He was also working there at the time.

When Anthony Carroll got his chance to question, he struck a deadly blow to the prosecution. He simply asked Daniel "when you left Hannan's yard after dinner on that Sunday where was the accused Patrick Hannan". Daniel replied "in the yard as I left him a few yards from the door". Then again what else would Daniel say about his employer and relation. But then he revealed that Patrick Coughlan was also in the yard that day.

It was still all too close for comfort despite what Daniel said. Both farms, Patrick Hannan's and Walsh's were at either side of the road to Quitrent mountain. To get from Patrick Hannan's to where Walsh was shot, was through several fields which were the disputed land. If Walsh had been shot from behind it would have been from someone standing in one of the disputed fields.

Guard Doherty was called again to give evidence concerning the investigation. He told how on the 19th of September he went to Patrick Hannan's. When asked if he had a gun, the initial answer he got was no. After further questions Patrick admitted to having a gun he did not own nor had he a permit for. The gun as we know already was John Shinnick's. When asked Doherty described the gun as a single barrel shot gun.

Carroll objected immediately saying "that is not evidence". The solicitor continued saying Hannan should have been cautioned when he was asked about the gun but he was not. He went on "that is the law, this is a new policy, and we are borrowing it from the French Republic". The judge though disregarded him saying it was evidence.

The next witness was Lieutenant Michael Joseph Burke of the Free State Army.

He was in charge of the military in Kildorrery until October of this year 1923. Burke went on to explain how as there was no guards stationed there at that time, he in effect was acting for both military and police matters in the village.

He knew Patrick Hannan as he had asked for a gun permit several times that summer. On the 19th of September he went to Hannan's and took possession of a shotgun and cartridges. Three days later Hannan came to him and reported finding a coat and hat hidden in hay.

The prosecution then asked Burke about the murdered man Michael Walsh.

He admitted to knowing him, as Walsh had come with several complaints. Burke then revealed that since Walsh had reclaimed the land he was under military protection for some time. Burke admitted to knowing all about the disputed farm but was not present in June when it was cleared. He said it was cleared on the 6th or 7th of June by a special infantry battalion. Since then he knew of several incidents on the farm in question.

Burke was however in Kildorrery at the time of the clearance and interviewed Thomas Fitzgerald. They were obviously suspicious of him at the time and searched him at the barracks. On him was several rounds of .45 ammunition and he was then held for a further two days. He made no signed statement during that time but Burke advised him to take the case to a civil court and not deal with it himself.

Carroll for the defence asked the witness several questions about Patrick Hannan. Burke said he believed up to a time that year that Patrick Hannan was a quite inoffensive man and he had approved his application for a gun permit.

Once the prosecution got their chance, Casey jumped at the opportunity of asking when Burke's opinion of Patrick Hannan had changed. Burke explained it was some time in August he then believed that Hannan should not have a gun. Casey continued but the Lieutenant refused to answer why he changed his mind saying it was a military matter.

Anthony Carroll was glad that the Lieutenant had not gone further as it may have incriminated his clients in a way that was detrimental to the case.

Commandant Guerin of the National Army Kilmallock gave evidence of having examined the shotgun which was produced in court. In his opinion the cartridge fired was not the usual type; it had three slugs or swandrop shots in it. This is how he accounted for the fact that only one shot was fired yet Walsh had been hit three times. Normally he said that shotgun used No.2 or No10 cartridges.

After another week in custody the five were back in court and further witnesses called. Patrick Coughlan was a fifteen year old lad who worked on Patrick Hannan's farm. He was questioned at length about making the hay and when the coat had been found. Carroll then moved to the day Walsh was shot. The witness recalled it well saying they all had dinner together at about twenty past two. Patrick Hannan, his mother and Daniel Hannan were present. The dinner was finished about twenty to three and Daniel left afterwards. Coughlan then left going to McGrath's farm which was close by. Sometime later he heard Walsh had been shot from a man Kennedy who was running to fetch the priest. He went back to Hannan's and Patrick was still there outside the house, he estimated the time to be after three.

When William McGrath was called, he had different times to previous witness. McGrath said Coughlan called to his house about two that day. It was about ten past he claimed when John Kennedy passed by running to get the priest. McGrath remarked that he had not heard a shot fired that day despite being about 700 yards from the scene.

Farmer William Clohane who was originally from Rockmills but recently occupied a farm in Tankardstown was called to give evidence. His farm was almost between Walsh's, Pat Hannan's and the land in dispute. Clohane said he had been out hunting with Patrick Hannan up to two the afternoon Walsh was shot. There was nothing shocking in this as Hannan had admitted the same in his statement.

The court hearings rumbled on weekly through December, all the time the five men were held in custody after each day in court. It soon became obvious that none of the five were going to be released any time soon. Christmas came and went. It was early January before more evidence would be heard. Why Anthony Carroll didn't protest further on behalf of his clients as they were now in jail for over three months.

The slow process started again in January of weekly sessions with more witnesses. More statements for the accused were read out going back over evidence that had been heard previously. In one statement by Patrick Hannan he admits to paying Thomas Fitzgerald £2 8s for a month's grazing for seven or eight cattle. That was of course before Michael Walsh regained possession. Inspector Sutton read several statements all from Patrick Hannan which were quite similar.

The next witness however was going to add weight to the motive for the prosecution. He was Thomas Mannix, manager for Castle Dairy near Kildorrery for several years. Mannix knew Michael Walsh as he had supplied milk to the creamery for years. He said John Hannan came to him in June 1923 and asked "would he join the ranks" but the manager refused to get involved. It went on "are you going to boycott the milk of Michael Walsh" but again he refused. John Hannan then threatened that several other farmers would stop supplying to the creamery. While this was going on in the office several other farmers waited outside in support of Hannan's demands.

The state solicitor was busy in January on other matters and more than once the hearings had to be postponed. On the 22nd of January the five were called at Mitchelstown Court after the district court business had ended. Same as the week before the State Solicitor Mr Casey was not in court when the time came. Inspector Sutton applied for the case to be adjourned again for another week.

Now Anthony Carroll finally took the opportunity and protested to the judge. He said the state either needed to proceed with the case or discharge the accused. Carroll even took on some of the blame for it himself but now he would apply to the Attorney General to deal with it.

The judge claimed to have no option on several occasions but to remand the accused. He then passed most of the blame to the state solicitor and his non appearances saying he was otherwise engaged in Cork City.

Carroll then appealed to the judge to discharge John Bermingham as there was no evidence against him and he was never mentioned in any statements. He said John Shinnick was in Lisdoonvarna when the murder took place and should also be discharged. He wanted the case brought to a conclusion for his client's sake saying they were brought all over the county every week and then back to jail.

Carroll left the court frustrated with the proceeding or lack of them that day.

He was not gone thirty minutes when Casey eventually turned up. The state solicitor then agreed that John Bermingham should be discharged but did not mention John Shinnick. He again applied for a remand for the remaining four until the following Tuesday. Casey was still confident he would produce evidence against the remaining four accused men.

When the court sat again on the afternoon of 29th of January, Carroll pressed for the case to be held again the next day. Casey again was the problem he could not attend so the case would still take weeks more. Carroll was keen to move the case on and have several days hearings together.

The first witness examined that day was Johanna Walsh sister of Michael Walsh.

She told how she had lived with him and both of them had never married. Her brother she said acquired the Tankardstown farm in 1902 and held it until March 1922. She recalled Sunday 11th of March 1922 when her brother's horses came into the yard from the Tankardstown farm. Her brother took back the horses and went to mass. The horses came back again but this time Thomas Fitzgerald was standing at the end to their boreen shouting. They later found a keep out sign on the gate of the farm. She said from that Sunday until June of 1923 Fitzgerald then had possession.

When her brother regained possession in 1923 the horses and cattle he had on the land were stolen. On the same day in July of 1923 all three of their farm workers left together. The defence declined to cross examine Johanna knowing they could gain nothing from it.

More witnesses were called that day in court. Mary Linnane the servant gave evidence as she had done at the inquest. Several men gave evidence of the whereabouts of Thomas Fitzgerald that day. It all however tied in with the statement he had given last September.

The case dragged on at the same slow pace which seemed to suit the prosecution and their lack of ability to produce evidence against the four men. In early February parish priest from Kildorrery Richard Aherne took the stand.

He had tried to intervene in the case previously when walls and houses in the village were tarred. He said Thomas Fitzgerald had denied at the time tarring the walls. The priest was not able to give any direct evidence nor did he admit trying to find a settlement between the disputing parties.

Michael Linnane father of Mary Linnane then told the court how he had worked for Michael Walsh from time to time over the course of thirty years. Michael told how he was still working for Walsh up to his death but had been threatened to stop. He recalled a Sunday in June 1923 seeing Thomas Fitzgerald driving Walsh's cattle and horses from the Tankardstown farm.

He then moved on to being in the trap with Walsh coming home from mass on the 16th of September 1923. He had already given this evidence at the inquest shortly after the murder. The inquest however was not interested in who done it the prosecution did.

Casey asked "after the shot was fired did you see anything or anybody". Linnane said he saw two men running along the ditch going fast. Casey asked did he recognise one of the men and he replied "yes sir". The court waited with baited breath for the answer of the next question "who was that man" "Thomas Fitzgerald the accused". The witness then admitted seeing the other man's face but did not know him.

Linnane was sure it was Thomas Fitzgerald he had seen running away with a gun. Carroll cross examined the witness asking why he had not identified Fitzgerald in previous statements but gained no information.

The following week John Hannan was sick in prison and unable to attend. The court was adjourned. It was just another setback in a case that seemed to go on forever.

Not much more happened in February that year, even March passed by with the men being remanded on several occasions. At a hearing in late March, Casey relented to the defence and John Hannan was discharged on the charge of murder. Casey warned that there could be other charges against him in the future. The other three were sent back to prison for yet more time.

Now there was three, Thomas Fitzgerald seen at the scene with a gun. Patrick Hannan was hunting nearby at the time. John Shinnick had been in Lisdoonvarna at the time but had lent a gun to Hannan.

On Saturday the 5th of April at Fermoy Courthouse there were revelations that could change the outcome for the case.

Casey wasted no time and got straight to the point, since the last hearing Michael Walsh's body had been exhumed. The Minister for Home

Affairs had authorised the exhumation and a post mortem had been carried out. They could now confirm that there were three entrance wounds but only two exit wounds. The location of that missing bullet had also been found.

Anthony Carroll must have been shocked as the defence had not been notified of these developments until now.

David Walsh brother of the deceased gave evidence of identification of the body for the exhumation. He even told how he saw the doctors start the examination when the coffin was opened.

The doctors Dr Barry Kilworth and Dr Michael O'Brien both gave evidence of having carried out the post mortem in September last. At the time they had found three entry wounds and only two exit wounds. Despite this there was never any embedded object found in the body. Two of the shots went right through the body and either of them would have been enough to cause the death. Anthony Carroll asked both doctors what sort of gun caused these injuries and both answered a rifle at close range.

The next witness had led the examination after the exhumation. He was Professor Arthur Edwin Moore a pathologist from Cork University College. Moore told the court he had twenty seven years experience of post mortems, specialising in gunshot cases.

On the 4th of April Moore had carried out the post mortem on Michael Walsh's body near Kildorrery.

He agreed with the doctor analysis of the gunshot wounds. The three on the back were punctured clean through he said. While the two exit wounds on the front were elongated with intestines hanging out. He had found the missing bullet lodged in a muscle near the hip. The bullet he found would cause the injuries found in the other two wounds. He could not calculate the distance the shots were fired at as the exit wounds had previously been examined. The bullet was produced in court as evidence it was a .303 rifle bullet.

Michael Walsh's grave in at St Mologga's graveyard.

The case was now again slipping from the prosecution. After all the time the guards had spent looking into John Shinnick's shot gun it finally turned out it was not the murder weapon at all. No rifle had been found that could have been it. The prosecution then seem to start the delay tactic again in the desperate hope more evidence could be found to support Michael Linnane's statement.

It was the 30th of April before any more evidence was heard. On that occasion Sergeant Irwin from Kildorrery gave evidence of having timed many distances in the area in the last few weeks. He listed out in court the places visited and how long it took him between the places. Patrick Hannan's house to murder scene across the fields at a good pace took 7 minutes 27 seconds. He cycled from Meadstown Cross to Buttevant that took him 58 minutes and 7 seconds. The list went on he had walked cycled or ran between many points and gave the times.

They still had nothing concrete to support the statement that Fitzgerald ran away with a gun. If they had evidence or could produce the gun Fitzgerald would have been on trial by now.

On the 13th of May the case was finally coming to a conclusion. There was still talk in court about John Shinnick's shotgun despite recent evidence. The prosecution went over the evidence and at last applied for the three men to be sent for trial.

Anthony Carroll then spoke saying in all his 35 years experience he never encountered a case like this. His clients were imprisoned now for over eight months.

The prosecution he said were "prowling in the dark from day to day". During his speech Casey clarified the charges against Shinnick were now conspiracy to murder, accessory before the fact.

Carroll went back over everything arguing that it was clear Shinnick loaned the shotgun but innocently. It was nothing more than an old ordinary shotgun used for shooting crows.

Despite the evidence Daniel Casey still clung to the fact that one shot had been fired with three projectiles so it must have been a shotgun. Casey also depended on the fact the three men had motive being enemies of Walsh.

After long speeches from both sides the judge came to a decision. He said there was no prima facie case against John Shinnick and he was discharged.

He then returned the remaining two for trial before a jury on the charge of wilful murder of Michael Walsh.

Despite the numerous court hearings over several months the public thronged to the courtroom for every hearing. Now with the end of the hearing of evidence the case spilled from the minds of the public. Months passed as the two men waited for their trial at the central criminal court.

On the 4th of November they were taken from Cork Prison and transferred to Mountjoy. This they assumed was in preparation for the trial. Carroll still represented them and he protested to the Chief State Solicitor and the District State Solicitor regarding the delays in the case.

Sometime later he received a reply that the state was to enter a nolle prosequi meaning charges were to be dropped.

It was not until the Tuesday 9th of December when the men were taken to the Central Criminal Court. They had to wait until the following evening before the case was called. It was the last case in the evening when the courtroom had been cleared of public and press before Thomas Fitzgerald and Patrick Hannan entered. In a matter of minutes the representative of the state said despite the evidence they felt there was not enough to go to trial. The judge then discharged the pair and they left after one year two months and four days in custody.

The pair now publicly announced their innocence in the case and complained bitterly about the delays in the case. The men could now say what they wanted and the state could not retry them on the same charges.

It was a troubled period in Irish history as everyone knows, men fought and died for independence of the country. The Civil war divided the country and even families in their beliefs. But in this quarter of Kildorrey men were divided and fought for the right to land. One died but who really shot him we might never know for sure. Nobody heard three shots fired that day, yet a rifle bullet was found in the body.

The state's failure to get to the bottom of it was as obvious as the motive behind it. It turns out maybe the crime that seems to be agrarian have a political element to it after all. Walsh took on the land around 1902 and was denounced as a land grabber. Thomas Fitzgerald returned from America and in 1921 took the opportunity to retake procession of the land during the war of Independence. He enlisted a following who believed in his right and boycotted Walsh. Only weeks after the Civil War Walsh it seems Walsh was able to use his influence with the new authorities to get the farm back. Fitzgerald was left with nothing and possibly looked at Walsh as a man who already had a farm. It was over forty years since his father had got into debt, yet Fitzgerald thought it must have been worth fighting for. Walsh seems equally stubborn in his rights but never did he think anyone was daring enough to shoot him in broad daylight.

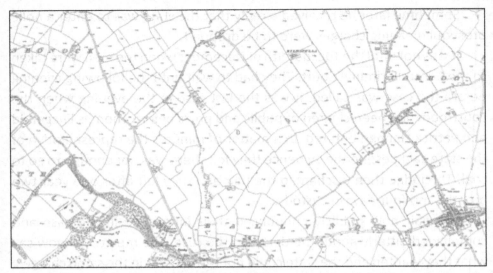

Map showing the route Walsh would have taken home from Kildorrery.

I Want You!
Meelin Newmarket 1931

A tiny ad placed in the Cork Examiner on Christmas Eve 1930 can't have attracted much attention and never would anyone imagine what it could possibly lead to. In this modern age of technology it's easy to track someone down, get their mobile number or even find out more information about them on social media. But nearly one hundred years ago it was much more difficult, especially if you no longer knew their address or they had moved on. Asking around the locality might work but if the person had left the area the last resort may be the newspaper. This relied a lot on luck that someone who knew the person might see the advert or that the person themselves reads every column.

In Victorian times lovers carried out secret correspondence in the personal columns but this personal ad was a little different. It read if Michael Walsh formerly of Meelin will communicate with Heffernan and Co., Kanturk he will hear something to his advantage. It appeared on Christmas Eve 1930 and several more times over the Christmas period. Heffernan and Co., Kanturk were at the time advertising agents for the newspaper.

When Michael Walsh walked into Heffernan's office in Kanturk sometime in January and enquired who was looking for him. They didn't know at first if it was actually him but a meeting was arranged between the parties. It is hard to see now how it was to his advantage.

PERSONAL

NOTICE —If Michael Walsh, formerly of Meelin, will communicate with Heffernan and Co.. Kanturk, he will hear of something to his advantage. 8346

Notice that appeared in the Cork Examiner, with thanks to Irish Newspaper Archives and Cork Examiner.

The person looking for Michael Walsh was Bridget O'Connell, well actually Bridget Walsh as she was his wife. Why she choose this method to contact him is strange because he was not formerly of Meelin but still lived there albeit now with his sister. Michael now worked as a farm labourer for a nearby farmer. The small village of Meelin less than five miles north of Newmarket was like any small rural village at that time.

Bridget and Michael had got married in Meelin in August if 1919. Bridget had originally come from near Boherbue south of Newmarket. However it was no secret in the area that the marriage was not a happy one from the outset. Michael was forty getting married and Bridget only a young girl of nineteen and over five months pregnant. Did they have any other choice but to get married, he would have been pushed into doing the right thing. Their first child was born in November 1919 but died not long afterwards. Most likely by this time Michael had left Bridget to fend for herself. She blamed his drinking to be the source of the trouble but maybe it was just a symptom. He seemed to prefer travelling around working in different farms labouring, but some said this was because he was difficult to get on with. He came back to her for a while a least and a daughter was born. Michael left her to bring up the child and never supported her financially.

The couple split permanently as they could no longer live under the same roof. This was shocking in rural Ireland in the 1920's. At least now they could try to have a happier life, while many couples lived under the pretence of happiness.

Their child was reared by Bridget's mother and Michael went to live with his sister nearby for some time at least.

Bridget on the other hand moved around more, where she was far less known. She went into service working in several places Kilmallock, Bruff and Kanturk. She assumed the identity of an unmarried woman and went back to her maiden name, O'Connell. It would have been much more difficult for her to find a job especially in service if she was married, respectable houses would have shunned her. She worked for a farmer called David Walsh but left in November 1930. Then she worked for a Mr Lenehan at Rossacon halfway between Kanturk and Newmarket but did not stay there long either.

The ad however brought the pair back together and after the meeting in Kanturk they stayed together in Jones Hotel for a few nights maybe this was the advantage Bridget alluded to. They agreed to try to live together again. They took up residence in a small house at O'Callaghan's farm near Meelin while Walsh worked for John O'Callaghan. After over seven years apart they now resumed their relationship as husband and wife but no matter how much they wanted it to work it was not going to be easy. It only lasted a matter of weeks before one left. They tried again but by late April the couple couldn't stand being under the same roof as each other.

On the 29th of April Michael moved out and took a job with Jeremiah Browne a farmer nearby, where he also got lodgings. Bridget was seen leaving Meelin with her belongings and a donkey and cart but she would return once more. Bridget stayed at either her mothers or sisters for a while and then she went to Kilmallock looking for a job.

On the 6th of May Bridget arrived in Newmarket by train and went to Meelin looking for her husband. She could have taken out another ad to find him but he may not have bothered replying again. This time she took a far more direct approach. Finding him in Browne's farm she went to the kitchen and called him out sternly "I want you".

The pair walked into Meelin and were heard arguing loudly by several passers-by that evening. They had nowhere to go to talk in private and everyone would have been aware of their circumstances and the disgrace it was.

She asked him about his wages and pressured him for money. He told her to come back on Sunday but that is according to her. Up to a few months ago she had not heard from him for seven years, now Michael was saying he might be able to buy a house in November. They didn't go into a pub together despite Michael having mind for drink. Everyone would have heard their business in there anyway. Instead Bridget bought a glass of Lemonade by going to the back door of Quinlan's Pub. It was May and the weather was warm.

Afterwards they walked towards Browne's; Bridget needed somewhere to stay for the night. There was no question of her going back to Browne's; he would not have wanted her there.

When the pair parted Michael walked the three quarters of a mile home to Browne's. By the time he reached there he was in intense pain and struggling to walk. On the roadside someone had to help him home and into the farmhouse. After ten one of the Browne's found him in the Kitchen in agony and helped him to bed. Walsh was begging for help and knew he needed it before his condition worsened. A message was sent to get a doctor and it was nearly midnight before the dispensary doctor arrived at Meelin from Newmarket.

Michael Walsh struggled up the lane that night on his way to Browne's.

He found Michael Walsh flat on a mattress on a bedroom floor in immense pain. He was suffering from muscle spasms but was quite conscious. Walsh had a frightening stare in his eyes and was petrified. The doctor knew there and then it was poisoning, and even determined it was strychnine from the symptoms. Within minutes his condition worsened dramatically and the doctor was convinced he would die in moments. Back then there was little could be done once the poison was in the blood stream. His face turned blue and his whole body stiffened up. The doctor then administered chloroform and asked for an ambulance to take him to hospital immediately.

It took four hours before the ambulance arrived and Walsh was taken to Kanturk hospital. There the medical officer Dr Collins found Walsh dead on arrival at the hospital.

On the 7th of May within hours of Michael's death the guards were investigating the circumstances and tried to figure out his last movements. Chief Superintendent Clinton from Bandon with Superintendent O'Sullivan from Kanturk were leading the investigation with guards from Meelin and Newmarket. The state pathologist was also notified so that the results from the post mortem would be available for the inquest which was expected the following day.

The following afternoon the inquest was held at Kanturk District Hospital by Coroner Dr M Ryan. Both Superintendents from Bandon and Kanturk attended. Supt O'Sullivan stated that he did not want to go into the facts of the case at this time as the investigation was ongoing. He merely wanted to establish how Walsh had died through medical evidence and formerly identify the body. He also applied to have the contents of the stomach sent for analysis and the verdict of the inquest postponed pending those results.

Michael Walsh's brother Jeremiah from Rowels near Meelin identified the body at the inquest. He said he last saw his brother alive two weeks before. There appeared to be nothing wrong with him then, he drank at lot but that was normal. Despite living reasonably near each other Jeremiah admitted they had not met for nearly ten years until recently. Jeremiah had first heard his brother was dead on Thursday morning from Jeremiah Browne. The farmer told him his brother had taken poison.

The doctor who attended Walsh that night Dr Verling gave the medical evidence. He told how a boy brought a message to him and he arrived at Browne's house at quarter past midnight. Walsh was in extreme pain with muscle spasms every fifteen seconds. The man was in dread of his life and asked the doctor to do something for him quickly. A few minutes later his whole body went into spasm and frothed at the mouth. His jaw was clenched so tight the doctor broke a tooth trying to apply a gag. The doctor told how he applied chloroform and then managed to get a tube into the stomach and pumped out the contents. This would at least remove the poison that was not yet absorbed into the bloodstream.

The convulsions stopped after 2am but the jaw remained tightly closed all the time. He called for an ambulance about one and it arrived at twenty past four in the morning. The doctor told how he knew immediately that night that Walsh was suffering from strychnine poisoning and was close to death from the symptoms. However he said despite the intense pain Walsh didn't want to die.

Dr Collins told how Walsh was dead on arrival to the hospital. The inquest was adjourned to await the results of the contents of his stomach.

The remains of Michael Walsh were at the morgue in Kanturk and left there on Saturday the 9th of May for the funeral. Bridget Walsh was seen at the morgue but when the funeral procession left she did not go with it and at least pretend to be the grieving wife everyone knew she wasn't. This would have further fuelled the rumours that she had in fact wanted her husband dead.

The Gardaí at this point were watching the movements of Bridget and she was followed around Kanturk. She was staying at Jones Hotel.

On Monday the 11th of May Bridget Walsh was arrested by Supt O'Sullivan, when asked for a statement she refused to say anything. The following Wednesday she appeared before District Justice Gallagher at Buttevant charged with the capital crime. No witnesses were called but Supt O'Sullivan applied to have her kept in custody until the next sitting of the District Court on the 22nd May. He said by then he was confident he would have enough evidence against her to make a case. At first the judge thought one day in court would suffice but soon learned that there could be up to 32 witnesses which he said would take at least three days. The superintendent also said that the analysis of the stomach contents would take three weeks. When asked again to make a statement Bridget Walsh refused but said she had no legal representation. She was then taken to Cork Gaol till the next court date.

When the court sat again on the 22nd the prosecution were now in a position to call several witnesses. The accused had since got legal representation, a solicitor David Ferguson from Kanturk. With the amount of evidence he was going to need his thirty years of experience. The prosecution was led by Mr Finlay and Mr Casey state solicitor, on behalf of the Attorney General.

Dr Verling again gave medical evidence as he had at the inquest. He thought Walsh was close to death that night but still believed there may have been a chance of survival. When asked by the prosecution "in your opinion did Walsh believe that he was going to recover". The doctor replied that Walsh knew he would die unless something was done for him.

The next witness had evidence that was conclusive against the accused.

Peter O'Toole Master of Science at the College of Science in Dublin was an analyst at the state laboratory. The analyst explained how he had received a glass from the Garda. In it he said was a white crystal substance mostly around the rim. Since analysing it he could now prove that it was strychnine 19/64 of a grain.

The prosecution asked what was a lethal dose, O'Toole replied that half a grain was the generally accepted minimum amount that would kill. This would equate to 30mg, as one grain is 65mg.

The witness continued and moved on to the contents of a ladies coat he had received from Detective Sergeant Reynolds. In the left hand pocket he found one crystal of strychnine a third of a grain so big he extracted it by hand. On closer inspection he found another fragment one tenth of a grain. O'Toole finished by saying he had yet to examine the stomach and organs of the deceased.

The next witness however would prove where Bridget had acquired the poison.

A chemist from Kilmallock James Horgan was sworn in. He said that Bridget Walsh had come to his shop on the 5th of May. She produced a note from her employer, it read "Dear Sir, will you please give the messenger some poison for dogs, as they have what lambs and sheep I have killed during the past few nights and oblige, David Walsh".

The chemist then asked her to confirm the story and she did. He asked again had Mr Walsh sent her and she again agreed he had. He told how he then sold her 10 grains of strychnine which cost a shilling. The chemist asked her to sign the poison register and she did so with her own name and also David Walsh.

Ten grains of strychnine was a hell of a lot for poisoning dogs, a fatal dose for a dog is less 1mg. So 65mg per grain, Bridget walked out of the chemist that day with enough poison for at least 650 dogs.

The next witness could prove however that the poison was not for dogs at all. David Walsh farmer at Rathranna near Kanturk confirmed that Bridget Walsh worked for him for two years till November of the previous year. He said that he had not set eyes on her since then. During her time with him she was known as Bridget O'Connell and he was led to believe she was not married. David Walsh also confirmed that he did not have sheep nor did he ever send a messenger for poison.

To further prove their case the prosecution called a handwriting expert Captain Quirke. He examined the note she gave to the chemist and compared it to a sample of her handwriting. He concluded in court the writing was similar.

An employee of great Southern Railways could prove Bridget's movements on the 6th. He recalled selling her a 3rd class train ticket in Kilmallock to Newmarket saying it was the only ticket sold to Newmarket that day.

To further prove Bridget's movements on the 6th Bridget Conway a publican in Meelin was called. Conway said that on that evening shortly before ten she heard knocking on her back door. Outside was a woman she did not know looking for a bottle of lemonade. Conway recalled asking her did she want to take it with her but the woman replied she wanted to drink it there. The publican then poured a bottle of lemonade into a glass and handed it to the woman. In front of her the woman drank most of it but left some saying she would take it to her companion.

The publican looked out as the woman walked away and saw a man moving out on the road. A few minutes later the woman returned with the now empty glass and handed it back saying nothing.

The publican said the next morning she saw a sugar like substance on the inside of the glass. She then put it on a shelf with the bottle and kept it until it was given to the Gardaí. Conway confirmed to the court that she had no strychnine of her own in the house.

**The pub in Meelin where Bridget bought the bottle
of lemonade that evening.**

As the prosecution had proved where Bridget was, now it was time to provide motive and nobody could do better than the next witness, farm labourer William Frawley from Gormanstown, Kilmallock. He had met her a few years earlier and said they became friendlier when she worked for David Walsh. He said they met Wednesday, Friday and Sunday nights.

Finlay for the prosecution got straight to the point asking "taking her for a single woman were you making love to her?" This was extremely direct language in court in a very Catholic Ireland. Frawley admitted he was, explaining that she never told him she was married. He was then asked about letters she had sent him but Frawley said he couldn't read but had received two from her. He also said his house had been searched by the guards who may have found the letters.

Several members of the Gardaí were called and gave testimony about the evidence especially the glass and how it was handled.

Supt O'Sullivan then explained how he had interviewed Bridget Walsh on several occasions and received a statement from her in Jones Hotel Kanturk before she was arrested on the 11th of May. That statement was then read out in the court. In it Bridget explained her marital status and claimed it was her husband who left her and at one stage had not seen each other for seven years.

She admitted going to Browne's house on the 6th to find her husband. According to her she told him that she was tired of going about the country and wanted to settle down and live like everyone else. He however said it was impossible until he saved enough to get a house. There in the laneway outside Browne's farm they argued bitterly for nearly an hour. After this they went to Conway's to get lemonade and she drank three quarters of it. The remainder she gave to her husband who said he didn't want it and would prefer water. According to Bridget though he drank some and handed it back saying "drink it yourself". She then threw away what was left and gave the glass back.

Bridget did not learn that her husband was dead until the next morning and heard the rumours that she had poisoned him.

On the second day of the hearing another witness was called to place Bridget's movements on the night of the 6th. John Ryan a farmer from Knockduff, Meelin had met her that night about eight. He said she asked him was her husband still at Callaghan's. Ryan however told her he had left the same night she had in April. She then asked him where would she find him and Ryan told her at Jer Browne's. The farmer then also identified the clothes produced in court saying it looked like what she wore that night but she also had a pair of gloves in her hand.

The next witness was Jeremiah Browne Junior; he told how he was sitting around the fire chatting after supper on the 6th May. His brother Joseph and Michael Walsh were also there, when a woman came to the door and loudly said to Walsh "I want you". He immediately went out with her saying nothing. It was after ten when Jeremiah was in bed and he heard footsteps outside and the door opening. He got up to find Walsh in the kitchen partially dressed in pain on the floor. He took him to bed and sent his brother to get a priest and doctor. Walsh became very frightened and was sweating before the doctor arrived. They stayed up that night with him.

The next witness was Mary Walsh from Rowels, Meelin, and wife of Jeremiah Walsh (who was Michael's brother). From her account she cannot have known Bridget very well, in the last twelve years they had met a few times. They had last met a few weeks before when Bridget and Michael lived at Callaghan's. On that occasion Bridget told her that Michael was leaving her again.

Mary told the court how she never saw Bridget again until after ten on the night of 6th of May. Strange that the women discussed where Michael was working and at the exactly same time unbeknownst to Mary, Michael was lying in pain. That night Bridget stayed at her brother in laws house and the next morning the women headed for Newmarket. Bridget had announced that she was going home wherever that was.

Mary revealed that it was in Newmarket when the pair heard Michael Walsh was dead or dying in Kanturk hospital. Mary didn't believe it but Bridget on the other hand started crying.

Walking along further they met Mary's husband Jeremiah who confirmed the story having heard from Jeremiah Browne. Mary's husband said it was poison and Bridget quickly interjected with "he poisoned himself". Mary however now turned to Bridget saying how she never mentioned meeting Michael the night before. Bridget claimed to have forgotten having met him.

The three then went back to make arrangements for a coffin and hearse. On the way there they met Jeremiah Browne and Bridget accosted him for talking about her. Afterwards the three went by train to Kanturk and straight to the Hospital. At the hospital Mary said Bridget was not upset to see her husband's body but seemed excited.

After declining to cross examine several witnesses David Ferguson questioned Mary Walsh about what was said when they met Jeremiah Walsh. Mary then reveals Bridget said to her husband "He poisoned himself; he would sooner have done it than live with me".

The district Justice having heard the evidence said he believed there was a prima facie case against Bridget Walsh. The charge was the capital crime of murder and he sent it for trial to the next sitting of the Central Criminal Court in Dublin. When asked if she had a statement to make her solicitor merely replied for her saying she wished to say nothing. Afterwards she was removed from court and taken back to jail.

That same week Meelin was rocked by another murder story. A native of the village, Superintendent John Curtin, was shot outside his own house in Tipperary town. He was only about 30 and his parents were still living in Meelin.

People still discussed how Bridget poisoned her husband and what drove her to doing it. From the evidence against her the talk was not if she was found guilty but merely when.

After nearly a month in jail for Bridget the case came before the Central Criminal Court in Green Street Dublin. It was unusual that in a time when murder was so uncommon those two cases from the same locality were in court.

When called before Justice Hanna indicted for the murder of her husband Bridget clearly entered a plea of not guilty. For the prosecution Mr Finlay was now assisted by Joseph Healy Chief State Solicitor. The defence had solicitors Mr Harrison and Patrick O'Grady.

Mr Finlay opened for the prosecution by giving the background to the case then went over the evidence that he would be giving. The prosecution were confident Bridget would be found guilty. He saw no other outcome but that Michael Walsh died by poisoning at the hands of his wife. It was also revealed that in the day of the crime Bridget Walsh had met her lover William Frawley in Kilmallock before leaving for Meelin.

One of the first witnesses called was sister of the accused Mary Brosnan. Mary told of the relationship between Bridget and Michael saying he never wanted to support her financially. Bridget placed the ad to get back in contact with her husband or else she would go back into service.

Doctor Collins from Kanturk was called to give evidence about the post mortem he had carried out. Death he said was certainly as a result of the strychnine poisoning. The judge then questioned about the dead man's liver and the doctor replied that there was no signs of cirrhosis of the liver as would be expected in a heavy drinker. The doctor said he was surprised Walsh had not died sooner. Larger doses of strychnine he said need to be washed out within three hours.

Several more witnesses were called that gave similar evidence as before. One witness William Frawley was called again. He claimed to accidentally bump into Bridget Walsh on the 6th May. The pair went to a pub where she bought a few drinks. Frawley revealed that Bridget wanted to meet him again on the following Friday.

Under cross examination however Frawley denied they were still in a relationship saying he was since seeing another woman and had no intention of getting married to Bridget. The judge interjected having evidence in his hand, the love letter written to him by Bridget. He said" I don't want to read these in court but obviously she was very fond of you". Frawley played it cool saying "she might be" and again denied any notions of marriage.

Again Supt O'Sullivan told how he received a statement from Bridget on the 11th of May. Harrison for the defence objected to it being allowed but was overruled and the statement was read. In it she had said arrangements were made to meet her husband again on the Sunday morning. She wanted money from him for their daughter and said to him "I don't know what I'll do with you". Bridget also mentioned it was her husband that told her to leave Callaghan's when they lived together.

Supt O'Sullivan was questioned by the defence and admitted that Bridget had done everything the Gardaí has asked and handed over her clothes as evidence.

When the defence got their opportunity Harrison tried his best to point the blame at Michael Walsh. He painted the picture that Michael Walsh was a difficult man to live with. His client the accused had only lived with him again to try to give their daughter a normal family life.

The defence put forward the case that Bridget purchased the poison at her husband's request. He had asked her on the 2nd May to get it for him when in town. She had never concealed any of her movements and gave him the poison bottle that night for rats. Harrison believed it was impossible for Bridget to put the poison into the lemonade without being seen by her husband.

For Michael to have done it was even more impossible to put the poison into the lemonade without her seeing it. Either way it happened in that few minutes and she had the better opportunity.

The defence then called the accused Bridget Walsh to give evidence. Harrison began by questioning her about her life up till her husband died. Bridget said her husband had left her after only a few days of marriage. He came back for a few weeks at a time but once she did not see him for seven years. Bridget said she supported her daughter herself by working in many places.

Now she claimed that her husband asked her to get poison before they left Callaghan's house. He told her to be sure to get it for him.

The judge asked her why she forged a note to get the poison but she had no answer. Bridget then went back to that night she met her husband. She handed him the bottle of poison outside Browne's and they walked towards Meelin. Bridget said she asked her husband why he left Callaghan's after she had. According to her he said he would rather hang himself than stay there. They argued along the way, Bridget said she asked her husband about money and he said he would have it for her on Sunday.

Getting on to the lemonade Bridget said her husband sent her to get it as he wouldn't go himself. In other places it has been suggested they would have gone to a pub but it was only for men. Yet Bridget had that very day been in a pub with another man.

Harrison asked her "did you interfere with the lemonade" she replied "No I had nothing to do with the lemonade". "Did your husband drink the lemonade?", but she said "I could not say". Bridget said after giving the glass back they headed back towards Browne's and parted fifteen minutes later. Then she went to Jeremiah Walsh's house and stayed the night. There she told them about her argument with her husband. Yet this was completely at odds with what Mary Walsh said previously.

Harrison asked her had she said "he poisoned himself, he would rather do it than live with me" to Jeremiah Walsh the morning after. Bridget now claimed she could not remember saying it at all. The judge intervened asking was she willing to swear that she had not and Bridget was willing to. It seems she would swear anything to avoid the hangman's noose.

When Finlay got his opportunity to cross examine the accused his questions were relentless and went on for some time. On several times he would catch her out. Bridget denied being in love with Bill Frawley saying "it was only a pastime to me". She claimed they were not in any kind of loving relationship at all but often met accidentally.

He then produced the letters and Bridget admitted they might be hers. The judge asked her why she said might and she gave in saying they were written by her.

Finlay read one out "Dear Bill, just a line hoping to see you tonight if you can forgive me. I should be so sorry for being cross with you. From B to

Bill." More letters between the pair were read out in court one contained the lines

> There is a tree I used to pass
> Every leaf as green as grass
> Not half so green as my heart is true
> I love but one and that is you

Bridget was now asked was she writing these to Frawley around the same time as putting the ad in the paper to her husband but Bridget managed only to say "I suppose so".

He went on questioning her about her relationship with her husband at the time saying if it was bad why he would ask her to get poison. Bridget was giving vague answers saying things were not too bad between them but not good either.

He asked her why in her statement she told the Superintendent that she stayed at her sisters between 2nd and 6th May as this was not true. Bridget finally gave in and admitted she had not told the truth but said she had nothing to hide.

Bridget claimed she was looking for work in Kilmallock but was asked why she bought the poison before looking for work. Bridget said if she found a job she would have posted it to her husband.

Finlay was ready for her and said but you didn't know where your husband was now working. Bridget however claimed she knew he was at Browne's but she had to ask a lad that evening thinking he was still at Callaghan's.

When asked how you knew a letter was needed to get poison but Bridget claimed her husband told her to get it in someone else's name. The questions then went on to the poison had she opened the package at all, she said she had not. Was the paper still around the bottle when you gave it to him? Yes. Can you give any suggestion as to why strychnine was found in the left hand pocket of your coat? I don't know how it could be in it.

Was the sole purpose of your visit to give him the poison? Yes. You came a distance of 40miles by train to deliver that poison? Yes but I meant to go to my sister. Here she could easily have said to get some of his wages because she had previously said she asked him for money that night.

Clearly Bridget wasn't telling the truth and her story was starting to show cracks under robust questioning. If Finlay could show the jury she lied about several small things, well then she could lie about more.

He continued asking her how she handed the glass to her husband, was she looking at him at the time. When asked about Jeremiah Walsh telling others she had poisoned Michael, she could not say why she had not denied it and told off her brother in law. And yet after that she went by train to Kanturk with him.

Finlay asked why she never told the Guards about buying the poison if she had nothing to hide but Bridget said the Gardaí had scared her. The he asked her why she did not attend her own husband's funeral, she said because of being followed by detectives.

Bridget Conway who had sold the lemonade to Bridget, leaves the courthouse, image courtesy of the National Library of Ireland and Independent Newspapers.

William Frawley seen outside the courthouse, image courtesy of the National Library of Ireland and Independent Newspapers.

After Finlay finished the judge asked several questions to her about whether she could have seen him take poison that night. He then moved on to the ad she put in the paper. Did she really expect to get her husband back and she replied she did. The judge was leading her "and practically a day after you wrote this love letter to Frawley". Bridget couldn't manage a reply but after still claimed she had wanted to get him back.

The defence needed anyone they could find to put doubt in the jury. Brother of the deceased Timothy Walsh was called. He said he was two years older than Michael and originally from Cummery Connell, between Meelin and Rockchapel. Harrison asked him bluntly were you ever in a mental hospital to which the reply was no. Then as if he had tricked him Harrison called Dr Fitzgerald from the Central Mental Hospital. Fitzgerald confirmed that in fact there was a man called Timothy Walsh from the same place admitted in 1898. The doctor failed to recognise him now as it was thirty years later and Timothy was only 22 then, having been there for six months. Harrison was not going to let it go and asked the doctor was another brother in the hospital since the poisoning. The doctor again confirmed this was true but denied it was shock as a result of the recent death. It was quite obvious what Harrison was trying to do, if he could prove insanity in the family the jury would doubt it was murder at all.

Harrison went on with his address to the jury trying his best to convince them of another possibility. The motive he said suggested by the prosecution was Bridget wanted to marry Frawley. Harrison suggested as Walsh had been missing for seven years that Bridget could have remarried. She could have applied to court saying he was missing seven years and presumed dead. Otherwise he said she could just have married Frawley, bigamy was far less a crime than murder.

Harrison put forward that Walsh was sick of it all and tried to kill himself and take her with him. There was no trace of poison on Walsh's pipe which he smoked while walking back with his wife. Now Harrison picked up on what the doctor said, the poison he suggested was taken later on in the evening; otherwise Walsh would have died earlier.

Joseph Healy state solicitor was to get the last word. He clearly outlined a woman having an affair with a man; she gets the poison, disliked her husband and had poison in her possession. This he said had one likely outcome and she could explain what exactly had happened. Her statement to the superintendent was riddled with several lies.

Healy concluded by saying" there was never a case clearer in the whole annals of Green Street Courthouse".

The jury retired at just after half one to decide the fate of Bridget Walsh. While they were gone Justice Hanna revealed he had received two letters about the case.

He called Mary Brosnan sister of Bridget to come forward and explain how it happened. She claimed her mother had asked a shopkeeper in Newmarket to write a letter for her. The judge wanted to know how the letter was sent in an official letter from the Oireachtas. Mary replied the envelope came from Dan Vaughan a local TD but claimed she thought there was nothing wrong with writing to the judge.

It was revealed that Dan Vaughan TD Farmers party for North Cork had in fact written a letter asking for leniency for the accused. The letter gave a character reference, saying Bridget had worked for his sister. She had an unhappy marriage and deserved to be considered in that light. Vaughan intended the letter to be sent to the Attorney General not the trial judge.

The story was that the letter was to be taken by Mrs O'Connell to the Solicitor Ferguson but she gave it instead to Mr Murphy. He in turn enclosed it with another letter and must have sent it to Justice Hanna rather than the Attorney General.

The judge made it clear that making communications with the judge in a case was clearly content of court and should be inquired into further. He did however accept entirely Mr Vaughan's explanation. He warned everyone that content of court is punishable by a fine or even prison sentence. He then threatened that Mr Murphy could be called to court but finally said it had not affected the case or had it.

At three the jury returned and asked the chemist questions relating to the poison. The chemist Mr Horgan told how the strychnine was in a bottle wrapped in paper. He said there was no possibility that of poison grains falling out onto the paper. He had secured the bottle with a cork before wrapping it.

This should have swayed the jury immensely, how then had the strychnine grains ended up in her pocket if she had not interfered with it.

At quarter past three the jury returned again and delivered a verdict of not guilty.

Bridget Walsh was then discharged from court, she left with her sister and a large crowd followed.

Why the jury chose not guilty clearly against the weight of evidence against her. There was still a lot not explained or did the jury just have sympathy for Bridget after the life she had with her husband. If she had been found guilty would she have faced the death sentence as a man most certainly would? Had it been a man being accused of poisoning his wife would the verdict have been different? Only six years before Anne Walsh from Fedamore Co Limerick had been executed for the murder of her husband. She was the only woman ever to face the death penalty since the foundation of the state. The last woman executed in Ireland before that was in 1902, so it was extremely rare for a woman. There were several other cases where women were sentenced by it was commuted at the last minute. So was the jury just unsure what to do with a woman on the capital charge.

Bridget outside the court with her sister, image courtesy of the National Library of Ireland and Independent Newspapers.

There were still a lot of unanswered questions as they left the court room that day but now it was too late. Why did she go all the way to Meelin that night to deliver a message to her husband who had done nothing for her all the years? Why would she bother asking him for his wages when he never gave her a penny. More likely scenario was she had given him one last chance in January but now she was done with him.

Still put simply it was never explained how if she was not guilty there was poison in her pocket. If she had given him the bottle he would never been able to get it into the glass without her seeing. Much more likely she had the advantage he didn't know she had the poison at all but clearly what happened between two people on the side of the road will never be known.

The blue poison bottle itself was only found fifty years after hidden in a hollow in the trunk of a tree. Where it was found was not in the direction Walsh would have walked home that night. It was however on the path Bridget possibly took to get to where she stayed that night. The case featured in RTE television programme Thou Shalt Not Kill in November 1995 featuring Cathal O'Shannon. In it O'Shannon was quite obviously shocked at the verdict of the jury.

Bridget smiles outside court after the verdict, image courtesy of the National Library of Ireland and Independent Newspapers.

Group photo outside the courthouse, image courtesy of the National Library of Ireland and Independent Newspapers.

Whiteboys or not!
Lisnagourneen Rockmills 1823

Rural Ireland in the 1800's life was hard for people. Many survived by renting a small plot of land but this was subsistence living at best. The use of common land made a big difference and meant people could have a cow or two grazing.

Landlords and farmers charging high rents to the labourers was nothing new but at least the common land was free to use. The landlords began to enclose the common land but did not lower the rents. Landlords and farmers changed their farming to cattle not only using the common land but forced the labourers from the land. For the farmers they had the added incentive that grazing land was not subject to tithes which was 10 per cent payable to the protestant clergy.

The only way labourers knew to fight back was with violence directed at the landlords and tithe collectors. Not only did they fight back but organised themselves into secret underground organisations. Counties Cork, Waterford, Limerick and Tipperary were the most active for several decades in the 1700's and into the 1800's. Members were required to swear an oath before becoming involved. Wearing white smocks on nightly raids they quickly became known as the Whiteboys. They were also called the Levellers as these groups knocked the fences enclosing what was once common land. Some styled themselves as Queen Sadhbh's children. In Irish mythology Sadhbh was Fionn Mac Cumhaill's wife and mother of Oisín.

Landlords and protestant clergy received threatening letters warning them of the consequences. In some parts mock gallows were erected and graves dug. Cattle on the once common land were often found in the morning with hamstrings cut or horses had their ears cut off. In the countryside many houses were raided at night with Whiteboys demanding arms or money to buy arms. Often they attacked the houses of farmers who now rented land from which labourers had been evicted.

The authorities were slow to respond at first taking the view that the landlords had made trouble for themselves. However by 1765 the Whiteboy Act enforced tougher laws to deal with the violence. Crimes against property by groups of more than five was now punishable by death, as was swearing oaths and membership of secret societies. This quelled the trouble for a while but it started up again and spilled over into the agrarian unrest of the early 1800's.

It was in this climate in North Cork in the 1820's not far from Castletownroche towards Rockmills lived Thomas Franks and his family in the townland of Lisnagourneen. Thomas's wife was Margaret Maunsell originally from Ballybrood, Co. Limerick. They had married 30 years before in 1793 when they were both 20. Two sons were born Henry became known as Henry Maunsell Franks and Thomas but it seems only Henry survived to adulthood. Thomas Franks farmed land but also acted as agent on the estate of the Earl of Kingston. The Earl held the bulk of his land in Roscommon and Sligo but also had parcels of land near Kildorrery and Mitchelstown.

The Franks family lived in a long thatched house that was very common in Ireland back then. At one end of the house lived a labourer called Edmund Galveen with his daughter Mary; they had their own entrance but also had a door directly into Franks part of the house. In the farm yard was another small house and an old man lived there, but apart from that nobody lived within several fields of the house.

On the evening 27th October 1822 Thomas Franks was at home with his son Henry, a neighbour Thomas Windham and a servant Michael Walsh. Between 8 and 9 they suddenly heard the sound of gunfire outside and instantly there was someone knocking on their door. Whoever was outside didn't wait for them to answer and lifted the latch on the door and charged inside. The Franks suddenly found three men in their house, one held a pistol and another a rifle. One of the intruders demanded Henry Franks to give them any guns he had in the house. Franks swore he had none but the three men were having none of it and kept up their demands. One of the intruders took turf from the fire and threatened to burn the house down if arms were not produced. The house was searched by the men and after twenty minutes no guns were found.

The man with the pistol went to the parlour and made Henry Franks get on his knees. He called for a book on which Henry was to swear but refused the common Prayer book demanding a holy bible be got. When it was brought to him Henry swore on the bible that there were neither guns nor ammunition in the house. While he did the intruder held the unusual brass barrelled pistol to his chest. Suddenly the three men disappeared as quickly as they had appeared.

The following day a man in the locality Jeremiah Sheehan was arrested at the Mallow Fair by a Mr Lowe. He was held at Mallow Bridewell where Henry Franks was brought to identify him. Henry Franks had no trouble recognising the man who had held a pistol to his chest just the night before. Sheehan had made no attempt to disguise himself and now he was charged with serious crimes.

It was not until the March 29th of the following year when the case came before the Cork County Assizes. Sheehan now stood charged with demanding arms from the Franks and administering an unlawful oath on him. These were serious charges and there was considerable public interest in the case.

The first witness called was Henry Franks. He gave a full account of what had happened in the house that evening and told how he could recollect the events perfectly well. Under cross examination Franks said he never saw Sheehan before the night in question. The defence asked several questions to Henry doubting his ability to recognise the accused. However Henry explained that he had ample opportunity to see the accused and was positive he was the same man. He also stated that none of the three intruders that night wore any form of disguise.

Thomas Franks was next called and sworn in; he could not identify Sheehan but saw a man with a brass pistol that night. Thomas then pointed out a man in court called Richard Butler as the man who held the pistol that night.

An elderly neighbour Thomas Windham was called as he was visiting the Franks the night of the disturbance. Windham recalled seeing two men, one with a pistol but was not able to identify the accused Sheehan.

The servant Michael Walsh being the only other in the Franks house that night was called to take the stand. Walsh recalled standing in the hall and seeing the two men with the guns. He went on to say how he saw one holding a pistol to his master's chest and demanding him to swear an oath. He continued saying how the man's face was visible with the light from the fire but when pressed could not identify Sheehan who sat in the courtroom.

The defence then got a chance to make their case which mostly consisted of alibis from relations of the accused. David Fitzgerald who knew Sheehan well explained how he had met the accused on the 27th. Fitzgerald said that half an hour before it got dark he went with Sheehan and Sheehan's brother Timothy to Mallow Barracks with a horse. The witness admitted that Sheehan was married to his sister. Then he went on to explain how the Frank's house seemed to him to be 8 or 9 miles away from the barracks.

Maybe back then there was doubt over what time it got dark but with modern technology it is easy to calculate. On the night in question dusk occurred at 26 minutes past five.

The next witness was another David Fitzgerald, uncle to his namesake who had just left the stand. The older Fitzgerald had met Sheehan between five and six that evening near his own house. He went with the accused to get a rope for him and then left him at Sheehan's house before returning home.

Timothy Sheehan had a similar story but was willing to go further. He recalled meeting the last witness that evening and leaving him at their house. He then swore when he and his brother got home their supper was ready. His version is that they both had their supper and went to bed around eight that evening.

Finally to further support their story the Sheehan's aunt was called to take the stand. She was at home that night when the brothers returned, she witnessed them both eat their supper and then saw the brothers go to bed. According to her she bolted the door that evening and was first up the next morning unlocking the door for the men to go to work.

Hearing all this, the judge summed up all the evidence with great accuracy before letting the jury retire to decide. They didn't find it hard to come to a verdict and soon returned to the courtroom with a verdict of guilty. The judge then got his chance again and told the now guilty man how he wished he could pass a harsher sentence. He told Sheehan how his life was saved merely by the fact that he had not removed arms from the Franks house that night. Had he picked up so much as a bullet that night he would now be facing a death sentence. The judge then passed his sentence on Sheehan giving him transportation for the remainder of his natural life. The prisoner was then removed from court to await the arrangements to take him to the prison colony which at that time was most likely Australia.

In the middle of all this or at least some time around then Henry Franks had arranged to get married to a Miss Kearney from nearby townland of Ballyvoddy which was adjacent to Rockmills. His intended bride was an heiress of a considerable farm and they were both widely accepted as being fine catches with everything going for them. Her father James Kearney had died several years before leaving everything to Miss Kearney. Marrying meant they would combine their farms and be even more comfortable and secure. However it was not quite as easy as that she had a half sister Ellen Kearney, by her father's first wife. Ellen was married since 1815 to a Mr Arthur O'Keeffe also of Ballyvoddy who conveniently managed her farm. Obviously enough O'Keeffe was opposed to the marriage as Franks would then get control of his wife's farm and his future could be in jeopardy. Miss Kearney was said to have been keen to get married and gain control of her farm or at least she thought she would, for really her husband would have control.

It seems to keep O'Keeffe on side and not wanting to see her step-sister thrown out of her house an arrangement was made before the wedding. O'Keeffe and his wife were to remain in the house they resided for the remainder of their lives. To facilitate this, the newly married couple would reside with the Franks. The Franks house however would need improving for the couple and a contractor was employed.

Some sources state that the house was in disrepair due to the further activity of Whiteboys in the area. Some even going so far as to say it was the harsh way Franks had dealt with evicted tenants on the estate which brought the trouble on the family.

Either way up to September 1823 the family took up residence with Thornhill's in the village of Kildorrery. Their own haggard and house were set fire to sometime in the summer of 1823 doing damage to the house. Thornhill seems to feel uneasy about having them to stay for too long and the family were keen to move home. They wanted the workmen to complete the job quicker but this seems unlikely. On the 1st of September the Franks move back home again. It lacks any kind of comfort without windows or doors but that was the least of their worries.

On the night of the 9th of September Henry Franks and his mother returned home from Kildorrery. The family all dined together and afterwards remained around the table. It's easy to imagine them there under the light of a candle most likely discussing the renovations on the house or the upcoming wedding. Thomas Franks got up and went to the door as he heard a noise outside. As he did the door burst in and a man struck him with a fist and shoved him back into his own house. Several more rushed into the room, one man was dressed in women's clothes and had a white cloth over his face, other members of the party had their faces blackened to hide their identity. One of the intruders kicked over the table knocking everything onto the floor and extinguishing the only candle. The gang immediately demanded guns which Thomas Franks said he had none.

The Franks family all ended up on their knees in their own kitchen pleading with the intruders and emphasising that no guns were in the house. Thomas Franks told them as he had also done a year before that he would go to Rockmills with them and get them guns there.

They were not happy with this and several of the men began breaking up furniture in the kitchen. The leader of the party who was dressed in the women's clothes called out to the others to do their duty. At this stage one of the others handed him a shotgun and he fired at close range into the chest of Thomas Franks who fell to the ground. When he fell several more of the men joined in and repeatedly beat Thomas on the head with a crowbar.

The leader called out again to his subordinates to "do their duty" and their attention was turned to Henry Franks. Vastly outnumbered he had no chance and received a few blows to the head. His mother intervened trying to protect her son and was warned off by the gang. Not taking the warning she too received a few blows to the head and she fell down on the floor as her husband had before her.

Lisnagourneen House at it is today.

Now with all three members of the family lying on the floor the gang continued with the crowbar passing it around the gang so each one could have a go. Meanwhile another one them started with a three pronged pike indiscriminately stabbing the victims. This continued for nearly an hour until they were satisfied that all three were quite dead then they began to leave. Henry Franks made some noise like snoring or choking, whatever slim chance of surviving he had was now gone. The gang came back with the crow bar and this time made sure he was quite dead before leaving.

The gang then left the place with many of them heading in an easterly direction.

Once he was sure the gang had left and the coast was clear, Galveen who lived in the adjoining rooms emerged from his hiding place. Having heard the commotion Galveen knew something bad had happened but was not prepared for what he saw in the Franks kitchen. He came upon Mary Myers who had been hiding under a table the whole time.

Edmund Galveen knew immediately that there was no hope for any of the Franks and ran to the gardener's house to tell him what had transpired. Afterwards he rode to Kildorrery as fast as he could to the army barracks and returned with several soldiers.

The police and local magistrates were informed. Search parties were sent out around the locality to try and apprehend anyone behaving suspiciously.

It was Thursday morning by the time the Coroner James O'Brien reached the scene of the ghastly crime to hold an inquest. He found that several of the local gentry had gathered to form a jury for the inquest. It was noted however that it was only the gentry that had come; none of the ordinary people of the countryside had come near the house. None of the gentry had dared go inside the cottage to the horrendous crime scene.

When the coroner did enter the cottage he found the three mutilated bodies still lying there since the murderers had left Monday evening. The jury was promptly sworn in. The jury consisted of Henry Green Barry, Richard Oliver Aldworth, George Bond Low, Thomas St John Grant, Garret Nagle, Henry and George Walker, John Heard, William Quinn Montgomery, Roger Sheehy Burke, Edmond N Norcott and Spotswood Boles. Nobody envied them the task that lay ahead.

Before they began to hear any evidence all the jury had to view the three bodies in the cottage. The inquest had only called two witnesses as they were present that night.

First up was thirteen year old Mary Meyer who had only been working for the Franks family for about ten days. She retold the events of Monday evening; she had been in the kitchen with the Franks family when the men burst in. Mary explained how the first man to hit Thomas Franks was of very large stature and wore dark clothes. The man dressed as a woman had a white cloth over his face and acted as the leader giving orders to the others. When the candle was blown out, Mary managed to hide under another table near the fireplace where she stayed and witnessed the dreadful deeds unfold.

She told the inquest how she first saw Thomas Franks shot, and then Mrs Franks tried in vain to protect her son and was killed as a result. Mary estimated that she had spent almost an hour under the table in dread of her life of being seen as no doubt they would have killed her as well. While under there she saw all three lifeless bodies on the floor being struck by the crowbar. Mary said one of the men wore a green surtout coat, which was a sort of smock overcoat worn by cavalry officers in the army and also had spurs on his boots.

The next witness was Mary Galveen whose father Edmund was a labourer employed by the Franks. She lived with her father in rooms adjoining the Franks house.

That evening Mary said she was going out to fetch water with a jug when she met a few men at the door. She got a punch in the face from one of the intruders and was forced back into a small room. Several men stood guard at the door preventing her escape. During her time in captivity Mary could hear the commotion from the Franks part of the house. She heard demands being made to Thomas Franks for guns and several times heard a man call out "do your duty".

After what Mary thought was half an hour one of the men came to her and asked her to fetch a candle. She went to the room where the Franks family were and saw the bodies on the floor. After getting a candle from the press and lighting it the men put her back into the small room again. Mary said while in the other room one of the men held her hand and asked that she not lift her head to look around the room. She told the inquest she had not looked around the room out of fear but had heard moans coming from Henry Franks who lay on the floor.

Mary was kept in the room for another half hour when she heard men washing their hands in a tub of water outside the room she was in. Then one of the men asked her how far away was the river before the gang left the house. Mary looked out as the men left heading easterly she said. She thought there was about sixty men in total but did not recognise any of them.

While the inquest was going on two men were brought into the room by a local magistrate George Bond Lowe. When Lowe heard of the murders he went and arrested the two Sheehan brothers who lived 8 or 9 miles west of the place. Their brother Jeremiah had been sentenced to transportation for life the previous year after demanding arms from the Franks family.

When he saw the bodies one of the Sheehan brothers touched the finger of Mrs Franks. He was asked before the inquest why he had done it and he replied "twas custom in the country". Sheehan then said it was an awful bad thing that had happened and wished who ever had done it would receive justice. It was generally believed at the inquest that neither of the brothers showed any sign of guilt for the dreadful scene before them. Both men were then separately asked about their movements on Monday night and were able to give reasonably good account. However the jury felt the brothers needed to be questioned further and required that they be detained.

The proceedings of the inquest were interrupted when a Thomas Arbuthnot entered with bloody leaves he had found. Arbuthnot had been out searching the vicinity and revealed to the inquest the evidence he had found was east of Frank's house. He said it was at a farm called Scar near Kildorrery which had been farmed by the Franks. The inquest then adjourned and took to the countryside looking for more evidence. They subsequently found blood west of the house in the direction of Doneraile. This led the inquest to the conclusion that the gang split in two after the ghastly deeds they had done to the Franks.

It was also stated at the inquest how the Franks had been put out of the farm known as Scart some time before by the Countess of Kingston. The landlord had however not evicted the tenants on the land and they continued to live there. Thomas Franks appealed the decision and because of some technicality managed to get it overturned. Only four days before the Franks were murdered Thomas Franks seized the lands at Scart from the tenants for the rents that had not been paid to him since he was evicted. While it was said that Mrs Franks begged her husband not to pursue the rents which he claimed were owed.

The jury of the inquest came to the verdict "that the deceased had come by their deaths by the hands of a party of Whiteboys, to the jurors at present unknown who on the evening of Tuesday Sept 8th 1823 forced into the house and then and there wilfully inflicted on them several mortal wounds with a loaded gun and an iron crowbar of which they died instantly".

Strange as it seems it was after the inquest that the clothes were removed from the bodies. On Thomas Franks it was found his body had been stabbed all over with a hayfork. So much force had been used that there was also holes in the floor where the pike had gone right through him.

There was a strong feeling amongst the gentry of the locality that those responsible for these dreadful crimes would be found and swiftly brought to justice. A meeting was held at Bowen's Court between the local magistrates. Their purpose was to determine the best actions to apprehend those responsible. It did seem however that the ordinary folk of the area were not going to be as helpful to the investigation as the gentry.

One woman did come forward with evidence after the inquest. She had been travelling home to Limerick from Youghal. On Tuesday she stopped at Castlelyons and sought refuge at a farmhouse but was refused. Her story was she slept outside and during the night men came and hid guns in a cock of hay in the haggard.

The Friday following the Inquest the funeral took place on the Franks family. It was again noted how a large number of the gentry attended but none of the labouring class were there, nor any tenants of the Franks.

On the 20th of September in Fermoy there was a special sitting of the court to deal with cases under the Insurrection Act. Such was the unrest in the country at the time that the Insurrection Act allowed for summary justice. This meant those accused could be tried and convicted by two magistrates rather than a jury. It even introduced a curfew at night; those found not to be at home were also punishable. The penalties were severe up to seven years transportation. At that time over 300 per year were transported for crimes such as this.

That Saturday in Fermoy William Mead stood accused of breaking the curfew. He had been arrested an hour before sunrise the morning after the Franks were killed. He had at the time a reaping hook in his hand and was not two miles from the Franks farm house. Mead however was lucky the farmer he was working for gave evidence that he had slept in his house that night. William Mead was acquitted and discharged from court but this showed how the law was going to track down the Franks killers.

That same day in court John Sheehan was charged with having ammunition which he denied and not being at home on the night of the 15th. During the evidence it was found he slept at a place called Wallstown, this was only three miles from where the Franks were murdered. Not being able to give a good account of his movements that night and no witness for his defence Sheehan was quickly dealt with. He was quickly found guilty and sentenced to seven years transportation.

Within weeks six men had been arrested on information from one of the Sheehan brothers who swore he was not in the house that night. The six men from the Rockmills area were taken to Doneraile and held in the jail there. The woman's clothes the leader had worn that night were found heavily bloodstained. It was felt that evidence like this would help prove the guilt of the men who had been arrested.

Despite six men in custody a proclamation was issued by the Lord Lieutenant of Ireland for the arrest of the Franks killers. It offered five hundred pounds for any person who gave information of the killers which led to a conviction. It was to be paid in one hundred pounds for each of the first five persons convicted.

The proclamation went on to offer a pardon to any persons who were there on the night but did not actually do any of the killing, so long as they gave information against those who had carried it out.

Maybe this was why one of the Timothy Sheehan brothers came forward with information but having knowledge of it also implicated himself. Instead of getting the pardon offered in the proclamation he found himself in jail.

In early December Timothy Sheehan who had been in custody for several weeks made his escape from jail in Doneraile. This signalled that he was guilty and worried of the consequences if it was proved. A reward of fifty guineas was offered for anyone who managed to arrest him.

It was not until the Cork Spring Assizes on the 9th of April 1824 that the case came before Mr Justice Torrens. Five men were now to be charged with the dreadful crimes against the Franks family, three Cremin brothers, Magner and O'Keeffe.

One of those accused stood out from the others, Arthur O'Keeffe. It was clear to all in court that he was not an ordinary country person like the others. Arthur wasted no time and addressed the judge with ease and confidence. He asked that the trial not go ahead and said it would only prove he was completely innocent. Arthur stated that the Franks were his friends and there was no reason he would want them dead. Arthur spoke for the other four who stood charged with him but failed to have the trial postponed.

The judge decided to hear the case the next morning.

Saturday the 10th O'Keeffe again tried to have the trial postponed. His reason now was that witnesses he needed for his defence had not been given ample time to attend.

After much deliberation it was decided to postpone the case against Arthur O'Keeffe but the case against three Cremin brothers would continue as planned. The other two men were then removed from the court so they would not hear the evidence.

The three brothers Patrick, Maurice and John Cremin now stood in the dock charged with the most serious of crimes. After several objections a jury of twelve men were sworn in before the case went on.

The large crowd gathered in the courtroom were left dumb struck when Edward Magner was called as the chief witness for the prosecution. Magner had already given a statement to the effect that he was there that night and involved in the murder. He began his evidence in court to that effect saying he recalled the night well and was present at the Franks.

He went back to explain how it had all come about. According to Magner he met with the Cremin brothers the May before. They asked him to help kill the Franks and he agreed. The witness said it was not until two nights before the Franks were killed that he received the message to be ready and again he agreed. It was on the afternoon of the 9th Magner said he was reaping corn at Thomas Barry's farm at Ballyduff till four. He left there taking a woman's cap and gown and he went home to collect a pistol. Two hours later Magner says he met with three Cremin brothers at Frank's kitchen garden as had previously been arranged. It was then Magner put on the cap and apron, he said Patrick Cremin was also dressed in a woman's shawl and apron.

Then Magner admitted being the one who charged into the house and demanded guns from Thomas Franks. The witness then went further and revealed he shot the pistol at Thomas Franks but said it was Patrick Cremin who struck him knocking him to the floor. Mrs Franks was screeching he said so they twisted the table cloth around her face while they finished off the two men. Magner said there were nine men in total in the gang that evening.

Under cross examination the witness admitted having taken the Whiteboy oath two years before. The oath he said was to do anything he was ordered to do which included killing men, women and even children.

The witness was pressed further and told how he had been tried and convicted before under the Insurrection Act. Magner said he really didn't want to leave Ireland so he found another way by turning into an informer against his accomplices in order to protect himself. When asked Magner said the crimes he had been involved in previously was the burning of four or five houses but said he would have burned more if ordered to. He then admitted to murdering the Franks and said he would have killed more if ordered. The killings Magner said did not affect him much; he slept that night and went to work the next morning as normal. The witness gave evidence which painted a terrible character of himself and he seemed to do it with little difficulty.

It's worth noting that while Edward Magner was not on trial as he had become an approver he was not free and was still being held in jail at this time.

The next witness called was Mary Myers who had also given evidence at the inquest. Mary told how she had previously identified the Cremin's and also admitted knowing them. Going back to the night the Franks were killed Mary said she witnessed a lot of men in the house that night but could recognise only the Cremin's seeing the three of them there. Mary explained how she hid under the table the whole time and went over all the dreadful happenings that evening. She told how Henry Franks begged for mercy after seeing his father killed but the intruders continued saying "you have no mercy to get you rascals". Mary also told how frightened she was that night knowing at any moment she could be next.

A doctor was called to give medical evidence of the Franks as he had found them after the killings. Dr Piddel described how Thomas Franks had been shot in the chest and suffered massive head injuries. The doctor said his skull was so broken the brains were coming out and it would have been easy to put his hand inside and remove fragments of the skull.

Henry Franks had a broken arm and also suffered from head injuries. His mother Mrs Franks was lying nearby with a handkerchief tied over her face. She had died by suffocation whereas the men had died from their head injuries.

With this the case for the prosecution was heard and the defence wished to proceed having no witnesses to call. But then a character witness came forward for the brothers, James Gould identified himself saying the Cremin's were his tenants. The farmer said he knew the family with over twenty years and they had never done anything out of the way that was worth recalling. Then he backtracked a little stating their father was done for sheep stealing and revealed he thought people from that part of the country were "bad boys".

The judge gave his speech to the jury before charging them to leave and find a verdict. His speech went on for well over an hour going over all the evidence again and where Magner's testimony didn't exactly agree with that of Mary Myers. He left the jury under no illusion that it was one of the worst atrocities he had come across in his career.

However he made it quite clear to the jury that it was up to them to decide for themselves.

The jury retired to consult and returned to the court room after about thirty minutes. The foreman read out their verdict finding the three brothers guilty on all counts against them.

When the judge went to pass sentence one the three brothers called out "it is the wrong charge", however it was no use. The judge continued and told them that they had only two days to live and make amends for their guilt. On Monday he said at Gallows Green all three were to be hung until dead. The brothers protested in court so loudly that the judge lost control of the courtroom and the three had to be removed still swearing their innocence to heaven and earth.

The following Monday 12th of April 1824 brothers John, Maurice and Patrick Cremin were brought to Gallows Green in Cork to receive their punishment. Maurice the youngest of the brothers was so sick he had to be brought to the gallows in a cart; the other two were able to walk themselves.

That morning their father had been allowed to visit his sons and only asked that they admit whether they were guilty or not. Later at the scaffold one of the priests kneeled before the condemned men explaining the consequences of not telling the truth now. All three declared they understood fully their fate but swore there and then that they knew nothing of the murders of the Franks family until the morning following the crimes.

They said "having nothing from man to hope for and less from god" and begged mercy from god for their prosecutioner. Their pleas of innocence were repeated by the condemned men right up until they drew their last breath. This made the majority of people present believe that the men were indeed innocent. Less than a minute later all three brothers were hanging lifelessly from the gallows, having never admitted their part in the murders.

The bodies were then cut down and taken for dissection at the local hospital. This was due to the Murder Act of 1751. The law stated that those found guilty of murder would not be allowed to be buried afterwards. The bodies were to be either hung from gibbets or dissected for medical research. This was the only way at the time hospitals could obtain bodies for such purposes. The law also stated that once found guilty of murder the hanging was to be carried out within two days. Only if the second day fell on a Sunday could an extra day be allowed. This obviously enough left no time for appealing the sentence or getting the sentence reduced. In cases such as this nobody could be sure until right before the noose went around their necks whether they were guilty or not. It was then that they were asked to admit their guilt and most at this point relented with nothing to lose and admitted their guilt. However those that hung without admitting, nobody knew for sure in some cases whether justice had been served or an innocent man hung.

Magner's evidence was always going to be suspect. Why would the Cremin's have come to him for assistance from a man who had already turned informer to protect himself? Either way it was now too late for the Cremin's but Magner had again managed to save himself at least for the time being.

By the time the Spring Assizes concluded in Cork that April seven men in total were executed at Gallows Green within five days.

In July 1825, the following year, Timothy Sheehan and Thomas Bourke were arrested at Rockmills for the murders of the Franks family and taken to Cork to await their trial.

Again Sheehan managed to escape from prison but was re-apprehended at Grenagh a few miles from Cork City.

Despite getting his case postponed there were still suspicions surrounding Arthur O'Keeffe and he wasn't off the hook just yet. Having it postponed might have saved his life but he still had to wait in agony to see what would happen next.

Not till the Autumn Assizes in Cork on 18th of August 1825 was the case called.

Now Arthur O'Keeffe and Thomas Bourke stood accused of the three murders before Judge Baron Pennefather. It was stated that O'Keeffe's case had been postponed but he was ready to proceed at the Summer Assizes the year before. However the crown prosecution at that time sought another postponement. Arthur O'Keeffe stood out in court and did not seem at all like most Whiteboys. Despite standing out O'Keeffe did not seem worried and stood in court talking easily to his lawyer and a group of his peers gathered around him. While Bourke on the other hand was not legally represented nor did he have influential friends like O'Keeffe did.

Before the witnesses were called, Sergeant Goold detailed the case for the prosecution. He noted how O'Keeffe had made claims to Kearney's land and would have suffered by the proposed marriage. He also told how the Franks were seen in the area as severe landlords showing little sympathy to their tenants.

Then Goold revealed some of the evidence that would be heard from the witnesses. He said on Sunday the 7th of September two nights before the Franks were killed a meeting was held in Power's house near Shanballymore to make arrangements for the murders. It would be proved the Sergeant said that O'Keeffe was indeed present at that meeting and agreed with what was being said. He went further still saying it would also be shown Arthur O'Keeffe was in fact the ringleader dressed that night in a green coat holding a whip. It was known in the area that O'Keeffe wore a green coat but was said to have never worn it after that night. Then he disclosed that when the police arrived on the scene form Kildorrery, O'Keeffe's dog was seen near the Franks house.

Now almost two years later it seemed the end was nigh for Arthur, after hearing from a few witnesses the judge could be putting on the black cap which meant only one thing. This surely knocked O'Keeffe's confidence in getting off once more.

The Sergeant felt that the last trial witnesses had held back on certain fact but was confident that justice would again be served.

The Sergeant then turned his attention to Thomas Bourke who he said had a shirt over his clothes that night, this was how the Whiteboys got their name. The shirt however was left at the scene and the gardener's wife had washed it and hung it out to dry. Now the Sergeant said Bourke was seen returning for the shirt the evening after the killings.

The prosecution then opened their case by calling Timothy Sheehan who was now an approver for the crown prosecution. Sheehan said on the Sunday before the killings John Cremin sent for him. When he went to the meeting he identified Thomas Bourke as being present that night. He told that night the Franks would be killed but Sheehan now claimed he had disagreed with this. Saying his family had suffered enough already, as his brothers had already been transported. The others at the meeting called him a coward and eventually according to himself he relented and agreed to them.

Timothy then went on to speak of the night of the killings; he said he never entered the Franks house until after Thomas Franks was dead. When he did Henry Franks was on his knees and his mother was trying to save her son. He even went so far as to claim he tried to help the surviving Franks family but could not and ran out again. While inside the house he saw two of the Cremin's and a man in a green coat with a whip in his hand. The man with the green coat Sheehan had also seen at the meeting Sunday night.

When asked to identify the man now in court everyone was sure he would point to Arthur O'Keeffe but he did not. He pointed instead to Thomas Bourke and everyone was stunned.

Under cross examination by the defence Sheehan admitted that he was warned if he did not give evidence he would face the death penalty. When asked "would you swear anything to save your life" Sheehan's reply was simply "I would sir". The questions went on trying to prove how Sheehan would say anything until the judge intervened and moved the proceedings on.

Edmund Galveen took the stand, as we have heard before he lived under the same roof as the Franks but in a separate annex. Galveen identified both the accused men saying he knew them well as they lived nearby. Edmund recalled the night well saying he had driven Mrs Franks home from Kildorrery.

Later while attending to his duties he encountered three men outside the house. One of these he said was Thomas Bourke, they were checking to see were the Franks family home. A short time later Galveen saw Bourke again, now with a white shirt over his clothes and a pitchfork in his hand. There were two other men with him one called Walsh and another O'Keeffe but he said not Arthur O'Keeffe.

He was then warned to close his door and go to bed with his family. Galveen's evidence then turned to what he heard because obviously enough for his safety he complied with the gang. He heard Henry Franks frantically call out that his father was killed. He afterwards heard a man calling out for the others to do their duty, this voice he recognised as Arthur O'Keeffe. Then he recalled having seen O'Keeffe in the yard earlier that night wearing a green coat and white trousers.

When cross examined by the defence Galveen said he was on his knees in his own house when he saw Arthur O'Keeffe close by, outside the window. He was then asked why it was over a year after the killings before mentioning Arthur O'Keeffe. Why had he not said it at the inquest the lawyer questioned? Also why was Mrs Kearney with him when he did come forward and give evidence against O'Keeffe? Edmund however denied being encouraged by the Kearney's and also said he never took any money from them.

The questioning then turned to the first time he saw the men that night checking were the Franks home. He was asked why he had not warned the Franks that there were three men looking for them. Edmund admitted knowing that the men were going to do something bad but said he only had fifteen minutes and was too frightened to tell them.

After the cross examination several of the jurors began asking their own questions to the witness. The first juror asked directly to the witness did he know before that night what was going to take place and got a short answer "I did". Then he was asked for how long before and again the witness replied "about three weeks". To this the juror was amazed and asked why he had not warned any of the family. Galveen then claimed three days before someone came to him and told him the plans were cancelled.

Mary Myers sworn in and gave similar evidence she had before. This time she identified Arthur O'Keeffe saying he worn a bottle green coat that evening. She saw him turn to go out from her hiding place under the table. According to her O'Keeffe did not come into the house until after the Franks had been killed. She heard him say "do your duty" and then "beat them on the heads".

Under cross examination Mary plainly admitted to swearing to not having seen Arthur O'Keeffe that night several times. She did this to save his life as she knew him and he had a wife and family but said she was now telling the truth. The Cremin brothers she said she did not know nor care about when she gave evidence against them.

One juror asked Mary plainly which evidence from her should be believed, what she said today or what she said on previous occasion. Mary was unable to give an answer to this question which was quite telling.

Edward Magner was sworn in and gave evidence as he had done before. He recalled being in the kitchen garden that night and seeing Arthur O'Keeffe there in a green coat. He also saw him in the kitchen that night.

When questioned by the defence Magner remarked how he had not good clothes when he worked as a labourer. He admitted to having got money in Dublin from a Crown prosecution lawyer, which he used to buy good boots and clothes. Magner also said he fired the shot at old Mr Franks and that the Franks family had never done anything to him. Magner then was asked about his past and freely admitted to having burned several houses and doing anything he was ordered to. He finished by saying "I would wade up to my neck in blood" which produced laughter in court from some quarters.

Magner continued his evidence saying Arthur O'Keeffe was the agent where his father lived and often seized the lands when the tenants could not pay.

Mary Galveen again gave similar evidence as she had before but said she was sure she had seen Bourke that night. She however never mentioned seeing Arthur O'Keeffe at all that evening.

The next witness called for the crown was himself a magistrate whose testimony there would be no doubt. It was Andrew Batwell. The witness said he knew Arthur O'Keeffe who lived near the Franks house very well. He recalled having often seeing Arthur in a green coat before that night but never after.

A policeman William Brett then took the stand and was sworn in. He recalled Galveen arriving at Kildorrery that night with the dreadful news. Immediately he set out for Lisnagourneen with a lieutenant on a horse which was about half past eight. Approaching the Franks house he saw a dog on the road, later he saw the same dog outside Arthur O'Keeffe's and believed it was indeed his dog.

The defence then began to call its witnesses which consisted of character references since they had no alibis. First called was a respectable man Mr Williams who said he knew O'Keeffe for seven years. During that time he had never know him to do anything improper. O'Keeffe's job was to act as agent for the landlord which made him unpopular by the tenants especially when he seized land from them. Williams noted that Arthur had never fled when he was under suspicion even knowing what the consequences could be.

When questioned Williams revealed that Arthur O'Keeffe told him once, he had a child with Mary Galveen. Was this the reason why Mary had failed to mention Arthur O'Keeffe in her evidence?

Next up was a man called George Smith who was Arthur O'Keeffe's employer. He related knowing O'Keeffe since he was a child and now employed him as assistant agent on three estates. He felt that his employee always behaved correctly despite being assaulted several times by tenants.

When questioned by the prosecution Smith admitted that he thought O'Keeffe was wrongly charged and he felt it his duty to help him. He had also lent money to his employee to pay for his lawyers. Several more witnesses were called to give references of O'Keeffe but only one was called for Bourke.

With this the judge summed up the evidence, it was now nearly six in the evening and the court had sat hearing this case since nine that morning.

About half past six that evening the jury left the courtroom to reach a decision. The half hour while the jury were out Arthur O'Keeffe did not seem the least worried with what could happen next. While Thomas Bourke on the other hand was extremely agitated

The jury foreman announced the verdict of not guilty against both the accused prisoners. Arthur O'Keeffe then asked for the opportunity to address the court and the judge allowed him.

He rose to his feet and had his say. "My Lord, in the presence of the King of Kings, the Lord of Lords, and the Judge of Judges. I acknowledge that I am as innocent as the charge made upon me this day, as the child unborn. As well might they have arraigned your Lordship, or the Bishop of Cork, at this bar as me and I declare in the presence of god that I would search out, and punish the perpetrators of that horrid murder, as soon as any gentleman in the country."

The judge Baron Pennefather replied "well, I am glad indeed that you say so, Discharge those men". And that was it O'Keeffe and Bourke walked free from court. As they did the police made their best effort to hold the crowds back but desperately failed. The crowd however were well wishers who embraced the now free men. Those that were not wishing them well were in hysterics with the emotions of seeing their relations free. The crowds continued to follow them down the streets cheering as they went along.

In 1825 the Earl of Kingston was before a Lords Select Committee and was asked about the Frank's murder. He denied it was on his estate but said the Franks had been tenants of his. He revealed that on several occasions his agents had been refused payment by his tenants as the Franks had already got the money from them. He even admitted that some of the so called gentry like the Franks did not want to pay their rent at all.

J.R O Flanagan writing "The Munster Circuit" gave a brief but good account of the Franks murders. He concluded by saying "I trust never again shall this peaceful neighbourhood be sullied by so terrible a crime". Alas on this one statement time would prove him so very wrong. In fact at the time of writing it in 1880 it had already occurred he just didn't know about it yet.

Street fight gone wrong
Kingwilliamstown (Ballydesmond) 1897

Tuesday 29th June 1897, the Feast of Saints Peter and Paul there was a large attendance at mass. As there was no work on this feast day, many young lads were around the village. They frequented the pubs and by evening had gathered at the handball alley in the village of Kingwilliamstown. First cousins Daniel and Edmund Connell played against Patrick and Denis Herlihy. While they were playing two brothers John and Timothy Corbett approached to watch the game.

There had been trouble in the past between the Corbett's and Connell's.

The previous year Daniel Connell had spent a month in jail as a result of a fight.

Daniel Connell ceased playing handball and said "I suppose it's me they are looking for". Words were exchanged between John Corbett and Daniel on the street. After a few minutes and with many onlookers Daniel was heard saying "I will fight you myself". He then struck John Corbett in the face with his fist and the pair began fighting on the street. The fight was not going to be a clean one. Soon Edmund was involved helping his cousin and so Timothy stepped in to help his brother.

The Police were quickly on the scene and arrested John Corbett and both Connell's. They were all brought before a local justice of the peace Mr Thomas Jones from Glencollins. The crime must have been seen of as petty and the men were discharged.

Brothers John and Timothy Corbett headed home to Glencollins. On the way home John began to feel weak. So the pair stopped at a friend Denis Murphy's house so he could recover. John Corbett had sustained several cuts on his head but thought nothing of them. Murphy however grew worried and convinced him to attend a doctor and get the wounds seen to. A good neighbour and friend Murphy tackled his pony and trap to take him eight miles to see Dr JJ O'Riordan in Boherbue.

The doctor dressed the wounds but did not think they were any way serious.

The brothers returned again with their friend Murphy after seeing the doctor. By the time they were back John Corbett felt much weaker. So Murphy again extended his hospitality and John Corbett stayed at his friend's house for the night.

During the night Corbett's condition grew much worse. In the early hours of the morning John Corbett passed away as a result of his injuries aged only thirty.

The police were informed and a priest sent for. Sergeant Healy arrived from the village knowing already of the fight the day before. News of John Corbett's death came as a huge shock to the area especially to his elderly parents Denis and Mary (nee Sweeney) Corbett. He had two other younger sisters Mary still lived at home and Nora.

The inquest was held on the 1st of July by coroner James Byrne. Twelve respectable men from the locality formed the jury who would decide how John Corbett had died.

Several witnesses that were outside the handball alley spoke at the inquest and the jury quickly came to their verdict. The jury found that John Corbett had died from compression of the brain and haemorrhage of blood. This was as a result of the head injuries he had sustained the evening before. Despite the Police searching the area for Daniel and Edmund Connell there was no sign of them. They obviously had got word John Corbett was dead and knew it was now a serious charge against them. On the 3rd of July though they changed their minds and turned themselves into the Police in the village.

On Wednesday the 28th of July the cousins were brought before a special court at Knocknagree before Resident magistrate McDermott. The charge was read to them "that on the 29th of June 1897 at Kingwilliamstown, Co Cork they did unlawfully, wilfully and feloniously and with malice aforethought kill and murder one John Corbett of Glencollins".

District Inspector Thomas Monson from Newmarket represented the crown prosecution. Mr Edward Beytagh solicitor from Kanturk represented the accused men.

The first witness called was Cornelius Fitzgerald a local National School teacher.

He told how between five and six that day he was with John Corbett at the handball court. Words were exchanged between them but he could not recall exactly what had been said. Fitzgerald witnessed the fight start and saw Edmund Connell strike Corbett on the head but did know with what.

Brother of the deceased man Timothy Corbett was called to give evidence.

He recalled being with his brother that day and going to the handball alley. Once the fight began he saw Edmund Connell strike John on the head with the edge of a stone twice. A similar stone was produced in court for all to see. Timothy told he also took up a stone and struck Edmund in defence of his brother. The police then arrived and the fight was broken up. Timothy recalled in court the dreadful night he spent with his brother. All night he stayed up at his bedside and he died at seven the following morning.

Carpenter Patrick Herlihy was called as he was playing handball with the defendants that day before the fight. Patrick was twenty six years old and married in the village with two young children. Herlihy described the row between the men and gave similar evidence about the fight.

Dr JJ O'Riordan from Boherbue told how John Corbett came to him at almost one in the morning. He observed two large wounds on the top of John Corbett's head and a small one at the base of the skull. At that time he did stitch & dress the wounds but advised Timothy to keep them moist with bread. O'Riordan said he cleaned the head wounds and had to cut hair to do so.

He then described the post mortem he carried out on the 1st of July with Dr Verling from Newmarket. A large blood clot was found under one of the wounds when they examined the skull. It had been pressing on the brain and was the cause of death in the doctor's opinion. He told how the wound and clot could have been caused by a blow of a blunt object such as a stone. District Inspector Monson then produced the stone and asked "could it have been produced by a stone like this", the doctor replied it could.

Acting Sergeant William Keaty of Kingwilliamstown told the court how he was on duty in the village that day with Constable Conran. The sergeant explained he was 193 yards away when the fight broke out at the ball alley. From that distance he saw Daniel Connell come out on the road and strike Corbett with his fist. As the sergeant approached the scene he witnessed Edmund strike John Corbett on the head but could not be sure if it was with a stone or not.

Constable Conran told the court how on the 9th of August the year before Daniel Connell had assaulted Timothy Corbett. Mr Beytagh objected to this but the prosecution said they merely wanted to show how there was bad blood between the men.

Mr Monson closed the evidence for the prosecution satisfied that a prima facie case existed against the pair. He asked they be returned for trial at the Munster Winter Assizes on the capital charge. He knew Mr Beytagh would apply for bail for his clients and asked that the application be refused. He said the men could easily abscond as they owned no property to keep them there.

Mr Beytagh on the other hand argued that the charge before the Assizes would be reduced to manslaughter. He pleaded for bail saying it was unjust to hold them till December on the charge of manslaughter.

The judge asked on quest "in the case of homicide when life has been taken have you ever known the accused parties to be admitted to bail?" Beytagh claimed he had on several occasions but the judge was not changing his mind.

Edward Beytagh didn't back down either and continued arguing for his clients. He went on that in law only those charged with high treason could be refused bail. The likely sentences they would receive in December was two or three months. It was unfair he said to keep them in jail for six months.

McDermott made his opinion clear saying I will not grant bail, if they want bail apply to the Queen's Bench for it. The case for the defence had been reserved until their trial in December. The two were taken for court to Rathmore barracks and were then transferred to Cork Gaol.

At the Munster Winter Assizes the case came before Justice William O'Brien at the city courthouse. Edward Beytagh had been right, the charge was reduced to one of manslaughter but they could still get years if found guilty.

When called Daniel and Edmund Connell pleaded not guilty. The case did not take long as it was no longer a capital charge. The jury came to a verdict of guilty but recommended leniency for Daniel Connell.

Daniel Connell was sentenced to four months and Edmund to nine months for manslaughter. The terms were lenient even by modern standards. The same day in court a man got six months for wounding a man, while another got six months for stealing oats.

Ten years later Mary Corbett married local farmer Jeremiah Riordan and they stayed at home with her elderly mother.

Map of the village of Ballydesmond.

Was it you did this
Banteer 1915

On Thursday the 21st of January 1915 a group of men returned to Banteer from a coursing event at Kanturk over three miles away. Most returned on the five o'clock train and rather than go home, most spread themselves between the pubs in Banteer - Lanigan's, O'Callaghan's and Deady's. Over the course of the evening the people that had cycled to the coursing arrived from Kanturk. Much of the discussion in the pubs concerned the day's events.

Sometime before nine a young labourer Michael Murphy left his father in Callaghan's and headed for home to Glen South with his sisters Catherine and Maggie and two men they were courting named Foley and Moynihan. Michael had cycled to Kanturk earlier that day and now took his bike home with him. The group went on hoping their father would catch up and maybe get a lift from someone heading to Glen South.

For some reason one changed their mind that night and wanted to turn back to find their father. The siblings argued between themselves but the two young courting would not have got involved. The group turned around though and headed back to the village.

Entering the village by the church they met a policeman on patrol who commented on the noise they were making. At the same time there was some commotion coming from outside Lanigan's pub.

The policeman turned around and headed towards the source of the disturbance. It was a dark night and street lights where unheard of in country villages. On his way there which was only about twenty yards away he apprehended a man fleeing the scene. This was a case that was clearly not going to need Sherlock Holmes.

A man was lying on the street in a pool of blood. There were others at the scene and one man was trying to hold up the casualty to check his condition on the street. Twenty two year old farm labourer Michael Murphy was on the scene quicker than the policeman. He recognised the man on the street as his father Laurence. William Kennedy held him, having seen what had occurred he knew he was bound to be in a bad way.

The Murphy siblings had argued on the road about what was delaying their father now they knew. By now his daughters had also arrived. Michael dragged his father over close to Lanigan's and a lamp was got from Mrs Lanigan to check his injuries. A doctor and priest were sent for. Father O'Connor arrived from the parochial house which was nearby. Shortly after Laurence Murphy was taken to the local Barracks and looked over in the day room by the constables. By that time there were no signs of life from Laurence and his head injuries were such that he was barely recognisable. Dr O'Leary arrived from Kanturk and said there was nothing he could do for the man. He had died as a result of fractures to his skull.

Rumours in the area were that the trouble began when Murphy had entered Lanigan's pub on his own at nine that evening. It was said to have been a discussion about dogs that had turned ugly and had led to a heated argument. One man had to be forcibly removed from Lanigan's and when Murphy emerged from the pub he was set upon.

The police made several quick arrests, one of the men Jeremiah Twomey was caught running away from the scene that night. The police had felt from the start he was involved the way he was fleeing. His brother was also arrested, so Jeremiah and Timothy Twomey, labourers from Fermoyle became the chief suspects. William Kennedy who had left Lanigan's the same time as Murphy that night was also in custody.

People in the area were shocked at how a simple dispute had led to this. There seemed however to be more to it but locals were reluctant to talk. The suspects were the same age as Laurence Murphy's son Michael. It was common for young men in their twenties to fight after drink. But why would a man of an older generation get dragged into it.

Laurence Murphy known as Lar Fox was a farmer living in a townland called Glen South about four miles south east of Banteer. Laurence had been married for twenty four years to his wife Mary Driscoll. They both originally came from near the village of Nad. He had eleven children and it turned out his wife was also expecting another baby at the time. Some of the older children already mentioned Michael, Catherine and Margaret had left home and worked nearby. Several young children would now grow up without their father. Lar was well known locally as a quiet family man who kept greyhounds.

The inquest held on 23rd January by coroner James Byrne in O'Callaghan's public house in Banteer. The jury of twelve men was made up of locals John Kiely foreman, Daniel Carroll, Patrick Meade, Denis Sullivan all farmers from Shronebeha. And John Kearney, Daniel O'Callaghan, Daniel Cotter, Jeremiah Cronin, Philip Mullane, Daniel Ahern, Timothy Connell and Denis O'Callaghan mostly farmers from Banteer area.

District Inspector Spears represented the prosecution while Kanturk solicitor JJ Lenehan was there listening to the proceedings for his clients, the accused.

Even though the police had a lot of information and had arrested suspects, this process still had to be carried out and move on to be investigated before a magistrate. The outcome of the inquest was a foregone conclusion.

The first witness called was Sergeant John Connors who came on the scene that night. He told how he was between the Church and the priest's house when he met Michael Murphy. Behind him he heard something going on in Banteer.

Michael Murphy gave evidence of identification, that the body was indeed his father. He had last seen him alive when he left Callaghan's pub on Thursday night. He headed for home while his father went on to Lanigan's.

William Kennedy from Shronebeha was called as a witness. He recalled talking to Laurence Murphy in the taproom of Lanigan's that night. Murphy then went to the bar and left a few minutes later. Kennedy said he walked out only seconds after the deceased man. As he walked out of Lanigan's he saw Murphy fall on the street and two men laying into him. District Inspector Spears knew he had enough evidence for an inquest but he decided to keep going. He asked did Kennedy recognise the men kicking Murphy that night and asked him to identify them. The witness identified them as Jeremiah and Timothy Twomey. Kennedy claimed he ran over and tried to stop them kicking a defenceless man on the street. According to the witness there was no one else there at the time despite many people being in the village that evening.

Defence solicitor took his opportunity to limit the damage for his clients. He asked William Kennedy if he had been arrested in connection with the case as it had been reported in the newspaper. The witness said he was arrested in a way but only to be questioned and was not charged with anything.

Medical evidence was given by Dr P J O'Leary from Kanturk. He said when he arrived at the barracks in Banteer Laurence Murphy had been dead for some time. He carried out the post mortem the following day finding several fractures to the skull. There were also many wounds to the face, jaw and ears. Significant haemorrhaging was found inside the skull because of the head injuries. The cause of death was pressure on the brain as a result of the fracture to the base of the skull. The district Inspector asked would a heavy nailed boot cause such injuries. The doctor agreed that it was indeed possible.

A juror asked the doctor would the first blow alone have been the cause of death. The doctor was unsure as Murphy had received so many blows. The coroner intervened saying "we have the cause of death". The juror however didn't give in saying "likely he was beat further than death".

The coroner summed up the case for the jury saying how it was unnecessary to mention any names. The purpose of the inquest was merely to find the cause of death he didn't want to go into who had done it.

The jury returned after only fifteen minutes saying their verdict was to agree with the medical evidence. The coroner announced an open verdict and Lenehan was relieved his clients had not been mentioned in the verdict. With the evidence against them they would surely be found guilty before a jury. The coroner expressed his sympathy to the widow and her children before the inquest concluded.

The police continued investigating the case despite having suspects arrested. It was the motive behind the crime that was in doubt. It was difficult to believe that a disagreement that night had escalated in just one night to murder. The two families in question lived in the same area within a townland or two of each other. They were both large families with children of the same age. A few years before Margaret Murphy worked for an aunt of the Twomey's called Nora Barry. While she was there a young brother of the suspects Hugh Twomey worked for his aunt. He left and was replaced by Michael Murphy. Was this the reason a dispute arose between the families? Catherine Murphy had remained working for Mrs Barry until the night her father was killed. There had in the months before been altercations between the Twomey brothers and Michael Murphy.

Murphy was killed right in the middle of Banteer.

It was almost a month later on Monday the 15th of February a magisterial inquiry was held in the circumstances surrounding the death. Brothers Jeremiah and Timothy Twomey were now charged with murder before resident magistrate Hardy in Kanturk courthouse.

Crown solicitor Anthony Carroll from Fermoy stated the case for the prosecution. He claimed evidence would show the attack on Laurence Murphy and that no argument broke out that night. It was a planned attack by the brothers who had it out for the Murphy's for several years.

Mr J J Lenehan solicitor from Kanturk had the tougher job representing the accused brothers.

Ellen O'Connor who worked in Lanigan's pub was able to detail the movements in the bar that evening. At seven that evening she saw Danny Murphy, Jim O'Brien and Bill Kennedy enter the bar. Then Jack Callaghan, Mick Riordan and Michael Sheehan arrived with two younger brothers of the Twomey's. Most of them left again after one drink.

Ellen went out to post a letter at nine and when she returned Lar Murphy was sitting at the bar with Jack Connors, Denis O'Connor (her brother), Jim O'Brien, Tim Riordan and Mick Sheehan. She then saw one of the accused enter but couldn't tell which, she simply said the foxy one. He didn't call for any drink but seemed to be looking for someone.

She returned from the kitchen to see several men rushing for the door. Her cousin Jack held Jim O'Brien back from hitting Lar Murphy. Murphy left the pub but the others stayed. Ellen got the lamp afterwards and went out onto the street. She saw Lar Murphy on the ground with his face covered in blood.

The next witness was Ellen's cousin John O'Connor a farmer from Killvoy.

He corroborated what she had said. While he was at the bar that night, Jim O'Brien called a drink for the men at the counter. Lar Murphy took a pint of porter from O'Brien. Afterwards Jim took a swing at Lar Murphy with his fist but John O'Connor prevented him from doing so. John thought if O'Brien had managed to hit Murphy he would have knocked him to the floor. Then he said Murphy backed away and left the pub.

Mrs Mary Lanigan, publican, Banteer took the stand. She recalled that night and gave evidence that mostly agreed with what her employee had said. Mary thought she had seen both Timothy and Jeremiah Twomey in her pub that night. She said they didn't normally come to her pub and that night they didn't buy any drink. The Twomey brothers only talked amongst themselves before leaving.

This evidence took almost a day in court and another date was set for the following Wednesday. The Twomey brothers were remanded back to custody and taken to Mallow barracks.

Two days later the court sat again to hear more witnesses. Another publican Daniel O'Callaghan recalled the 21st of January. Michael Murphy was there about half eight when the accused Twomey brothers came in. They called for no drink but had words with Michael Murphy. As a result of this the publican said he asked them to leave saying don't come back here again tonight and Timothy went. Jeremiah he said however needed to be shoved out. Even then Jeremiah came back in by the back door and had to be forcibly removed for a second time. The publican believed though that neither of the Twomey's was under the influence of drink.

Another employee in Callaghan's that night was called. Peter Clifford saw the altercation between the Twomey's and Michael Murphy that night. He described it as a loud conversation and reckoned a fight would have broken out but the Twomey's were thrown out.

Daughter of the deceased Catherine Murphy took the stand. When she saw a man lying on the street that night she did not know at first it was her father. She said his face was covered in blood and mud and was unrecognisable. It was only when they got the lamp she began to think it was her father. She recalled doubting it and asking her brother Michael was it their father at all. It was Jeremiah Twomey she said replied to her saying "its Larry all right".

At one point in the questioning of a witness Crown solicitor Anthony Carroll let slip his confidence. The witness smiled instead of answering his question. Carroll remarked "you won't be smiling when you're before Justice Kenny".

Constable McNamara had been at the barracks when the accused were first taken into custody. He had taken statements from them and proceeded to read them out. At the time Timothy accounted for the blood on his clothes. He said that at Willie Lehane's the day of the coursing he cut his finger and it bled quite a bit.

Lenehan objected to the constable reading from his notebook as it was not a signed statement but he was allowed to continue. The constable had asked Jeremiah "where did you go when you came out from O'Callaghan's". Jeremiah claimed that he went to Quinlan's but when asked who was there he could not give names. He had said while in Quinlan's he had no drink but was in the tap room. After leaving he saw a man was shoved out who then walked towards the chapel gate. While the man walked away he fell back on the poll of his head.

It seems confusing at first Lanigan's Quinlan's but it was the same place. Mary Lanigan's maiden name was Quinlan; she had married Thomas Lanigan years before. Her father Michael had run the pub for years but died two years before in his eighties. As is often the case in small villages a pub could be known as many names other than the name over the door and the older name would remain in use.

The constable also had a statement in his notebook signed by Timothy Twomey.

In it he explained how he missed the train and ended getting a lift to Banteer from his uncle Dan Lehane from Dromcummer Beg. Timothy claimed he was crossing the street that night when he saw a man "partly fired out of Quinlan's". He saw the man fall on the street and hit his head but didn't go to him. Instead Twomey said he continued on to Sheehan's for fags and then posted a letter. Afterwards he saw a crowd gathered around and heard a man was dead. He left for home alone and when he got home his brother Jeremiah was there before him.

Sergeant John Connors gave evidence as he had at the inquest. He now described how he was reasoning with Murphy and Moynihan on the road that night when he realised something was wrong in the village. When he came on Jeremiah Twomey running away he said to him "what's up". Twomey said a row had broken out and he was running away as he did not want to be involved in it. The sergeant explained how Twomey was let go and was not arrested until later that night. At the same time Michael Murphy asked Kennedy had he been the one who assaulted his father but Kennedy denied it.

After hearing from the witnesses the magistrate Mr Hardy felt that there was a case to answer. He returned it for trial before a jury and the accused would be held in custody until then. It was only a month away though as the Cork Spring Assizes were due to be held in March. The brothers more than likely didn't see it this way, if found guilty it meant that month was to be their last. By April they could very well be swinging from the end of a rope. If the prosecution could prove at all their actions were premeditated this was the most likely outcome for them.

When it came before Justice Kenny at the Cork County Assizes in March the prosecution were confident they had a solid case against the Twomey's. After all one of the brothers had been apprehended at the scene of the crime. They could also identify the body when even the dead man's own children were unsure.

This was no drunken brawl. That night the Twomey's had been to more than one pub without drinking. It was as though they were looking for someone and draw the Murphy's into a quarrel.

After being thrown out of O'Callaghan's they moved on to Lanigan's, then they waited outside for their prey to emerge. More was known by those at the bar in Lanigan's that night. Was Jim O'Brien involved or was it just pure coincidence that he picked a fight with a man who was killed minutes later. William Kennedy had been seen with Jim O'Brien and the two were friendly. Yet Kennedy went out after Lar Murphy and others remained inside. He tried to stop the kicking, according to himself. Was he aware of a plan beforehand and couldn't stand by?

As good and all as Anthony Carroll was at prosecution the Attorney General himself Mr Jonathan Pim now represented the accused. The prosecution also had Sergeant Mc Sweeney, Mr Reardon and Anthony Carroll. While J.J Lenehan still represented the accused with solicitor Joseph O'Connor and a Mr Atkinson.

The Attorney General opened the case and went into the background of it. The prosecution now put forward for a motive that the Twomey's and Murphy's were in a dispute for years. Pim claimed it stemmed from when Hugh Twomey left his aunt's and Michael Murphy replaced him. Later both Catherine and Margaret Murphy also worked for Mrs Barry. The dispute began with words but over the years grew into hatred that ended in violence.

He then went over the events on the night in question in Banteer which we have heard before. Mr Pim however asked the jury why were the Twomey's outside Lanigan's looking in the window before Lar Murphy came out. He also asked the jury to carefully listen to all the evidence but said who else could have done it but the Twomey's? Who else had a feud with the Murphy's?

Michael Murphy was called as witness for the prosecution. He told how there was never any trouble with the Twomey's until he took the job at Barry's. Then there was a change they clearly did not want him there but at first they just didn't talk to him.   He recalled being in O'Connell's on St Stephen's night before. That night Timothy Twomey tried to start a fight with him but he walked away with his sister. He recalled being in O'Callaghan's pub on the 21st of January with his father and sisters. Jeremiah Twomey came in that night at eight and said to him "what did you do to my brother in Gortroe". Murphy told him he had not done anything to him but Jeremiah claimed his brother was beaten in Gortroe because of him. The Twomey's challenged him to come outside but the publican intervened and threw them out. When Jeremiah got back in the back door he said "come out now Tim wants you".

Michael then moved on to events later that night. He explained how at first he did not recognise his own father as his face was swollen and covered in blood. When he did recognise him he said to Kennedy "was it you did this" but the reply he got was "what do you mean by that you bastard".

Catherine Murphy daughter of the dead man told how she worked for Barry's. She then spoke about the 23rd of December she was at Barry's with Timothy Twomey.

His father Patrick came in and said he did not want his son to have the leftovers of Moynihan. This was clear he did not want his son involved with her.

Daniel O'Callaghan, Ellen O'Connor and Mary Lanigan also gave evidence for the prosecution as they had done before.

William Kennedy was the only man who actually saw what happened on the street that night. When Atkinson got his chance to cross examine he jumped right into it with questions. First he asked the witness about conflicts with past statements he had given. Then he asked why he had been arrested the night Murphy was killed. Kennedy denied ever being charged with anything saying he was released the next day. He did reveal he was friends with Jim O'Brien who was in his house when he was arrested.

Atkinson needed to try harder to bring Kennedy's evidence into doubt. So he directly asked "are you not a notorious bully in Banteer and have you not been convicted every month?" Kennedy replied admitting he was convicted a couple of times. Again Atkinson was prepared and read out the convictions Kennedy had got. On August 1909 he was charged with drunk and disorderly and again on May 1913. The following year August 1914 he was done for assault and December 1914 drunk. The solicitor said to the witness "your character is such that I can call you a drunken rowdy?" Kennedy didn't seem bothered saying "you can if you like".

The Attorney General then questioned the witness about the events on the street that night. Kennedy said when he told the Twomey's to stop kicking Murphy they did but Timothy turned back and kicked once more. Justice Kenny asked where the Twomey brothers were when Murphy fell. Kennedy said at either side of him.

Constable Thomas McDonnell told the court how he had met Jeremiah and Timothy Twomey that night about nine at the chapel gate. He then went into the details of finding Murphy on the street.

Sergeant Connors gave evidence as he had before and he now explained why he had arrested Kennedy. That night he believed Kennedy was with Jeremiah Twomey and involved in the murder. Kennedy he said was found at home that night but at first resisted arrest. He was released the following afternoon.

The doctor P.J O'Leary gave medical evidence as he had at the inquest and magisterial investigation.

Several witnesses from Gortroe were called to verify the story how Timothy Twomey tried to start a fight on St Stephen's night. Afterwards the prosecution ended its case.

Atkinson spoke for the accused men saying he had never come across such a baseless case as this. The claim of a feud between the families he also dismissed saying one of the Murphy girls walked home from a dance with Timothy last year. He said Kennedy was the only witness and could not be trusted. Atkinson then proceeded to tear apart the evidence Kennedy had given saying it was riddled with contradictions.

He also claimed that the prosecution failed to call the men who drank with Murphy in Lanigan's that night such as Jim O'Brien. His clients characters he said "were above reproach" and was sure they would be found not guilty.

He then called witnesses for the defence. Robert Barry was called; he was married to Hanorah Twomey, aunt to the accused. Robert said Hugh Twomey had left him of his own accord for a job with better wages. Michael Murphy did not replace him but worked for him sometime afterwards. He also claimed that Margaret Murphy was good friends with the Twomey's when she worked for him.

Father of the accused men Patrick Twomey gave evidence for his sons. He told how Timothy was 22 and Jeremiah 21 years old. Patrick denied saying to his son "you must not have the leavings of Moynihan" in front of Catherine Murphy. What he recalled saying that day was "this is no place for flirting with the man sick in bed upstairs. He claimed he was on good terms with Lar Murphy saying they helped each other at harvest time. His wife Bridget then also gave similar evidence about her sons.

On the second day of the trial Joseph O'Connor spoke for the accused men.

He referred to how the Attorney had tried to establish motive the day before because of the lack of evidence. Now O'Connor tried his best to bring doubt into the motive saying there never was a feud at all. He was sure the jury had the measure of Kennedy and would not believe what he said. O'Connor then called Kennedy the lowest form of humanity suggesting he was involved. He put forward the notion that the crime was committed by the men Murphy argued with in Lanigan's.

On the other hand the Attorney General got the last word. He admitted to possibly getting the origin of the feud wrong but was sure there was animosity between them. He dismissed the defence's suggestion that Kennedy had killed Murphy. Even worse he said was their suggestion that Kennedy was setting up the Twomey's.

He asked the jury who were the Twomey's looking for in Banteer that night? Why were they waiting outside Lanigan's looking in the window? The attorney General didn't suggest that the Twomey's set out to kill Murphy that night, just that they wanted to give him a hiding and went too far. The Attorney General saw no other possibility than the Twomey's had killed Murphy.

As was always the case the judge summed up before letting the jury go and decide the fate of the accused men. The judge explained the difference between manslaughter and murder for the jury. He did ask though why more witnesses had not been called by the prosecution and even suggested the motive against the brothers was weak.

It was ten past twelve on the second day that the jury retired to deliberate. Only fifteen minutes later they returned with the verdict of not guilty.

Jeremiah and Timothy Twomey were then free to walk out of court instead of a death sentence had they been found guilty.

Timothy Twomey the eldest in his family left Ireland for Boston in 1926. People in the area were slow to forget even if he had been found not guilty he was still some way implicated in it and knew what had happened. At least starting out in America the record was wiped clean so to speak. His younger siblings Hugh, Julia, Ellie and Matthew also moved to the Boston area in the 1920's. Younger brother Patrick remained in the area married a local girl but died in 1923 aged only 28.

William Kennedy also sought to get away from the area. He joined the Irish Guards during WW1. He later transferred to the 4th Battalion of the Guards Machine Gun Regiment. He was wounded in action and died as a result in November 1918.

For the Murphy's however Mary was left to bring up her young family with the help of her adult children. The youngest Patrick and Elizabeth aged only four and two at the time. They would hardly remember their father at all.

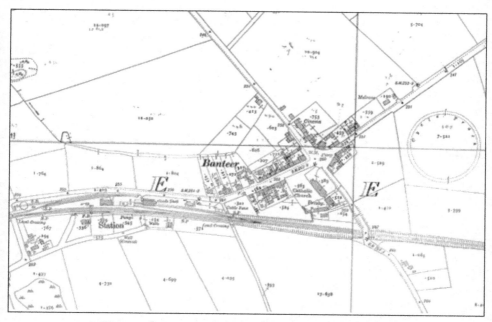

Village of Banteer where the killing took place.

Village of Burtneek where the killing took place.

Disappeared in town
Rathgoggan, Charleville 1909

On Monday the 12th of July 1909, sisters Anne and Bridget Gayer left their home in Feenagh Co Limerick and headed for Charleville nearly 10 miles away. The elder sister Anne had celebrated her 21st birthday just four days previous, while the younger Bridget was only two weeks shy of being nineteen. They both lived with their mother Kate, a widow of a few years who was a small shopkeeper in Feenagh. The night before her mother suggested going to Newcastle West but Bridget wished to go to Charleville. Her mother gave in and allowed the sisters to go to town.

It is not hard to imagine the sisters heading off to town in the donkey and cart with great excitement dressed in their best clothes. It wasn't often they got to go to Charleville; Bridget wanted to exchange a pair of boots she had bought the Easter before. They most likely had an extra few bob in their pockets to spend on account of their birthdays.

Having left Feenagh at eight that morning the sisters arrived in Charleville sometime after eleven. It's no surprise that they didn't often go when it took over three hours compared to a car journey that takes twenty minutes today.

When they arrived in the town they stopped outside Lynch's shop as that was where Bridget wanted to change the boots. Anne waited outside for her for some time.

When Bridget emerged she told her sister that she had changed her mind about the boots. They didn't have the ones she wanted after all only dearer ones, so she would have to keep them. Then she told her older sister she wanted to just go a few doors down the street to Galwey's hardware shop to get a brush. Anne wanted to go with her but she insisted on going alone and not leaving the cart unattended. Before going she told her older sister to feed the donkey and not to leave the trap alone for fear someone might take something. Anne complied and fed the donkey watching Bridget head off down the street.

Charleville as it appeared back then, Image courtesy of the National Library of Ireland.

When Bridget did not return at first Anne thought nothing of it but as time went by, she presumed there must be some reason. Anne looked for her sister in Galwey's shop but it turned out she had never been there. She then searched all over the town and at about three went home alone thinking she had just missed her sister somehow and she might be at home before her. When Anne went in to her mother's little shop and her younger sister wasn't there she became more worried.

Back then people were not as contactable as they are today, so not being able to find Bridget, her mother and sister presumed there must be some logical explanation. They were from a big family, Bridget had three other sisters and three brothers. Ellen married to another Feenagh shopkeeper, William Scanlan, and they only lived two doors up the street. Katie married to shopkeeper Timothy O'Connor in Newcastle West and Mary Anne a nun in Nebraska. It was possible Bridget met with or went to one of her local sisters' houses.

But with the inability to contact anyone all they could do that evening was head back towards town looking for her. More members of the family gathered and headed to Charleville. At least it was July and not getting dark soon.

Despite their best efforts that evening there was no trace of Bridget to be found in Charleville. They asked passers-by had anyone seen her but got no information. Eventually the family contacted the police who assured them they would look into the matter.

Early the next morning the family were up and preparing to set off for town again. Now there were more members of the family and in-laws to help in the search. Ellen and her husband William who lived only two doors down the street went to help in the search. William remarked that she may have run off with a lad to America and would not make contact until she landed there. With that the family made inquires at the train station but again there had been no trace of her there. They spent a long fruitless day asking everyone in town but went home to Feenagh with no information.

Days passed but the family did not give up hope, thinking that there must be some logical explanation despite the fact she had just seemed to disappear without a trace.

Every morning Ellen and her husband came and checked had a letter arrived with information but none arrived. They now began to cling to the fact she may have run off to America but had no money they knew of. A telegram did arrive from a brother in London but it just confirmed she had not gone there.

On the 20th of July children playing in a meadow field half a mile south of Charleville came across something. They knew immediately something was drastically wrong. Concealed in a dyke under a bush they saw something suspicious. The kids ran to tell a labourer working nearby, who then got more help before reporting the finding and the Gayer's worst fears were realised.

The police were immediately alerted and arrived on the scene quickly. It was indeed the body of a young woman and from the very start there was no doubt but it was foul play. An attempt had been made to conceal the body with long grass ripped from a nearby ditch, with a bush place on top. Her clothes were up over her knees and it was obvious she had been dragged by the feet for several yards from the spot where she had died.

The body was taken to Market House in the town to await an inquest.

The reaction in the normally quiet town was one of shock, who could possibly have done this to such a young woman. Superficial examinations by doctors found five stab wounds in Bridget's back near her spine. A post mortem was also organised for the following day as the results were needed before the inquest.

Where no information was forthcoming before the discovery of the body, now people came forward and gave the police a few clues. A young woman had been seen leaving the town and meeting a man who had come from the opposite direction to her. The pair were seen talking before going back towards Ballysallagh Crossroad near the Holy Cross Graveyard and were seen taking the road towards Buttevant. The theory now assumed was that the pair were heading to the train station but the man convinced her to go in the opposite direction which ultimately led to her doom.

Now the search was on to find out the identity of the man seen with Bridget Gayer that afternoon. Everyone in the town was talking about it, nothing of the like had happened for some time. If the people of Charleville were shocked at what had happened so close to town, those in the tiny village of Feenagh were even more so. Feenagh was a peaceful place and the people there struggled to come to terms with what had happened. Everyone knew both the Gayer's and Scanlan's well. William Scanlan grew up on a farm half a mile from the village where his mother Margaret still lived. He had spent time in America and had joined the Army there. During his time in the Army Scanlan saw action in the Cuban War of Independence. Having left the Army Scanlan moved back to Feenagh to settle down. He received a pension from the American Army which was quite considerable amount in rural Ireland at that time. Scanlan had married Ellen Gayer in 1907 and they had a baby William the following year.

The police were under immense pressure from the people of the town to catch the killer and set about their investigation of identifying the man seen with Bridget nearly nine days before. On Tuesday night just before ten Sergeant Purcell with two constables Brennan and Dukelow set out to arrest the man they believed had killed Bridget Gayer.

Leaving Charleville they headed north towards Feenagh in the summer darkness.

At a place called Ballyagran the police met a car with four men heading towards Charleville. They stopped the four men who said they were travelling to town to see about Bridget Gayer. One of the men was thirty two year old William Scanlan brother-in-law of Bridget. There on the side of the road the police arrested Scanlan who said only "let ye prove it".

He was taken to his home in Feenagh and you can imagine the shock his wife got when the police entered her house with her husband. Never mind to think of her husband being accused of murder but the murder of her own sister.

The police searched the house for any evidence of Scanlan being the killer while he was present. Several items were taken by the police and also articles of Scanlan's clothes for further inspection. It was late when they left with the accused man but despite this his wife and in-laws were out on the street in shock and disbelief. William remarked about his in-laws "there they are now, ask them all about it, it was ye that got me into this with yeer talk". His mother-in-law quickly replied "we said nothing except that you were away the day Bridget was missing".

The police arrived back at Charleville barracks at nearly five on Wednesday morning. Getting Scanlan arrested and into the barracks under the cover of darkness was convenient for the police as the townspeople would wake up to the news a man had been arrested. During the day their job could have been more difficult if an angry mob gathered.

Later that evening before an inquest had even been held William Scanlan was charged before resident magistrate Mr J St George. Several witnesses gave statements but at this point there was no actual evidence against Scanlan.

When the statements had been heard St George asked the accused if he had any questions. Scanlan quickly replied "no your lordship, I have nothing to ask, but I'd like to tell how it was, why I was missing that day". The magistrate rebuked him with "you can't make a statement but you can ask a question". Such was the law then that the accused was never allowed to speak or explain their side.

A witness Ellen Donoghue was called, she saw a young woman walking up and down outside Holy Cross Graveyard. She said it appeared like the girl was waiting for someone. She saw a man emerge from the graveyard and join her. The man headed towards Buttevant rather than the railway station and the girl was heard asking him why he was going that way.

The witness was able to describe what Bridget was wearing that day but was not sure if the man she saw was indeed Scanlan. She remarked that it looked like him but she found it hard to be sure. When asked, the witness said she saw the pair heading down the Buttevant road holding hands. Clothes that Bridget and William wore that day were then produced. Ellen could identify Bridget's clothes and said the man's clothes looked the same but was not sure.

At this point the police applied to have the accused remanded into custody for a further eight days and the judge agreed. It was late that evening when Scanlan was removed from court. Despite this a large crowd had gathered outside. The police knew they could not hold Scanlan in the town such were the feelings against him. It took a large escort of police to take the accused to the train station where another crowd had gathered. The mob was curious to see the accused man but it was obvious they bore no sympathy for him but quite the opposite. Scanlan was put on the train and taken to Cork Gaol to await his next court appearance. Meanwhile the police would search for more evidence and find witnesses to build the case against William Scanlan. If more evidence could be found they would then be able to send the accused to trial at the next Assizes in Cork.

At noon the next day the inquest was held by Coroner Byrne to investigate the events surrounding Bridget Gayer's death. Again the courtroom was packed and the coroner had no trouble at all finding a jury of twelve men.

It must have been extremely difficult for her but Ellen Scanlan; older sister of Bridget identified her remains for the inquest. Ellen said she had last seen her sister alive on Sunday evening the 11th of July.

Dr John Cremin told how he had visited the scene of the crime and carried out a superficial examination there assisted by Dr Hayes. Later at Market House the doctors carried out a post mortem. The wounds were not in fact stab wounds as they first seemed but bullet wounds. They had found three bullets from a pistol in the body and this accounted for all the wounds. The body he said showed signs it had been dragged face down some distance but there were no signs of violence on the head, neck or face. Back then one could not mention sex or rape in court so the doctor merely said; there were no signs of violation. One bullet went through a lung and the heart and was found in the chest wall. The lungs were holed in three places and two of the bullets broke ribs leaving bones in the lungs.

Dr Hayes said that any one of the bullet wounds would have proved fatal and could not have been done by the deceased. He also noted how he had seen the clothes before they were removed and at the back some of the clothes were scorched. The three bullets were then produced and shown to all twelve of the jury.

The coroner said it was not necessary for the purposes of the inquest to go into all the facts. As far as he was concerned they merely needed to prove how she died. He suggested that the jury find a verdict that Bridget Geyer died from gunshot wounds.

The jury agreed with the coroner and found that Bridget Gayer died as a result of bullet wounds inflicted by some person, or persons unknown. The foreman then said he wished to pass his deepest sympathy to the family. He said that they were appalled by the crime but wished to disassociate the people of Charleville from the crime. Before the inquest finished there was some discussion on where was the best place in town for bodies under such circumstances. Bridget Gayer's body had been taken to the Market Yard but some felt it should have been taken to the courthouse. The Coroner finished by saying it was up to the townspeople to erect a morgue.

Later on Thursday evening the funeral took place from Market House Charleville to nearby Holy Cross Graveyard. It does not need to be mentioned here how big the crowd that gathered for the funeral.

On Wednesday the 28th of July, William Scanlan was brought from Cork Gaol and escorted to Charleville by train. He was taken to the courthouse where the police escort had difficulty getting their prisoner through the crowds. A hostile mob had gathered outside booing and jeering at Scanlan as he entered.

Scanlan led from court, with thanks to Irish Newspaper Archives and Independent Newspapers.

The court began at eleven thirty, presided over by Mr J St George resident magistrate. Anthony Carroll crown solicitor represented the prosecution while Mr Rodgers Fox from Kilmallock was for the accused.

That day in court only heard the testimony of one witness, Michael McCarthy, who lived at Main Street in the town. McCarthy unlike most witnesses had been to court before, three years previously. On that occasion he witnessed a crime which also features in this publication.

He started by telling how on the 12th of July he was employed carting goods between the railway station and the town. McCarthy recalled seeing William Scanlan that day between eleven twenty and half past. He pointed Scanlan out in court saying "that's the man I saw". It was between Robert Daly's gate and the Ballysally Graveyard. McCarthy said the pair walked towards the Graveyard and Scanlan entered. The witness then said once he had passed by he looked back and saw the woman waiting outside the graveyard.

When questioned by the defence solicitor, McCarthy told how he had only given information the Thursday before. Fox asked why he had not come forward earlier when he heard a girl was missing but the witness never heard she was missing. McCarthy said he saw Scanlan leaving court the week before and recognised him; it was the next day he went to the police with information.

Mr Carroll for the prosecution then applied to further remand the accused until the following Wednesday. The judge and Mr Fox both agreed after some discussion to the application. Before the prisoner was taken away the judge said, he hoped there would be no ugly scene outside. The case he said was sub judice meaning under judicial consideration and should not be discussed elsewhere.

No matter what the judge said it wasn't going to make any difference as a mob had already gathered outside. The police struggled in keeping the crowd back. The crowd followed as the prisoner was conveyed to the barracks. Many even waited outside the barracks and again followed when Scanlan was taken to the train station. The police escort needed their own train carriage to transport the prisoner. As the train stopped at Buttevant, Mallow and Cork crowds were there to catch a glimpse of the man accused of such a dreadful crime.

A week later on 4th August the court sat again, the crown prosecution wanted to determine the movements of Bridget Gayer and William Scanlan on the 12th of July.

Anne Gayer was called to the stand and sworn in to give evidence. First Anne explained how she was older than Bridget by two years. She had three brothers two of whom John and Daniel worked in London, while James worked in Croom as a harness maker. They also had three more sisters; Mary Anne was a nun in Nebraska and the other two married, Ellen to William Scanlan the accused man. Kate Gayer was married to Timothy O'Connor a shopkeeper in Newcastle West.

Anne then spoke about the day before her sister was shot. Bridget had asked her not to tell James she was going to Charleville the next day. Anne heard James return home at eight that Sunday night and heard him talk to Bridget about Scanlan.

She then went over the events leading up to her sister's disappearance. She retold how she fed the donkey as her sister went to a shop. That was the last time she had seen her alive. Anne told how she searched the town that day before going home to her mother. When she got home that night Scanlan had not yet arrived home. She saw him return between eight thirty and nine and she told him how Bridget had gone missing. Scanlan dismissed her saying she was gone to America or some place. He did however say he would go to Charleville searching but his horse was missing a shoe. While Anne stayed up waiting for news of her sister and her mother's return. William Scanlan and his wife Ellen went to bed two doors down the street.

Despite staying up Anne was ready to go to Charleville at five the next morning. She told how it was William Scanlan she went with and spent the whole day searching for Bridget but found nothing.

Anne recalled being at home on the 20th when the dreadful news arrived that Bridget's body had been found. William Scanlan was present at the time and he offered to go to town and identify the remains. Scanlan had previously told her that on the 12th he had attended Cahirmee fair. Nowadays Cahirmee fair is held in Buttevant still on the 12th July, but back then it was held at Cahirmee fair grounds about two miles east of Buttevant. The defence solicitor Mr Fox chose not to question Anne at all.

The next witness was the mother of the deceased Kate Gayer. She recalled to the court how Bridget was friendly with Scanlan before he ever got married. Early in 1907 he rented a house from her in the village of Feenagh. From then on she said he was coming to her house. Around that time he asked for Bridget's hand in marriage but she laughed him off as she was not yet even seventeen. It was a few months later two matchmakers arrived at her door Patsy Meehan and John Power. They arranged a match between Scanlan and Ellen who was working in London then. Scanlan had told her he had £40 pension from America. Once the match was arranged Ellen was sent for from London, there was no mention how she felt about the situation.

The mother also recalled how when Bridget was missing Scanlan sent his wife every morning to check had a letter arrived from Bridget. She said he would often come to her during the day asking was there any news of Bridget. At that time Kate said she was counting down the days till the ship arrived in America and Bridget would send a telegram home.

James Gayer brother of Bridget retold the events leading up to 12th July.

The summers evening before he sat outside on the pavement reading with Scanlan on one side and Bridget the other. He had asked her where she was going the next day but she said her mother was going to Newcastle West. Neither did Scanlan reveal that he was going to Cahirmee fair.

It was the day after Bridget disappeared that James arrived in Charleville.

He met with William Scanlan who was out searching the town. Scanlan told him he was sure Bridget had gone to America and would go to Queenstown to make inquiries at the shipping agents. He never got to Queenstown however as he was arrested that evening.

James finished by saying how Bridget and Scanlan were friendly before Ellen returned from England to marry him.

A young lad John Madigan aged sixteen from Feenagh was then called and sworn in. His father John too was also a shopkeeper in the little village of Feenagh. On the morning of the 12th of July the lad had helped Scanlan to catch his horse in a field nearby about nine in the morning. Scanlan told him he was going to Cahirmee fair but asked that he not tell his wife. It was half eight or nine that night before he met Scanlon returning home. He was asked to take the horse to the blacksmith as it had a shoe off, he did as asked but the blacksmith was gone to bed.

A neighbour from Feenagh Kate Cronin told how Scanlan had borrowed her husband's saddle on July 12th. He told her before leaving he was going to Cahirmee to sell his horse and if he did not he would spend the day there.

Several more witnesses were called and told how they had seen William Scanlan heading in the general direction of Charleville town on the morning of 12th July. He could however had turned off and headed towards Buttevant and then the fair.

The next witness placed Scanlan closer to the town that day. Cornelius Connors a labourer from Smiths Lane in the town told how he was working at Binchy's farm close to the town that day. He recalled bringing the hay into the farmyard when a man rode in. He asked could he leave the horse there for a short time but Connors told him it would be in the way. He then allowed the man to put the horse into a stall. Connors said this was between eleven and eleven thirty. When asked was that man present the witness pointed out Scanlan to the court.

There followed several more witnesses who had seen the accused man in the vicinity of the town around that time. Bridget Stanton recalled sitting outside her own front door that day and saw Scanlan walking quickly past in the direction of the graveyard. She could describe what he wore, a dirty grey suit, boots and a coat a little lighter than the trousers. About twenty minutes later he passed back this time with a girl, she then thought to herself he must be her father. Scanlan was after all over forty and more than twenty years older than Bridget, who was a good looking nineteen year old.

Bridget Stanton's husband John also gave evidence. He had been working in the garden that day and saw everyone passing by. He saw Scanlan pass twice, once alone and with a girl the second time, this was just after noon as John had just heard the church bell ring. John described the girl as a brave strong looking girl with a proud walk.

The last witness that day Edmund Garvey thought it was strange they were holding hands when he saw them outside the graveyard. It turned out that the cottage Garvey lived in was built on the field where Bridget wad found. The court adjourned until the next day to hear more evidence against the accused man.

Where Bridget and William were seen heading that day.

When the court sat again the next day another large crowd gathered outside but for the first time there was no protest against the accused. Those that were there just stared at him in a curious silent way. Scanlan's wife sat near him in court wearing black.

The first witness that day was Mrs Motherway who lived on the Buttevant road. On the 12th she saw a man and young girl pass by her, holding hands. She looked back and the man was helping the girl over a ditch into Mrs McAuliffe's meadow. Mrs Motherway watched them walk across the field towards the railway station. She had already identified the man as Scanlan at the police barracks.

Several more witnesses had seen Scanlan in the area that day. One saw him heading towards Buttevant about one, galloping and beating the horse with the reins to go faster despite the horse looking tired.

Edward Watson from Charleville met Scanlan on the 19th of July and asked him about the missing girl. Scanlan's reply was that she was a good looking girl and it must have been some business with a young fella. Watson was being vague but was asked what words the accused used to him. Finally he gave in when pushed and told that Scanlan said "some man must of tried to get the better of her and that in case she should show the white feather he had done her in". Then the witness said Scanlan put his hand on his shoulder and said "dead men tell no tales and if you take notice of me she will be found in a ditch or dyke". It was the day before the body was found that Watson had met Scanlan.

The case was again adjourned and Scanlan remanded in custody till the next hearing set for the following Tuesday. When it did resume on the 10th of August the prosecution had moved on from placing the accused at the scene to finding a motive for the awful crime.

John McAuliffe a labourer from Ballybane recalled an event November or October the year previous. That night in Feenagh he said he heard music coming from Gayer's house. He heard Bridget playing and he went to ask her for a dance. A man objected to him dancing with her and he now recognised that man as William Scanlan. McAuliffe went to leave but before he did he turned to Scanlan and said "one woman at a time was enough for him". He then saw the pair together on at least three occasions near Feenagh.

Constable Dukelow was called to give evidence of the arrest but revealed much more. On the night he arrested Scanlan when they went back to Feenagh Scanlan spoke to several people while in police custody. Now Dukelow could recall what he had said that night and it revealed his state of mind at the time. To John Madigan he said "Johnny, do you remember the time you met me in Buttevant and you know we were not home in time when the girl was missed and her mother had left before we came home. If I am guilty, I am willing for the rope".

The constable also heard what he said to his wife that night and told the court "Ellie, if anyone can prove they saw me talking with Bridget that day, I am willing to take the rope". His wife however replied "wisha don't say that".

The prosecution still had nothing more than circumstantial evidence and had not produced the murder weapon in court. They did however make attempts to trace the gun used. A pawnbroker from 6 Nelson Street one Robert Parker took the stand. He stated that earlier in the year around spring time he sold several revolvers. He recalled selling one of the same type a pin fire .32 Belgian revolver to a man who afterwards headed to the train. The price he got for it was only £6 6s as the man complained it would be much cheaper across the water. Robert felt the man was local but had returned from America. The three bullets found in the body were produced and the pawnbroker agreed they were of the same type.

After this the prosecution solicitor Mr Carroll applied to have the case sent forward for a trial at the next Cork Assizes. Carroll said they had traced the movements of Scanlan that day and his denial of being in Charleville told its own story.

The defence solicitor Mr Fox knew there was little he could do but agree with the application. When asked if he had anything to say Mr Fox spoke for him but the judge wanted to hear from the man himself. Eventually Scanlan replied "I will say nothing". The judge then sent the case to trial and Scanlan was taken back to Cork Gaol.

It was December at the Cork Winter Assizes when William Scanlan was indicted for the murder. He was now before Judge Wright and the prosecution was led by the Attorney General Redmond Barry, assisted by several other kings Counsel solicitors including Anthony Carroll. Just after ten thirty when asked how he pleaded William Scanlan stepped forward and clearly said "Not Guilty".

The Attorney General went over the case in minute detail giving a speech that took most of the day. Then several witnesses were called giving mostly evidence that had been heard before. They included members of the family and people that could place Scanlan in Charleville around the time despite his denial of this.

When the defence got their opportunity they tried obviously to tear apart the case. Their claim was it was all circumstantial and had stated no clear motive. Mr McElligott senior counsel for Scanlan however stated they had no evidence to call, but said there was nothing to connect him directly with the killing. Scanlan he said had been away in America for several years. Having never been to Cahirmee fair before he lost his way and this accounted for the fact he ended up in Charleville. He couldn't however explain how Scanlan was seen holding her hand. McElligott said "I suggest to you that this whole case is rotten with inconsistencies on the part of the Crown, I do not propose to call any evidence in this case. I rely entirely on the evidence of the Crown to procure the acquittal of the prisoner". He also stated that Scanlan was never seen with a gun nor were any bloodstains ever found on his clothes. Finally he asked the jury to return Scanlan to his wife and now fatherless family. (As if she would have him back now either way)

Still they clung to the claim that Scanlan had been in Buttevant at one that day and said he could not have killed and concealed the body in that time. The Attorney General got the last word and he now faulted McElligott speech. He asked the jury: Why if Scanlan lost his way did he never ask for directions? Why did he stable his horse in Charleville if he lost his way? What was Scanlan doing for over an hour in Charleville that day?

At five in the evening of the second day the jury retired to decide what to do with the accused. Over an hour later the jury returned asking were the shots heard at Mrs Motherway's cottage. The judge replied that the distance from where the body was found to that house was 340 yards and said there was never any doubt but Bridget Gayer was shot. The jury went again to talk it over until the foreman returned at quarter past eight with the news that they could not agree. The judge encouraged them to try again but by ten it was the same thing, one juror could not give a verdict.

After ten that night the judge didn't give a long speech for once but asked did they believe or not that the man who went into the field was William Scanlan. Again the jury tried again but came back at half past ten saying there was no chance of a verdict.

The jury was sent away and Scanlan remanded back to custody, the case would have to be heard again.

Feenagh, Co. Limerick, showing (indicated by a x) the home of William Scanlan, now on trial at Cork Assizes for the murder of Bridget Gayer.

William Scanlan's house in Feenagh, with thanks to Irish Newspaper Archives and Independent Newspapers.

The following week the case came up again and despite being a second time people still thronged the courthouse. It took some time to select a jury. Before lunch it was announced by the Attorney General that a witness could not attend. The Crown Solicitor verified that a key witness Michael McCarthy who placed Scanlan at the graveyard was too ill to attend. After much discussion in court the case had to be adjourned again. As the Assizes were almost complete and Christmas approaching the case would have to wait till spring of the following year. Scanlan must have been relieved that he would escape the hangman's noose and spend Christmas in jail.

Village of Feenagh as it is today.

The case was not called before the Spring Assizes and after spending all that time in jail Scanlan still would have to go through the whole thing again, as would the family.

At the Cork Summer Assizes in late July 1910 William Scanlan was again charged before Justice Boyd. Now the prosecution had more witnesses than before that both saw him heading to Charleville and in Charleville on the 12th July over a year ago.

Sergeant James Purcell was called and announced the sad information that Michael McCarthy had died only days after the last postponement. Mr St George was then called and told he had taken a statement from McCarthy the August before. After much deliberation this evidence was allowed by the judge and the statement was read out.

John Madigan a car driver from Feenagh was called. Scanlan previously tried to use him as an alibi claiming to having met Madigan in Buttevant at one that day.

Madigan first mentioned a conversation he had with Scanlan the week before the fair. Scanlan had told him he would not bother going to Cahirmee Fair to sell his mare as she was not in good condition. Madigan confirmed he had met the accused at the fair but said it was about two in the afternoon. When questioned Madigan agreed that two was a strange time to go to a fair saying any man going to sell a horse would go at seven in the morning.

Later in the day it was revealed that Mrs Motherway had also passed away since the last trial. Her evidence was key as she had seen a man and woman enter the field and was most likely the last to see Bridget alive apart from the killer. Again despite protests from the defence the judge allowed her previous statement to be read out and allowed as evidence.

It now looked like Scanlan's time was up and when the judge charged the jury he looked very nervous. The jury left before twelve but returned an hour later to ask questions about the times Scanlan had been seen. As the judge answered the accused man looked agitated and held his cap tightly to his face.

Just after one the jury came back again and said there was no chance of a verdict that day. The foreman said that motive or lack thereof was what they could not agree upon. The judge said however motive or not six witnesses place him near the scene that day and those facts they should act on. The foreman revealed that one member of the jury did not believe Scanlan was in Charleville at all that day.

This only annoyed the judge who said six witnesses swore he was and again asked they find on these facts alone.

The jury left again but returned at two saying they could not agree a verdict. The defence solicitor said he was ready to go to trial again but the judge was not in agreement. The case was again postponed till the next Assizes and hearing this Scanlan smiled in court but was then quickly removed. We can only imagine how the Gayer family felt seeing Scanlan leave the court, it's harder still to think how Ellen felt.

It was the 5th of December 1910 when for the third time the case was heard before a jury at the Cork Assizes with Justice Kenny. Several persons from the jury panel were excused having sat on the previous trials. As before William Scanlan again pleaded not guilty and it was noted he looked better now after some time in prison. He was quite composed and maybe felt after being here before he would not be found guilty.

As before almost fifty witnesses were called and gave mostly the same evidence as they had several times now. The prosecution took over two days and again argued about the testimony of the witnesses that had died since. The judge again allowed the evidence and their statements were read out in court.

It was Wednesday the 7th December before the defence was allowed to make its case. The defence had previously mentioned witnesses who had met Scanlan in Buttevant at one that day. Yet when it came to it these witnesses Tom Cronin and John King were never called. Despite a long speech the defence still had no witnesses or alibis for their client. They did mention again a partial letter which had been found at the Gayer's allegedly to have been written by Bridget as it seemed to be her handwriting. It mentioned a Mr Mahony and "my American order". The defence tried to hint Bridget was corresponding with this man and planned to emigrate with him.

It was Sergeant Moriarty who replied for the prosecution not the Attorney General. He commended the defence and how they carried out their duty for the accused.

However Moriarty said Scanlan failed to provide a single witness to prove his innocence.

He said there was no evidence that Bridget was in contact with a Mr Mahony and even less that he had done it. Why was Scanlan in the vicinity on that day was it just pure coincidence? He also discussed how the sisters had come to Charleville that day through Ballyagran. Yet he said Scanlan took a longer route through Newtownshandrum and arrived in town by Smiths Lane. Was this planned he asked so the parties would not meet beforehand? Having spent over an hour in Charleville the defence he said had failed to prove where Scanlan was yet the prosecution had six witnesses for this period. He claimed that Bridget had deceived her own family of where she was going that day and had made secret plans. He said Scanlan showed himself to be even more cunning and deceitful. The sergeant also said that she left home that day with the intention of never returning. It had been proved he said that she had a double set of clothes on that day in the month of July as she could carry no luggage. His address to the jury went over every witness and he summed up the case brilliantly. When eventually he sat down there was a huge applause in the court room.

The judge in his address seemed confident that the case which had been long was finally coming to a conclusion. He admitted how difficult it was for the jury to come to a verdict on a capital charge. The judge cast some dispersion on Bridget's character asking what she was doing that day with a married man. He also pointed towards the intimacy and illicit relations between the pair. The fact that Scanlan still denied being in Charleville that day was pointless when it was proved otherwise. He again went over the witnesses' evidence which now had been heard many times before. It was half two when he released the jury asking them to defend not just the public's interest but the innocence of the accused if they found it. He asked the jury to decide on the facts and if they believed Scanlan was the man who entered the field with the girl. Through all this Scanlan was said to have maintained his composure in court and was paying attention to the proceeding. He still seemed confident he would be found not guilty and would soon be a free man.

The foreman returned fifteen minutes later and asked for maps of the area, these were handed over and he returned to the jury. The foreman returned again at nearly four and handed a slip of paper to the clerk.

The question was then asked "have you agreed to your verdict gentlemen". Scanlan looked now like a man who had completely lost that air of confidence he once possessed and had lost all hope.

The foreman replied "we have" and now Scanlan knew this was different than before. "How say you Mr Foreman" and guilty was the reply. It was then asked were they all in agreement and the foreman replied that they were.

"William Scanlan you heretofore stood indicted that on the 12th day of July in the year of our lord 1909, you unlawfully, feloniously, wilfully, and of your malice aforethought did kill and murder one Bridget Gayer, against the peace of our Sovereign Lord the King, his crown and dignity, that indictment you pleaded that you were not guilty and for trial put yourself on God and your country, which country has found you guilty. Have you anything now to say why judgement and sentence of death and execution should not be awarded against and passed on you according to law".

232

WILLIAM SCANLAN.   BRIDGET GAYER.

Yesterday, at Cork, William Scanlan was found guilty of the murder of his sister-in-law, Bridget Gayer, near Charleville, and was sentenced to death.

Image courtesy of the National Library of Ireland and Independent Newspapers.

The now guilty party William Scanlan was shocked and could not manage to utter a single word from his mouth. The judge however proceeded after a brief silence in court.

He addressed Scanlan saying there was no doubt from the evidence that he killed the girl.

Then putting on the black wig he said "It is hereby ordered and adjudged that you William Scanlan, be taken from the bar of the court where you now stand to the prison whence you last came, and on Wednesday the fourth day of January 1911 you be taken to the public place of execution in the gaol in which you shall be there confined and be there hanged by the neck until you be dead and that your body be buried within the walls of the prison in which the aforesaid judgement of death shall be executed upon you and may the Lord Almighty have mercy upon your soul".

William Scanlan stood there in grave shock he didn't smile this time, just staring at the judge with his hand covering his face. Then one of the guards tapped him on the shoulder and he turned and was taken down, out of the courtroom for the last time.

A petition was lodged with the Lord Lieutenant on Scanlan's behalf to beg for a reprieve against the sentence of death. Over the Christmas period it was reported that Scanlan was still confident his petition to the Lord Lieutenant would result in him evading the hangman. He was said to not have given up hope at all, he was behaving himself in jail and eating his meals.

By early January the reply from the Lord Lieutenant was that he saw no reason to interfere with the normal course of the law no matter how difficult it was. Scanlan was now resigned to his fate and there was no other possible outcome.

On the morning of the 4th of January he was up early attended to by several members of the clergy. He then went to mass at seven in the prison chapel. At just a few minutes before eight the sound of people gathering outside his cell indicated to Scanlan that his time was nigh.

Outside was the Governor, Deputy Governor, Sheriff and prison surgeon as well as numerous wardens. Scanlan then blessed himself with holy water before his hands were bound and he was led out. The condemned man was then taken to the death chamber arriving there just before eight.

There the executioner John Ellis and his assistant William Willis had made their final preparations. Ellis had been an executioner for eight years and was at the time the chief executioner. He would be involved in over 200 executions before his own untimely end.

On this occasion Ellis had calculated a drop of seven foot six inches, the noose was quickly put around his neck and fixed before the white cap was pulled over his face. Outside the bell rang to indicate that the condemned man was on the scaffold. He made no final admission which was normally expected of the guilty party. Once the bolt was pulled death was said to be instant as the executioner had planned.

As the execution had been carried out in private those waiting outside learned that Scanlan was gone when a prison guard came to the gate. Years before executions were carried out in public for all to see and a black flag would have been raised afterwards.

An inquest was held afterwards by Coroner John Horgan. It found that death had been according to the law. His death was recorded as dislocation of vertebrae and severing of spinal cord caused by judicial hanging. William Scanlan became the last man to be executed by the British legal system before Ireland obtained independence.

In the tiny village of Feenagh Co Limerick life never went back to normal for some. Ellen Scanlan continued on the trade of shopkeeper, after all Scanlan had only got the shop as part of a marriage settlement. She reared William junior who was less than three when his father was executed. Mrs Gayer kept her shop close by and Anne continued what was now a family tradition and married a shopkeeper Thomas Reidy a few years later.

Bridget final resting place was close to where she had met William that day.

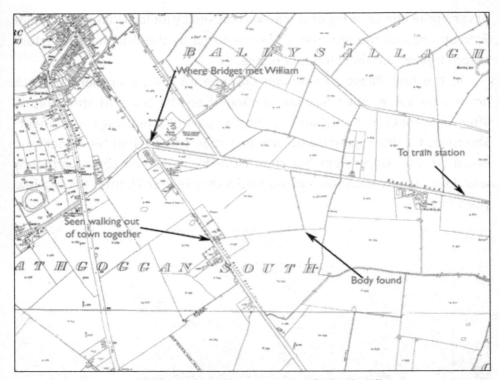

Where Bridget met William

To train station

Seen walking out
of town together

Body found

Map showing the area south of Charleville.

Hold Them, I'm Killed
Railway Station Charleville 1906

Charleville railway station opened in 1849. It was on the Great Southern and Western line from Dublin to Cork. The station itself was one mile from the town and right on the border to County Limerick. It's actually situated so close to the border that the northern tip of the platform is in County Limerick.

Like any train station at the turn of the last century it was a hive of activity. There were many men and women employed, station master, porters, booking clerks and signal men to name a few. In Charleville the station was so far from town many men from the area made their living as carmen conveying people, cases and goods to and from the town.

It was in this hive of activity the story begins in September of 1906. That day several carmen were employed drawing grain from the station in their horse and carts.

As one cart approached the station a man got on without permission of the driver. It was a childish prank and he was shoved off by the driver. Taking offence to this, he got a lift from another cart but continued shouting abuse at the driver who had thrown him off.

Nearer the station the insults turned into a scuffle between the pair. One sought revenge for being thrown off while the other wanted to avoid the conflict. The station master was quick on the scene and separated the two. It was his job to ensure all operations at the station ran smoothly, men scuffling outside the station, was the last thing he needed.

He knew the man driving the cart and was aware he was loading grain that day. The other man he did not know what business he had at the station so he marched him out of the train station. The man headed towards Leahy's pub which was nearby. When leaving he made a remark threatening to return and seek vengeance. The station master was a busy man and had no time to dwell on such troublemakers.

A few minutes later the man was back with an accomplice. They were seen pacing up and down near the station masters house armed with sticks waiting for their prey. Whether he wanted revenge with the carman he argued with or the station master is unclear.

The carman was still employed at the granary loading grain and was not aware of what was going on. It was the station master that quite literally ran into them. He ordered the two men out of the station and like before he only got abusive language from them. This was not down some dark alley in the middle of the night it was plain for everyone passing to see. Several of the other Great Southern and Western Railway employees took notice wondering what would happen next.

The two men set upon the station master; one went in with his fist and struck him. The station master was seen falling back defencelessly. He hit the ground with such force; his head was seen almost bouncing from the ground. A local carman Michael McCarthy had seen what happened and rushed to the scene. McCarthy used equal force to what he saw used on the station master. He lashed out with his whip knocking one of the attackers and then hit the other to prevent them going any further.

By now more employees were arriving on the scene, one of them Daniel Twomey was a clerk in the station and the son of the station master. The station master Thomas Twomey was injured from the fall but managed to utter the words "hold them, I'm killed". One of the attackers William Ward, better known as Manning in Charleville, tried to flee knowing he was in trouble and had gone too far. Daniel Twomey pursued him and caught hold of him and brought him back to the scene. Between the men they held the two attackers until the police arrived to arrest them.

Amongst the few that were there they knew William Ward a cattle drover but the other man Timothy Casey was not known by those at the train station. The pair were taken to the police barracks in the town. Later on they would be charged with assault on the station master before a local magistrate.

Thomas Twomey didn't go back to his endless list of duties. After the fall he had he wasn't feeling himself at all. He was taken to his bed in the house provided as part of his role.

Those that had witnessed the fall knew that it was serious. A doctor was called but could do little but monitor Twomey regularly and confine him to bed. At first the doctor Henry Bouchier Hayes believed he would make a fast recovery. He saw him the next day and Twomey was in an excited state but his temperature was normal.

By Friday the doctor knew it was more serious, Twomey's temperature was now over 38 and he was very restless. The head injury started to bruise at the back of his head. Hayes realised Twomey was suffering from concussion.

Three times a day the doctor came to see Twomey but as the days wore on his condition did not improve. In fact his condition grew steadily worse until a week later on evening of Tuesday 18th he lost consciousness and died.

The following day Wednesday the 19th, the inquest was held in Charleville by coroner Byrne and a local jury of respectable men.

The first witness called was the head porter at the train station Patrick Monahan.

He recalled seeing the station master separate the carman O'Grady and Ward. Fifteen minutes later he saw Ward return with another man carrying sticks. He heard the station master order them off the station as they had no business there but they refused to leave. Monahan told the court how when Twomey fell both men went to kick him while on the ground but Michael McCarthy intervened.

Dr Henry Bouchier Hayes told how he had preformed the post-mortem. He said death was caused by inflammation of the brain as a direct result of the fall Twomey had received. The jury found their verdict in agreement with the evidence that had been given that day. The coroner expressed his sympathy to the Twomey family and told how well known he was and liked by so many.

On Friday the 21st the pair appeared again at a special sitting of Charleville court.

District Inspector Cruise represented the prosecution while the accused had no legal representation. It sounds farcical but Ward and Casey were now allowed to cross examine the prosecution witnesses. Normally the accused would not be questioned and would only be asked by the judge if they understood the proceedings. This time however we hear a lot more from the accused men and they desperately try to shift the blame. They needed to be very clever to ask questions that would not implicate themselves.

Cruise opened by saying how the case had taken a grave turn, since Thomas Twomey had died two days earlier. The charge was no longer one of petty assault but now was murder.

The prosecution called the local carman Michael McCarthy who had intervened that day. McCarthy recalled the 12th when he was at the train station with a load of butter at about ten to five in the evening. He saw Twomey with the two accused men; he took the stick from them and threw them down. He could not hear what was said but presumed Twomey was trying to get them out of the station. McCarthy said he had no idea violence was going to break out; he would have intervened sooner if he had realised it.

He then saw Ward strike Twomey in the face with his fist while Casey ran into the station master with his head and knocked him down. McCarthy claimed while he fell Ward struck him yet again. Ward interjected saying "there is a lord above you, I was fifteen yards away".

McCarthy however continued his testimony saying as Twomey fell Ward struck him with a stick. He must have picked it up off the ground just before. McCarthy heard the great thud as Twomey's head struck the ground. He now ran to the scene and went straight in striking Ward with his whip with enough force to knock him. Casey he said was still going to kick the station master. McCarthy lashed out again preventing it by also hitting Casey several times with the whip.

**Where the stationmaster was struck down
between his house and the station.**

By now the head porter and Dan Twomey had arrived. Between them the men were held. He heard Twomey say "hold them, I'm killed" but the attackers said nothing.

Ward then questioned McCarthy; it was difficult as the men knew each other before the incident. Ward began "how far away was I when he fell?" the reply "you were alongside him not a foot away".

"Where did I get the stick?" "you got it on the ground". Ward went on asking were the sticks not thrown away by Twomey but McCarthy recalled seeing them on the ground. Ward was not used to this as a solicitor was and must have found it difficult asking questions about himself. He accused the witness of lying saying "tell the truth". McCarthy was adamant and said "I'm telling the truth" but Ward disagreed. Ward asked "Was I toss playing with you that day", McCarthy agreed he was. "Did I not win a few shillings off you that day" the witness said "you did".

It got more farcical as Casey now questioned the witness. He asked several similar questions about the sticks but McCarthy stuck to his story. Casey then asked "had not you me on the ground when the stationmaster was in the house" but the witness denied it.

Then John O'Grady was called and explained how the argument between himself and Ward had begun that day. The witness described the scuffle that had taken place and how the station master had broken it up. O'Grady went to load grain and when leaving saw the two accused men outside the station cottages. He was about 100 yards away when the violence broke out. He saw Casey run at Twomey with his head and knock him down. O'Grady recalled seeing the last witness Mickie McCarthy intervene and come to Twomey's aid.

Ward cross examined "did you see the whole thing", "yes I did". "Did you see him hitting him (Casey) and me with a stick", "no I saw him hit no man". Ward kept asking how far away was he, had he a stick in his hard and several more times did he see Twomey hitting them. None of the answers he got suited him, O'Grady was as sure of himself as the first witness and would not be swayed.

Another employee of the railway station was called; William Bryan worked in the parcel office. That day he had left the office when he heard loud talk outside. When he went out Twomey was trying to get Ward off the station. He heard Ward walk away saying "remember Twomey, I' am single handed now but I will be double handed soon".

One would think Ward would decline to cross examine but he didn't. He asked several questions but again none of the answers helped his case. Casey knew there was nothing to gain and declined to question the witness.

Patrick Monahan and Daniel Twomey were also called and gave similar evidence.

Dr Henry Bouchier Hayes explained how he had attended Twomey everyday after the assault until he died. He assured the prosecution that everything that could be done to save his life was; he was also assisted by Dr McNamara. There was no doubt at all he said that the injuries Twomey sustained were from hitting the ground very hard. He said this resulted in swelling in the brain over several days and caused his death.

At the end of the day after hearing the evidence the judge would surely have sent it to a trial at the next Assizes. District Inspector Cruise felt he wanted to be sure of that and had more witnesses to call. He applied to have the men remanded in custody until another court hearing.

It was a week later on Friday the 28th that the case was heard again in Charleville.

The public were again not allowed in the courtroom throughout the proceedings.

David Mahony was the first witness called that day. He told that it was him who had given a lift to Ward that day after he had been ejected by O'Grady. This occurred half way to the station from Charleville. When he gave Ward a lift, he shouted abuse at O'Grady calling him a "Bruff bailiff". Mahony also told how he had seen the scuffle between Ward and O'Grady which was broken up by the station master.

A statement Ward had given was read out in court. In it Ward admitted to the events leading up to the trouble with O'Grady. Ward claimed that Twomey emerged from his house and snatched Casey's stick out from under his arm. Having surprised Casey from behind Twomey struck Casey several times according to Ward. The station master then did the same to Ward running after him. While running after one of them Ward said Twomey took a stumble and fell over. Ward also claimed to never having raised his hand to Twomey that day despite many witnesses now saying otherwise.

Casey also had given a similar statement. He claimed they were only waiting around the station that day for a lift. He said Twomey came from nowhere and attacked them with their sticks. Casey's version was he did not know how Twomey fell over.

After hearing this District Inspector Cruise applied to have the pair returned for trial at the next Assizes in Cork. Obviously the accused men's statements were not believed as the application was approved by the magistrate and the men were sent to jail to await their trial.

On Thursday the 6th of December the pair was brought before Mr Justice Wright at the Munster Winter Assizes in Limerick Courthouse. Timothy Casey and William Ward were now charged that they feloniously wilfully and with malice aforethought killed and murdered one Thomas Twomey. At least by now the accused men had got legal representation and no longer needed to question the witnesses themselves. Ward had a solicitor Mr Cullinane while Casey was represented by a Mr Elligott.

Both men pleaded not guilty despite the weight of evidence that would be called against them. The Attorney General opened and went through the case before calling witnesses to prove the men were guilty. He said it was especially cruel that Twomey had been killed while carrying out his duties for GS&WR. It was his duty to ensure the smooth running of the railway station and deal with issues.

He claimed that because Ward was issuing threats to return and arming himself with a stick, showed it was premeditated to harm either Twomey or O'Grady. Because of this he argued the charge should be murder against the two men as they had set out to do harm that day.

Whether it was O'Grady or Twomey that Ward intended coming back to tackle did not matter. It was his intention to cause harm and resulted in the death of a man.

The proceedings in court that day were the same as had been heard before. Except several more carmen appeared all giving the same story. Ward and Casey attacked Twomey; none of them saw Twomey strike the accused at all.

During Michael McCarthy's evidence there were some questions about how much money he had lost earlier that day playing toss with Ward. The defence tried to discredit McCarthy but he remained steadfast in his story.

Once the prosecution was finished calling witnesses, the defence solicitor read out his client's statements. The defence then called carman Timothy Downing. He had a slightly different story saying Ward never struck Twomey but admitted Casey ran at Twomey.

Mr Cullinane then applied for an acquittal for Ward on the strength of only one witness. He gave a speech for his client.

Elligott instead of denying his clients part in it, he claimed the force Casey used was reasonable. He still clung to the story that Twomey had attacked them first.

The judge reviewed the case again before letting the jury do their part. Justice Wright explained to the jury how they might reduce the verdict to manslaughter. He did mention that had McCarthy not intervene the pair would most likely have kicked Twomey to death.

The jury retired at half four having heard evidence all that day. It was only fifteen minutes later when they returned with their verdict, guilty of manslaughter. The jury recommend mercy for the guilty men. Sentencing was deferred to a later date in the Assizes.

About a week later the pair were back in court again, at least they had known their lives no longer hung in the balance. The judge Justice Wright gave them five years each penal servitude.

Did he fall or was he pushed?
GSWR North of Buttevant 1873

Late on the evening of Thursday the 3rd of April, a Great Southern and Western goods train came to a natural halt on the Cork to Dublin line about two miles north of Buttevant. At first the train guards were not surprised at all; it just ran out of steam and came to a slow stop. Most likely it had broken down and could go no further. If it had broken down though, once stopped the engine driver or fireman would have jumped down to see what could be done. One would imagine they would then go and inform the nearest signalman of their predicament and seek assistance.

The train came to a halt and it was suspicious that neither the engine driver nor fireman was anywhere to be seen. The two train guards jumped down and discovered the train appeared like the Marie Celeste. Unnoticed to them it had travelled some distance on its own steam, quite literally.

One of the train guards headed north along the track to setup a signal to inform oncoming trains and while doing so found a hat twenty yards behind the train. While the other guard remained checking the train for traces of the driver or fireman.

The guard set out north again to place another signal further away and he found a body on the track 100 yards behind the train. The face was covered in blood and the body was still warm. He knew the man was dead. The guard pulled the body off the line in fear another train would pass. He then went back to tell the other guard and between them they confirmed the body was that of the engine driver.

One of the guards then headed south for the nearest station, which was Buttevant. Once the news reached Buttevant, the station master there set out for the scene with a fireman who had been heading to Dublin. The abandoned train was then brought to Buttevant station, where blood was noticed on the steps to the engine. The fireman who drove it there noticed the fire shovel had been left in the firebox and had been consumed by the flames. The hammer normally used by the fireman to break the coal was nowhere to be found.

Meanwhile the station master had headed north from the scene and found the missing fireman in the house of a signalman at a level crossing near Imphrick Church. The missing fireman Timothy Nagle had arrived there almost naked. Nagle explained it saying the engine driver had fallen off the train and he jumped after him. He had landed in a bog hole and took off his wet clothes and left them by the track. The signalman had given him dry clothes which he now had on.

The station master took Nagle on to Charleville. Later Nagle claimed that the engine driver had closed the door of the fire box on his hand. Nagle as a result said he tackled the engine driver and in the struggle the driver fell from the train.

The Engine driver was Archibald Wall from Mallow better known as Archie. He was 45 and had been a driver for many years. Timothy Nagle was twenty four and also from Mallow. Normally Archie and Timothy were not on that route. An engine had broken down in Mallow and their engine was tasked with going to Limerick.

The goods train had left Limerick for Cork on its return journey at half six that evening. Goods trains often travelled slowly and it passed Charleville about ten when there was some delay shunting in the station.

The inquest was held on Friday by Coroner Daly in the Mallow train station. The body of Archie Wall had to be brought from Charleville for the inquest.

Dr Parsons Berry told what he had found while carrying out the post-mortem. He found signs of violence on the body. Under the left eye was a deep cut with a fracture to the cheek bone. The nose was broken and there were other cuts to the face. He found bruises to the temple, back of the head and neck but the skull was not fractured. The doctor thought the injuries had been caused by a blunt instrument.

A juror wanting to get to the point asked would a fall from the train cause the injuries but the doctor said it was not so easy to say. After more questions though he admitted they were unlikely to have been caused by a fall. He also revealed that the blood on steps would not have been caused by the head hitting them but the blood dropped from above.

John Ryan told the inquest how he was one of the railway Police in Charleville. He was called to Charleville station that night and found Timothy Nagle lying in the waiting room. He questioned him about what had occurred but did not arrest him. Nagle told him the same story about the driver shutting the fire door on his hand and that was how the shovel ended up in the fire. Ryan then inspected Nagle's hand but did not see any mark or burn on it.

Dr Berry was then recalled to look at Nagle's hand in front of the jury. He found a small wound on a finger on the left hand but it was not a burn.

Ryan continued his evidence saying he asked Nagle how far did the train go on from when the driver fell off. Nagle told him once the driver fell he tried his best to stop the engine but it was about 100 yards before he got it stopped. Ryan asked Nagle that night why did he not alert the two guards as to what had occurred. According to Nagle he searched for the driver but could not find him, it was then that he got wet in a bog. Nagle told him he saw a light in the distance, so he took off his wet clothes and headed for the light.

John Quirk told the inquest that he was the fireman on the mail train that stopped at Buttevant that night. He went to the train stopped on the track and brought it to Buttevant to clear the track. He found the brake was not on and the train had stopped due to the steam being shut off. Otherwise he noticed nothing mechanically wrong with the train. It was only when he got to Buttevant that night that he noticed the blood on the steps.

The crossing north of the scene where Nagle ran to that night.

After hearing several witnesses the coroner felt more investigation was needed and adjourned until the following Tuesday. A juror suggested that all twelve of the jury should travel to where the body had been found. The District Superintendent of the GSWR said he would make a train available to them on the following Sunday. Timothy Nagle was taken to Cork on the evening train. Large crowds gathered to catch a glimpse of him.

The following Tuesday the inquest sat again in Mallow. Several more witnesses were called. Many were employees of the GSWR. More than one witness told how Nagle and Wall often had disagreements at work and it was even reported to the management suggesting they be separated. One witness saw Nagle strike Wall on the legs with the shovel several weeks before.

Peter Heligan the signalman who lived north of the scene told how he met Nagle on the crossing that night about quarter past eleven. Nagle had no trousers, coat, jacket, shoes or socks on. The fireman told him then that both he and the driver had fallen from the train. Nagle believed the driver was badly injured or dead. Nagle asked the signalman for a bed and some dry clothes. The signalman was worried that the track was blocked with the stopped train. Nagle told him that it wasn't as the train had been taken on to Buttevant, but at this point Nagle should not have known this.

They heard the mail train approaching slowly from Buttevant and Heligan knew the way it was slowing down it would stop at his crossing. Nagle remained in the house and asked the signalman to tell no one that he was there. When the Buttevant station master Mr Cashel came from the mail train he said the driver had been found but the fireman was still missing. The signalman knew he couldn't cover it up and replied "you need go no further, I have him here".

The county inspector asked Dr Berry about the spatters of blood on the brass work over the fire box. The inspector recalled counting 49 spatters there and more on the handrails. Evidence also showed how clothes had been found in several different places and some were away from the track. A policeman that had walked the line said there was no place on the track where jumping off the train could one land in water. It was also proved that the hat found twenty yards behind the train was the hat of Archie Wall.

It was suggested but could not be proved that the clothes were wet because Nagle had attempted to wash them to hide the blood. Nagle's solicitor however suggested though that if he wanted to hide his clothes he could have burned them in the firebox. More likely was that he first fled the scene and then thought of his clothes.

The coroner summed up the evidence for the jury and asked them to weigh up all the evidence. He noted how the police theory was that Archie Wall received a blow of the shovel and then the shovel was thrown into the fire. Then either Wall fell or was thrown from the train.

The jury only spent thirty minutes deciding and returned a verdict of manslaughter against Timothy Nagle. The fireman had already been arrested by the police. This was enough for him to be sent back to jail to await a trial.

It was in late July when the Cork Summer Assizes sat that year and Timothy Nagle found himself charged with murder before a jury. It only took two days in court for all the evidence to be heard but very little new evidence was produced. The inquest had taken two days which was unusual then. The fact the inquest had found a verdict of manslaughter was not the norm.

Now Sir Colman O'Loughlan prosecuted and maintained that Archie Wall died by repeated blows of a heavy steam shovel before being thrown off the train. The evidence though remained circumstantial as the guards on the train had seen nothing that night. This was despite the fact one guard was in the carriage behind the engine and the other at the rear of the train.

It seems the best the defence could do for their client was to claim the charge should be manslaughter rather than murder.

The judge tried to sum up briefly.

After only a very short deliberation the jury returned with the verdict of guilty of manslaughter. The judge addressed the prisoner saying he agreed with the verdict but remarked that it was a lenient one. When sentencing he took into account that Timothy Nagle was a young man of twenty three years of age. However he said it remained a serious crime and sentenced him to twenty years penal servitude.

At the end of it all we still did not know why Nagle came running up the track that night without his trousers, socks and boots on. Was it a case of going back to the most basic human instinct of fight or flight? We have the evidence of the fight so to speak but then Nagle ran. He must have waited in the shadows watching what the guards were doing that night and then decided to rid himself of the evidence, the clothes. By running and trying to hid that night he just made himself look guilty no matter what had happened. Nagle would be a middle aged man in his forties when he would be a free man.

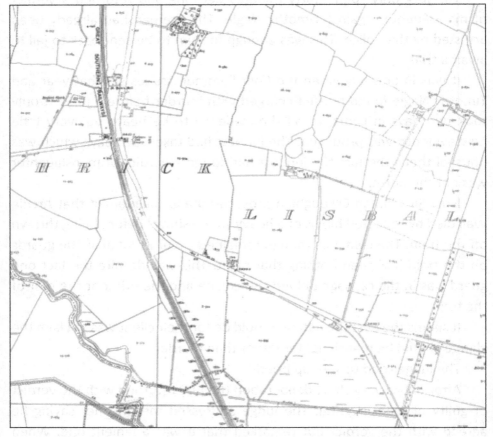

Map showing stretch of track and level crossing.

A watery end
Bannagh, Castlemagner 1847

We all have our own image of Ireland in 1847 and it is all pretty similar - a devastated countryside, widespread hunger and emigration. Not everyone had it so bad though, those with land could only complain of having a reduced income.

With the countryside in such a state, not much can have been thought of the disappearance of William Sheehan in March of that year. He had left Castlemagner on the 13th March to travel to his brother's house in the townland of Bannagh on some business and was never heard of again.

Weeks passed without any report of William, had he been the victim of some desperate crime? Crime in the country had certainly risen as people were driven to do anything they could to survive. Or had he just fled it all and emigrated like so many were doing at the time? When people asked his brother Denis Sheehan or Denis's wife Kitty they suggested he had left the country or enlisted in the army.

Such speculation was ended in late April by a fisherman, when a body was found in the river Blackwater near Killavullen. The man that found him did not know the identity of the body and how would he? Sheehan was from Castlemagner sixteen miles away on the other side of Mallow. Nothing was found on the body except a key tied to the inside of his clothing for safe keeping. Despite this fact it did not take long for the body to be identified as that of William Sheehan. When it was identified the body was taken to the police barracks in Killavullen and the family were notified.

It was clear from the start it was no accident, his body still bore the signs of a violent death. The skull was beaten in and fractured in several places.

Once news reached Castlemagner, people's suspicions were aroused. It had been known that there was a dispute between William and his brother Denis. William had been travelling to see his brother the last time he was seen. It seems William had sold his interest in a farm to Denis for £50 but the money remained outstanding. William had taken Denis's horse to recover the debt and it was to be sold the very day he went missing.

The bridge at Killavullen where the body was found.

An inquest was held on Wednesday the 21st of April by Coroner Richard Jones in the village of Killavullen.

Michael Bouchier told how on the Monday before, he was fishing on the Blackwater at Ballymacmoy near Killavullen. He saw a hand raised in the middle of the river and once he discovered it was a body he went straight for the police.

Elizabeth Barry a servant of Denis Sheehan's was the chief witness at the inquest. She said that she saw William Sheehan cross Bannagh bridge and turn up the boreen towards his brother's house on the 13th of March. Elizabeth told how normally William lived at his brother's house and slept in a room off the kitchen. However William had recently been staying at his sister's. Elizabeth had been sent on several occasions to deliver messages to William. Earlier on the 13th she went to William with a message from Denis saying that William Lane would buy the horse.

That day Kitty Sheehan sent her out to drive a cow into a stubble field. She returned to the house but Mrs Sheehan insisted she go back to the stubble field and watch the cow. It was over an hour later before the servant was permitted into the house where there was no trace of

William Sheehan. She had seen Mrs Sheehan return from the river which was nearby.

When she returned to the house, Mrs Sheehan was washing two shirts. Also in the house she said was a beggar man, her husband had gone out. She noticed the floor was wet and sops of straw had been thrown about the place.

Dr Tuckey gave the horrid details of the post mortem he had carried out on the badly decomposed body. The scalp in places was bare to the bone and the skull fractured. He must have shocked the inquest telling that the brain was still intact inside the fractured skull but was putrid. The doctor concluded Sheehan had been killed by a blunt instrument before being thrown into the river.

A farmer William Morrissey was called to give evidence, as he was married to Sheehan's sister. Morrissey said William Sheehan had slept at his house for three nights before going missing.

A constable from the Castlemagner area was produced. He had questioned Denis Sheehan about the whereabouts of his brother after going missing. Denis had told the constable that William had gone to Buttevant to enlist in the Dragoons.

He told how the brother's father had left a farm at Bannagh jointly to them and they worked it together until Denis got married about two years ago. William agreed to give up his claim to the farm in exchange for £50 in promissory notes payable in stages. The notes were not paid by Denis when they fell due and William was forced to take action.

Sometime in early March goods belonging to Denis Sheehan were seized. These included the horse, a cart and oats. Morrissey said he heard that Denis Sheehan was very put out that his goods had been seized and angry with his brother.

Normally an inquest had no interest in who had done the killing and would come to a verdict on murder by persons unknown even when there was clear evidence. But it was up to the jury themselves what their verdict was. The coroner could only assist them to reach that verdict. In this case the jury felt strongly and returned a verdict of murder against Denis Sheehan and his wife Kitty. The coroner then issued a warrant for their arrest and as a result the couple were taken to Cork Gaol.

The bridge at Bannagh, near where William Sheehan's body was thrown into the river.

The body had travelled along the river over the course of several weeks. It found its way to the Blackwater and even passed through the town of Mallow unnoticed. Whoever had thrown it into the river might just have gotten away with it if the body was found further along and was never identified.

After the inquest and despite Denis and Kitty Sheehan being arrested the trail goes cold. There is no record that the couple ever appeared before a magistrate never mind an Assize Court. Maybe it was lack of actual evidence against them but certainly the motive was very strong indeed. It was an advantage for the couple to have William out of the way to let them run the farm and keep their possessions.

This all occurred in a time when a fraction of the sum they were in dispute about would have fed a starving family.

A boy telling stories.
Kilburn Doneraile 1848

During the period of the famine a wave of crime swept across the countryside of Ireland. It was expected and feared that large scale rioting would occur but didn't. Instead it was isolated crimes. People were driven to doing things they might not otherwise have to get by. For a starving person stealing from someone with plenty was no crime at all, but punishable by transportation.

Near Doneraile, two cows belonging to a man called Mr White were missing presumed stolen. On Monday 24th of January 1848 a young man of nineteen Richard Ryall called to a man in Doneraile asking for some advice. Richard told this elderly man Benjamin Penn he had information about Mr White's cows and asked what he should do. Penn said he should go to Mr White and tell him what he knew about the cows. Young Ryall agreed and left saying he would go and inform Mr White what he knew.

The following Wednesday, young Ryall was back at Mr Penn's house again. This time though he said he had another story to tell. Penn was dubious asking was it a lot a lies like those he told about Mr White's cows the Monday before. Richard began by telling him that on Monday when going to Mr White's he passed his father on the road. He went back to see what delayed his father and said he saw his father enter the widow Murphy's house. Richard said he was on the road and he witnessed his father kill Mrs Murphy with a garden shovel. Benjamin Penn didn't quite believe it as it sounded very farfetched. Richard Ryall was this time more insistent saying go up and see Mrs Murphy sitting there on her usual place on her chair. The door he said was locked with a padlock and if his father was searched the key would be found in his father's boot. He even said that his father had gotten seven pence from the widow's house and given it to him.

Richard didn't want to go to the barracks because his mother was in town so Penn went and fetched the constable to his house. The young lad then gave the same account to Constable Bentley. At first Bentley was suspicious of there being any truth to the story but needed to check it out.

He took Richard to the barracks and locked him up while he and Penn set out. The widow's house was in the townland of Kilburn about a mile south of Doneraile. What he found there was what Ryall had said, the door was padlocked.

Once the door was broken in, the constable found the widow Johanna Murphy sitting in her usual place with her quilting frame in front of her. A shovel and a bill hook lay on the floor beside her. The old woman's face was covered in blood; she had several deep cuts to the face, neck and one bigger wound on the forehead. The room bore the signs of a frantic search, papers were thrown about and a box had been broken open.

Humphrey Ryall was found later that day and arrested by Constable Bentley. He protested his innocence and claimed to have been at work on Monday when the murder was said to have taken place. Everything Richard Ryall had said so far about the widow Murphy was true except the key to the padlock was not found on his father.

The constable suspected the son and duly searched him finding the key in his pocket.

Now it was Richard Ryall who had placed himself in the frame.

Johanna Murphy was over seventy years of age and lived on her own in a small house near the lodge to Kilburn House. She had a daughter in America which may have led people in the area to believe she had a little more money than most. She was normally seen sitting at her chair in her small house with a quilting frame before her working away.

Richard Ryall was only sixteen years old from the townland of Streamhill North of Doneraile. He lived with his mother Hanora and father Humphrey, There was also a younger brother Patrick and sister Norry. It seems he had fallen out with his father and was maybe trying to get revenge. How much worse could it get trying to send his father to the gallows? Richard was known for being an informer and had several months before given evidence against men for stealing. They were most likely jailed after being found guilty on his evidence, one was even said to have died in jail. Richard got a reward, which was said to be as much as £10. He would have had to travel to Cork for the Assizes and was provided for by the police as he was a crown witness.

Johanna Murphy's house was near the lodge to Kilburn House.

Did Richard think he could pull it off once more and this time blame one of his family?

The inquest was held in the Market House, Doneraile on Thursday the 27th January by county coroner Richard Jones. He was assisted by local justices of the peace. Both father and son were still believed to be in custody, but the inquest shows that only one was guilty.

Catherine Collins told the inquest she called to the widow's house on Monday last for a drink of water. There she saw a boy who she could now recognise as Richard Ryall. He was sitting by the fire talking to Mrs Murphy when she left that day.

Patrick Ryall who was only fourteen years old and brother of the accused was called to give evidence at the inquest. He saw his brother Richard put a billhook belonging to their father down his trousers on Monday morning and covered the handle with his jacket. The young boy said he never saw the billhook at home again but recognised it in the barracks. Patrick recalled his brother returned that night and gave him seven pence to buy meal. He told that Richard had neither employment nor means to getting money. Their sister Norry Ryall came forward and agreed with what young Patrick had said.

Ellen Shanahan told the inquest how she was Mr Whites lodge keeper and had lived next door to Mrs Murphy. The Tuesday of the week before Richard Ryall called to her house and asked did Mrs Murphy live alone. Innocently Ellen said she did live alone but said sometimes people stayed with her at night. How could she have known the young fella's intentions?

The local doctor Reardon, told that Mrs Murphy died from the injuries she had sustained on the 24th of January.

Having heard the evidence, the jury duly found a verdict of murder against Richard Ryall. His father Humphrey was afterwards released from custody and Richard was sent back to the barracks. It seems Richard had no awareness of the seriousness of what he was being accused nor the likely consequences.

The next assizes held in Cork would be in spring which would normally take place in April. Little did Richard Ryall seem to realise that within three months he could be hanging from the gallows despite his young age.

The Cork Summer Assizes sat that year from the 1st of April till the 1st of May one of the longest due to the many cases to be dealt with. By the time it finished the judge had sentenced 180 to be either transported or jailed. A case of murder was one of the most serious crimes but it would only take one day in court, maybe because of the volume the Assizes had to deal with. Still though in the capital crime the jury had to satisfy itself of his guilt before he could be sentenced to death. Mr Bennett represented the crown prosecution while Richard Ryall now found himself on the other side but had a Mr O'Dea to plead his case. Despite the fact that Richard had experience of being in court before as a witness, he still seemed to have no grasp of the reality of the situation.

The prosecution now maintained that when Ryall went to tell Mr White about the missing cows he passed the house of Mrs Murphy near the gate lodge. He made enquiries about the old woman the week before and then returned the following Monday to carry out the deed. They felt it was a clear case of premeditated murder and he tried to cover it up by blaming others.

The police had carried out their investigation which now provided the witnesses for the prosecution case. It cannot have been hard for the police to find witnesses; nobody would have wanted to see Richard Ryall back walking the countryside after what he had done.

The local parish priest James Daly was called to give evidence. Being so high in status in the community what he said would have been held in so high regard back then and was beyond doubt. Fr Daly said on Monday 24th of January he met Richard Ryall on the road between Doneraile and Charleville. Ryall told him he had seen an old woman killed that day by Maurice Roche. The priest doubted him, but Richard said Roche's shirt was covered in blood. Again the priest said he questioned Ryall who said he could not have done it as he had no blood on him.

Richard even told the parish priest his name and where he lived. He said he saw Roche kill the woman while he looked in the window. The priest though didn't think much of what Ryall said and didn't even ask who the woman was, thinking it was a just a fabrication.

Constable Bentley recalled clearly what Richard Ryall had told him that day. He said it was when he returned from the scene of the crime, he searched Richard. Having found the key on him Richard replied "that's one of the keys my father gave me". The constable afterwards arrested the father but found no key on him. Bentley also told of the week before the murder when he went with Richard Ryall to a magistrate's house where Richard gave information about who had stolen cows.

There were several witnesses who could put Richard Ryall near the widow's house on the day she was killed.

Patrick Ryall again gave evidence against his older brother as he had at the inquest. That Monday morning Richard told him he was taking the billhook to Joe Leary who needed it. That same billhook he now recognised in court. He said it was five that evening when his brother returned and gave him seven pence. Patrick also said his father had been home that Monday all day.

Patrick told how on the following day his brother told him to go to the Constable in Doneraile. He was to tell him that the widow Murphy had been killed by Maurice Roche with a shovel. Patrick did not go to Doneraile and inform the police.

Their sister Norry (Hanora) Ryall also gave similar evidence but said Richard had a row with his father on Tuesday night. It ended with the father slapping his son who resented it. Afterwards she heard her brother by the fire angrily utter "he'll never strike me again".

Humphrey Ryall was also questioned that day in court, it began "did you kill the widow Murphy?" and he replied "wisha I never killed a chicken". The questions continued but Ryall maintained he never knew the widow Murphy nor had he spoken to her in his life.

Humphrey admitted the trouble he had with his son. On the Monday night the widow was killed, his son returned home in awful form he said. When he came in he called his mother "an auld thief" and Humphrey struck him. Richard threatened to report him for hitting him. The following night the son tried to choke his father in the bed. Humphrey went on to say Richard was trouble out late at night playing cards. The father even revealed "he is the biggest blackguard in that part of the country" which produced laughter in court.

When the prosecution case closed they felt confident in getting a conviction against the young man, that the crown had once provided for when he gave evidence against others.

The best solicitor O'Dea could do for the defence was to give a long speech as he had no witnesses to call. There was no one to give Richard a character reference and if they did it possible would make him look worse. O'Dea warned the jury of the grave consequences of finding him guilty on circumstantial evidence alone.

After a long day in court, it was eight that night when the jury returned with their verdict of "guilty of murder". The judge did not announce his sentence that day Richard had to wait several weeks till the end of the Assizes. On the final day of the Assizes, all those found guilty were brought to court again to hear their punishment.

Judge Ball addressed him "Richard Ryall you have been found guilty of the foulest murder ever recorded in the annals of crime. You murdered a poor defenceless old woman deliberately without provocation". The judge then went on about how Ryall had been a crown witness and that he was willing to see his own father be accused so he could gain from it. Justice Ball admitted that Ryall's actions were depraved in the extreme.

Ball continued "such being the character of your offence the law cannot suffer you to live, your days are numbered and they are few". The judge then did not put on the black cap as was normal but still he announced Richard Ryall was to be hanged on the 3rd of June.

Richard had only a month to live and had burned his bridges with his family. He seemed oblivious to what was going on around him. His own fate or his betrayal of those around him didn't seem to bother him in the slightest.

By early June there seems to have been some sympathy for Richard Ryall because of his young age. His age had been quoted differently in many places but now he was using it to his advantage. It was claimed he was only seventeen and should be saved from the hangman. The legal system was also blamed for encouraging or bribing witnesses to give evidence, which Richard had previously gained from. The motive suggested for the crime was now hunger or insanity. He was also now recovering from "jail fever" which we now know as typhus, which was at epidemic levels in Ireland then.

For some of these reasons it was decided to give Richard a reprieve from his sentence for fourteen days. The truth though was Richard Ryall was nineteen years old; he had been born in Streamhill and baptised in November 1828. However his execution was now set for Saturday the 17th June outside the County Jail.

From some quarters there was some sympathy for Ryall's fate. Another reprieve was applied for and it was assumed he would now not receive the death sentence.

The Thursday before a petition was sent to try to prevent the execution going ahead. It was not received in Cork until after midday on Saturday. By then thousands of men, women and children had gathered in the vicinity of the county jail. Every wall, tree or anything that could be climbed on was to afford a better view. Such were the masses of people a boy fell from a tree into the river much to the amusement of the mob. What was the county jail is now part of the UCC campus but back then it was surrounded by fields on the outskirts of the city.

Even before any movement from the jail, law and order had broken down in the crowd. Several fights broke out as the crowd became bored with the wait. At one that day the soldiers arrived to prevent more trouble breaking out, but it was an hour later before orders were received to proceed with the execution.

After two Richard Ryall was led to the scaffold with the rope around his neck. The scaffold was erected at the entrance to the county jail. He shook hands with the governor and thanked him for the kindness during his time in jail.

When he climbed the scaffold he called out aloud "may the lord have mercy on my soul".

The executioner began his final preparations and was about to put the rope over the scaffold when Ryall interrupted him. He said "don't pull that up till I see Dr Beamish, I must speak to him". While Beamish was sent for, a priest tried one last time asking Ryall to tell the truth while he could. Ryall however made no confession that day.

Dr Beamish arrived at the scaffold and shook hands with the condemned man. Again Ryall thanked him for his help in jail. He now asked one last request before he was put to death. That the clothes he had gotten from the nuns be given to his mother for his younger brother.

It was said that his young brother and sister were amongst the crowd that day.

The executioner then continued where he had been interrupted before. The white was pulled over his face the rope thrown over the frame and tied. Then the executioner left the scaffold and pulled the bolt to release the drop.

What the crowd saw next must truly have shocked them; the method used at the time was the short drop. Ryall was seen struggling on the end of the rope for nearly five minutes while the crowd quietly witnessed what they had come to see that day. He was then left hanging there for another hour before his body was placed in a coffin, to be buried on the grounds of the jail.

Afterwards the executioner was recognised by the mob, which began booing and hissing at him as he was leaving. To escape without injury, the executioner had to be escorted away by an armed guard.

Patrick and Norry Ryall, the brother and sister in the crowd that day were said to be seriously affected by what they had witnessed. Richard

Ryall had tormented his parents but the only person he showed any kindness to was his younger brother, to whom he had given the seven pence and asked for the clothes for him.

I know who ye are
Monanimy Upper, Killavullen, 1826

On the Sunday 12th of March 1826 William Sheehan went to bed with his wife. They had six children and as they had a farm, there were also servants living with them. William farmed 60 acres in the townland of Monanimy close to Killavullen. He held the land from Myles Linehan who in turn rented most of the townland from the landlord.

During the night the occupants of the house were woken by the sound of breaking glass in the kitchen. A man climbed in the broken window and found himself on a servant boy who was sleeping on the kitchen table. A maid who was also sleeping in the kitchen was woken by the noise too.

The intruder threatened them with their lives if they did not lie still and cover themselves with a blanket. Once on his feet in the kitchen the intruder opened the door and two more entered while another kept watch outside. The pair who had come in were armed with bayonets and lit a candle from the fire.

Meanwhile Sheehan and his wife in the adjoining room had locked themselves inside. The men banged on the bedroom door asking him to come out saying they only wanted a few pound. Sheehan had no intention of letting them in despite the leader's threats of getting the blunderbuss. Between the three of them the door was lifted from the hinges and the men forced their way in. Sheehan tried to defend himself and struck one of the intruders in the face but that just made things worse.

He was overpowered and within minutes was lying dead on his bedroom floor. Sheehan was said to be a big strong man but he was no match for them. His wife became hysterical and the men demanded the money they had come for. A safe box was found in the bedroom and quickly broken open when the wife was not forthcoming with the key. Once the contents of the box were obtained they quickly left. It was as if they had known it was there.

An inquest was held the following day Monday the 13th by coroner O'Brien. The servant boy gave evidence as did William Sheehan's widow. The maid who was in the kitchen that night was not able to tell much of what had occurred. Based on this evidence the jury returned a verdict of wilful murder against some persons unknown.

It was believed that one of the intruders received a blow from Sheehan as he desperately tried to defend himself and his wife. The wound was said to have bled a lot at the time before they had made their escape. Surely now the police could search the area and find a man with a mark on his lip.

It was also known to have been carried out by locals. Sheehan had sold a horse a few days before. People would have known the money was in his house, the intruders had not come by chance. Not long after the inquest the police arrested local man Denis Neale, on suspicion of being involved, but he did not give away the names of the others.

March was a bad month to be caught for any crime but worst of all murder. The Spring Assizes were coming up in early April and justice was swift to deter others. Saturday the 1st April 1826 was the Cork Assizes Saturday before Justice Baron Pennefather.

Timothy Tobin a servant boy of barely eleven years of age amazed the crowded courtroom with his ability to answer and his composure. Tobin told how he had seen Denis Neale several times before that night but did not know his name then. He saw him at a fight in Killavullen and at Mass.

That night he was sleeping on a table under the kitchen window when at two in the morning the window was broken in and a stone struck him on the knee. A man climbed in the window on top of him. That man he said whose face was blackened seemed to be the leader of the gang. He saw them at the bedroom door threatening to shoot but said Sheehan was not letting them in. Tobin heard Sheehan telling them that they were blackguards and he would not part with a penny. Sheehan also said he knew who they were. Tobin witnessed the bedroom door shoved in and the man whose face was blackened stabbed Sheehan in the chest. Then he said they beat his head with a stone and stove in his skull. At the same time he saw Neale looking for the money and threatening Mrs Sheehan. Tobin believed that Neale was wearing an old coat torn at the sleeves and shoulders. The boy was not sure of the colour but thought it was made of frieze.

A juror asked young Tobin "do you know what will happen to Neale if you are to be believed?" The young lad was aware saying "he will be hung". The juror then asked what if he was telling lies and Neale was hung for it. Tobin replied "oh I ought to be hung myself".

Anne Sheehan the wife of the dead man was called to give evidence; she could not recognise any of the men who were in her house that night saying she had lost her senses. She admitted to being woken by the sound of breaking glass but that stones were also thrown through her bedroom window at the same time.

While her husband defended the door one of the men shoved the bayonet through the door and stabbed him. They then quickly broke down the door and gained access. Once in the bedroom she said one man struck her on the hand with a stick and demanded money. She showed the bruise on her arm saying how she could still barely raise it.

Anne told how she refused to give the give the key of the box and they threatened to kill her. The box was broken open and the man whose face was blackened grabbed the money and left. Anne knew there was £17 in the box, quite a sum in the 1820's. Before leaving one of the men turned to her and hit her again. This he told her was for delaying them as they had far to travel. She said that from where young Tobin was on the kitchen table he would have been able to see into the bedroom.

Under cross examination Mrs Sheehan admitted she did not recognise Denis Neale despite him living near her. Anne did recall a man in the house that night with a torn brown coat but could not tell if it was the accused or not. She told how that night one man said to her husband "you do not know me".

The chief of Police Mr Crossley gave evidence of arrest telling how he found Neale at home in bed. When Neale got out he threw aside a coat, Crossley told him to bring a coat but several times he replied saying it was torn. The chief said he became suspicious and insisted that Neale bring the coat, which was brown and torn at the elbows and shoulders. Right then in court the accused displayed his coat. It was brown and torn at the sleeves and shoulders. He showed both the front and rear of the coat like a man who had nothing at all to conceal.

This completed the evidence of the prosecution but there was no evidence called for the defence. Neale obviously had nobody who could prove his whereabouts that night.

With that the judge addressed the jury summing up all that was heard before letting them come to a verdict. The jury returned after a matter of minutes with the verdict of guilty and the judge then addressed Denis Neale directly. He admitted that Neale may not have struck the deadly blow but told him "The law says if several persons associate for the commission of crime that every one of them is answerable for the crime committed, that the hand which gives the wound is not more guilty than the man whose presence aids"

He then reminded him of the terrible crime he had been involved in and the consequences of it. He said "Little time now remains for you in this world, and I trust that before you leave it you will repent" The judge then implored on him the importance of repenting even at the 11th hour.

The judge proceeded and sentenced William Neale to death which would take place on the following Monday. There was no time or facility for an appeal in the 1820's the law stated the execution shall take place within two days.

On Monday the 3rd Denis Neale was led out of the jail at twelve thirty and taken to where the scaffold was erected at Gallows Green.

Before ascending the scaffold Neale asked for the Sheriff saying he had a statement to make. He told how he was convinced that if he did not tell the truth he was destined for hell. Neale then said he was not at Sheehan's house that night nor did he know anyone who was but he forgave his prosecutors from his heart. He even mentioned the coat saying that if he was a guilty man he would not have come to the trial with the torn coat for this is how he was identified. It didn't matter now the law had taken its course and it was far too late.

He then climbed the scaffold and as the executioner adjusted the rope Neale shut his eyes tightly and called out asking god to have mercy for him. Seconds later the drop was released and Neale struggled at the end of a rope before becoming a lifeless body.

It was less than a month in total from crime to execution but never was there a mention of the names of the other men.

Is that you?
Newberry House, Mallow, 1816

On the 18th of November 1816 Colonel Charles Newman travelled to Mallow. He went to Delacour's Bank or Mallow Bank as it was known and exchanged an order he had received for cash. From there he travelled on to Dromore House and dined with his older brother. Later that evening he arrived home with servant James Lucey and went to bed. The colonel was a man of over seventy years who had retired to his family's estate after many years in the army. He had been a lieutenant Colonel in the 8th Dragoons and served in Flanders during the war of the French Revolution.

In the middle of the night the elderly Colonel was woken by some noise and called out "is that you James" to his closest servant but received no reply. The intruders had not planned on the old man waking and had to do something drastic quickly before the alarm was raised.

He was found on Monday morning in bed with black marks around his neck from strangulation. The indentations of fingernails could still be seen. The bedroom had been turned over and several items were missing from the house - the bank notes he had got the day before, a gold watch, his pistols and items of clothing.

It seemed the house had been broken into as no one else lived with the Colonel except for his servants. The lobby window was broken and a ladder had been used to gain access.

Once the news got out, his brother Adam Newman arrived from Dromore to see what had happened to his brother. He met a servant who had blood on his shirt but could explain it. The servant claimed a horse had reared on him and his nose had bled. Newman's suspicions became aroused even before the inquest was held. One of the servants then began to give information about what had occurred. James Lucey and Daniel Clifford were taken into custody.

It did not take long for them to confess to what they had done. Lucey even told where he had hidden the Colonel's wallet with the money.

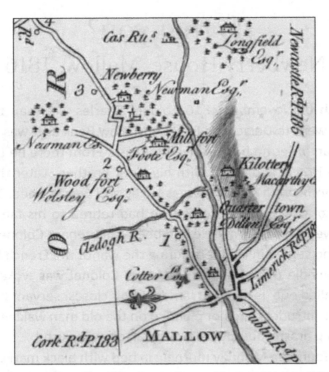

Period map showing Newberry house in relation to Mallow.

Newberry House as it is today.

The coroner David Tuckey assisted by several magistrates held an inquest at the house on the following Tuesday and Wednesday. Crowds came to hear how the Colonel had died.

Before long four were arrested in total. Three were servants of the Colonel's and another man Thomas Dorgan acting as the intruder. His cook Catherine Cooney was also arrested on suspicion, she had been working for him for nine years.

On Saturday 12th of April at the Cork Spring Assizes the following year, James Lucey and Daniel Clifford were charged with the murder and burglary of their master.

It was told how Lucey had been to the bank with the Colonel and knew about the money. Lucey was his favourite servant and the Colonel was said to have been very good to him. Not much evidence was needed to prove their guilt as they had already given confessions, Lucey was struck with remorse and told everything at the time even where the booty was hidden.

The jury were left with no option but to find them guilty of murder. The judge then set their sentence of death for the following Monday at Gallows Green. Both men were about thirty years of age and had been married for several years.

The crowd assembled at Gallows Green on the 14th was much more than normal. It was estimated at between thirty and forty thousand.

As they were marched from gaol to Gallows green the men were praying. Clifford read the prayers from a book. Once at the scaffold the men prayed with a priest for several minutes before taking their final steps. At the scaffold the men did what everyone expected them to do before they left the world, they made their confession. Both men admitted their part in the crime and accepted their punishment. They held no bad feeling to their prosecutors or anyone else.

The final preparations were made. The men stood on the platform and continued to pray. When the platform was released and the pair dropped the praying fell silent and after a short struggle they were dead. The now lifeless bodies remained hanging there and what the thousands had come to see was over.

After a while the bodies were cut down and removed for dissection to the county infirmary. The law at the time stated that a convicted murderer could not be allowed a Christian burial.

Captain Moonlight
Doonesleen, Kiskeam 1881

In Ireland in the 1880's tenants were unable to pay their high rents due to falling global produce prices. Some landlords reduced their rents while others just evicted. This sparked off the land war with the aim of a fairer deal for the tenants and options to purchase. The agrarian unrest led to violence in many parts of the country. Even the word boycott came about in Ireland at this time, within months it was commonly used.

In North Cork it was no different to any other part of the country. By night armed gangs roamed the countryside, threatening those that could pay their landlord. They disguised themselves with masks and behaved like the Whiteboys had decades before.

By the autumn of 1881 in North Cork many believed the worst of the trouble was over and looked forward to a period of relative peace but it was not to be.

On Monday the 3rd of October, several men gathered at Daniel Hickey's farmhouse in Doonesleen a few miles south of Kiskeam. They had come that day to help Hickey bring home the last of the harvest. In exchange he had got in a half barrel of porter and held what was traditionally known as a harvest home.

The singing and dancing was interrupted when a nearby farmer called Connors burst in with his wife and children. He told how he had just received a visit from Captain Moonlight and his gang. They had asked Connors had he paid his rent and the farmer said he had not. Before leaving the gang threatened him to pay no more than Griffiths Valuation.

A little later two of Hickey's helpers went out of the farmhouse. They could make out the armed gang assembled nearby outside John Hickey's house.

One of the men at Hickey's Patrick O'Leary called inside the house for the revellers to quieten down. He then let out a whistle and when he did a shot was fired almost immediately in response. The shot went over their heads. Patrick O'Leary and his friend Daniel Dennehy scrambled to get inside the house for cover. As they turned to go another shot was fired and this time it struck O'Leary. He managed to struggle back inside the farmhouse but was in immense pain.

A few minutes later Captain Moonlight and his gang burst in bold as brass like nothing had happened. The gang all wore masks except the leader. He wore an orange striped trousers and black army jacket with a soldier's helmet. A bayonet hung at his side and he held a revolver in his hand.

He warned Hickey about paying his rent as he had to Connors earlier. As the gang were about to depart a brave woman piped up from the party goers. She said to captain moonlight "you are departing this house leaving a corpse behind you".

The leader then went to the room where Patrick O'Leary was thrown in agony. With the light of a candle the leader inspected the wound and said young Patrick would be fine. Dismissing it he said a cure could be got in Mallow or Kanturk of ointment or the like. Before leaving he mentioned that they mistook O'Leary for a detective.

The house emptied out and someone sent for a doctor which took hours to arrive. There was not much could be done for him, the woman who spoke up was right, Captain Moonlight was leaving a corpse behind him.

Patrick clung on to life that night but was in terrible agony. Once the doctor arrived the next morning he realised the bullet had passed through his right kidney, abdomen and struck his hip. It was not until five on Tuesday evening that Patrick O'Leary's suffering ended when he passed away.

The story that got out first was that Hickey's farm had been boycotted and O'Leary was shot for helping out. Some said he had been running away when shot.

On Thursday of that week the inquest revealed that story was false. Coroner James Byrne held the inquest in Daniel Hickey's farmhouse. It was revealed that Patrick O'Leary had gone to Cork to attend the Charles Stewart Parnell demonstration in the city the day before he was shot. His father was the president of the Knocknagree Land League; the gang had shot the wrong man.

The jury was made up of twelve local men given the task of deciding how Patrick O'Leary met his death. On the jury was Daniel Mahony foreman, James O'Keeffe, Robert Howard, Jeremiah Herlihy, Daniel O'Sullivan, John Ring, Edmund Fitzgerald, John Lane, James Quinn, Daniel Murphy, William Cronin, John O'Keeffe and Patrick Hickey.

It was Fr O'Leary from Boherbue that first addressed the coroner. He said there was a rumour going about that the police had shot O'Leary. He denied that he was the source of the rumour. The priest then argued with sub inspector Martin for some time on the issue of the source of the rumour.

The inquest finally began when Daniel Hickey told of the gang coming to his house the Monday before. He recalled Patrick O'Leary was singing at the end of the table but did not notice him leave the house. Hickey it seems had not even seen him return to the house after being shot. Hickey described the leader's clothes in detail and said the rest of the gang had their coats turned inside out, with masks on their faces. He heard the leader say he would not have shot Patrick but thought he was a detective. The coroner remarked that it was a strange place to find a detective.

Daniel Dennehy who was a servant at Hickey's recalled being outside with O'Leary that night. He heard one of the gang say "what was that" then Patrick whistled and the gang fired.

Dr O'Sullivan from Boherbue described what he found when he attended O'Leary on Tuesday morning. Patrick was in bed in a pool of blood. He located the entry and exit wounds of the bullet near the ribs. He concluded that the bullet had hit the right kidney, intestines and the liver. The doctor said Patrick was quite conscious at the time and could answer any questions put to him. He was suffering from intense pain.

County Inspector Barry remarked more than once that he thought it strange that people in the house could not detain the gang until the police arrived. Dan Hickey replied that he had no firearms, saying if they came again he would let them go. Fr O'Leary defended them also saying they did not think at the time Patrick was so seriously wounded. Even a juror intervened and criticised Barry's comments saying it was easy for him to say that now but the gang numbered over twenty in total.

The jury had no trouble coming to their verdict "that the deceased Patrick O Leary of Tooreenglanahee in the parish of Nohovaldaly died from the effects of a gunshot wound inflicted on him on the night of Monday 3rd October at Doonesleen by some person unknown".

After some discussion amongst the jury they added the rider "that the persons in Daniel Hickey's house could not arrest the armed party without endangering their lives."

A juror added that he believed the police were not involved in the shooting but it was suggested that their bullets should be compared to the one that hit O'Leary. County Inspector Barry was willing to produce any bullet but again remarked that the people should have detained the armed man. The inspector hoped with the assistance of the clergy and public to bring the guilty party before the justice system.

Once the inquest finished that day the burial was held straight after. Patrick O'Leary's remains were taken to Nohoval graveyard near Rathmore. The funeral cortege consisted of almost two thousand people.

The Friday before the shooting tenants, had been told by the agent Mr Vernon to pay their rent. Many had not on account of notices and threats issued by "Captain Moonlight". The estate in the area was the property of a Lady Chinnery. All the houses in the estate had their roof slated and the landlord charged higher rents for them.

About the same time a man named Thomas Lyons was arrested near Kanturk. Despite the initial rumours it turned out to be unconnected. He had attacked a house with an armed gang but had only broken windows.

It was obvious at the inquest that nobody was going to identify anyone of the gang because they knew they would be visited in the night. Not a month before in Kiskeam three brothers ignored the warnings and paid the price with a late night visit. They however escaped with their lives.

Rumours continued about the shooting of Patrick O'Leary, some said he was a moonlighter himself and should have been out with the gang that night. This makes no sense though with the disregard the gang treated his wound that night one even said "get four pence worth of ointment and that will cure him". If they had known him or if he was one of them surely they would have been a bit more concerned.

All over the countryside the police searched for many different Captain Moonlight's and arrested many gang members. None of the country people assisted the police with their enquires and kept quiet on the matter. Inspector Barry's attitude was always that someone in Hickey's should have apprehended the gang that night. The truth was more likely that the country people although threatened by the moonlighters were still on the same side more or less. There was more mistrust toward the police than the moonlighters. If the gang wore no masks that night the outcome would have most likely been the same. That is probably why nobody was ever caught for the shooting of Patrick O'Leary.

Spent on drink?
Bregoge, Buttevant 1873

On the evening of Saturday the 15th of March 1873, Norry Hayes went to visit her elderly sister Mary Carroll in Bregoge near Buttevant who was sick. When the door was locked she became suspicious as the old woman was weak and did not often go out. The sister tried the door several times to no avail. Eventually she managed to shove the door in by kicking it.

What she encountered inside was a shocking sight indeed. Her sister Mary lay on the floor in a pool of blood. Her skull was horrifically fractured and blood still flowed from the wounds. The crime had only occurred a short time before and an iron bar lay on the floor beside her. The bar was normally used for hanging the pots over the fire, now it was covered in blood and hair.

Once she got over the shock of the scene, the sister ran for help. The first person she met was an old man, Ned Roche, and he went back to the house while she ran to Buttevant. On her way there she met her sister's husband Henry and told him what she had found. He had been working that day in Buttevant and must have been on his way home. He now made for home with haste and Norry headed for Buttevant to raise the alarm.

The police and a doctor eventually made their way to the house. The doctor carried out an examination of the old woman, while the police inspected the scene. They discovered the iron bar was covered in blood and the woman's hair. The motive seemed to be robbery as a strong box was found forced open and the contents were missing.

Despite the apparent motive one of the first things the police did was to arrest Henry Carroll. The police were also looking for two other men Maurice Keating and William Roche who had been seen hunting near the house that day. Mary Carroll was known as a thrifty woman by the locals who had saved a few pounds over the years.

William Roche was easily located and arrested but Keating was not to be found on Saturday or Sunday despite the search.

Sunday evening County Inspector George Barry arrived with a detective to take charge of the inquiry. More men were deployed to search for Maurice Keating and the murder scene checked again for clues. By then the police knew there was no evidence against Henry and he was released

On Monday after a manhunt for Keating he handed himself in at the barracks in Buttevant. His clothes were found to be bloodstained and he had tried to conceal it. Keating claimed his father had cut him the Friday before to account for the blood. The county inspector picked a long hair from his coat that could have come from Mary Carroll's head.

It was not until the following Tuesday the 18th that the inquest took place in Buttevant Courthouse. Coroner Daly presided over the inquest with a jury of twelve local men who had been sworn in. A resident magistrate Captain Coote and county inspector Barry were also present.

The first witness called that day was Norry Hayes, who had discovered her sister's body.

She told how that day she came from her home in Knockloona to visit her sister.

Ned Roche was also questioned and recalled seeing Norry running towards him screaming her sister was killed. They then met the husband who ran off towards the house in a state. Roche said Mrs Carroll was known in the area as a woman who had managed to save a few pound. It was also well known that she and her husband got on well and there was no trouble between them.

Henry Carroll told the inquest his wife was about sixty eight years old. He was working for Dr Sheehan in Buttevant that day, but his wife asked him to come home early. Henry claimed she had told him Keating had been about and she was in dread of him. He did reveal though that Keating had never actually done anything to them and had no actual reason to be in such dread of him.

Henry admitted to receiving a few pounds from America and gave some of this money to his wife. He thought she might have had two pound in silver in her box but was not sure. He said on the way to work that day he met Maurice Keating and William Roche with two greyhounds. Henry thought to himself that his wife was safe from Keating that day as he was otherwise occupied.

A twelve year old James Barrett from Buttevant called to Mary Carroll's house at one on the day she was killed. He found her washing at the time but had seen Maurice Keating hunting only two fields away from Carroll's.

Brother of the dead woman, Jeremiah O'Sullivan revealed his sister told him two months before that Keating had threatened to kill her. Keating himself asked why she would not have said that to her husband if it were true. But Jeremiah replied saying well she said it to me.

It was proved that day there was no evidence against William Roche and he was released from custody. As soon as this was announced Roche was sworn in to give evidence.

He said while hunting with Keating that day, he told him to go home which he did, leaving Keating alone near Carroll's house. In fact he said when they parted about one, Keating headed in the general direction of Carroll's house.

The next time he met him was six that evening in Buttevant when he bought Roche a pint of porter and he also bought one for Con Logan in McDonald's public house. He recalled that the porter was paid for with a two shilling coin. Later he also saw Keating buying more porter for other men.

James McDonald told how Keating and Roche had several pints of porter that evening and glasses of whiskey also. James thought Roche had paid with a two shilling coin but Roche clarified the matter.

Another publican Bridget O'Donnell said she sold Keating porter that night and he also paid with a two shilling coin. Con Logan was called but admitted he was drunk that night and could not recall much of what happened. He admitted drinking with Keating and Roche but was not sure who paid for it, this produced laughter in court as it wasn't him that paid for it.

Patrick Lynch Walsh was called to give medical evidence having examined the body the morning after. He described massive fracturing to the skull in medical terms and found the brains coming out. In court he produced several pieces of the skull which were over three inches. This showed the terrible battering Mrs Carroll had received. The doctor said the iron bar would have inflicted these injuries. He had also examined the blood stains on Keating's clothes and said lime had been rubbed on the stain to try to hide it.

Maurice Keating intervened saying how his father cut him on Friday night and that was why he had blood on his clothes. The coroner stopped him from going further saying "I'll advise you not to make any statements at present my good man". Keating took the hint and replied "very well sir"

By the end of the day the coroner revealed that several more were to give evidence but were not there that day. A juror suggested adjourning to another day to hear them. Daly who had been coroner in the area for the last fifteen years had never had a case like this before. He said the inquest would sit for several more days if he felt it needed to. It was the resident magistrate Captain Coote who announced that Maurice Keating was remanded to custody and the inquest was adjourned till the 26th of March.

It was unusual that the inquest was adjourned until the following week to allow the police more time to investigate. The jury could have easily come to a verdict of how Mary Carroll met her death. They did not need to know who done it, that was up to the police to investigate.

On the second day of the inquest, more evidence was produced against Maurice Keating.

Young Barrett this time went further saying he actually saw Keating at the corner of Carroll's house that day. The boy was asked why his story changed so much since the last day. The room was shocked when the boy said his father told him what to say and not to tell the truth. Sub Inspector Mullarkey said footprints had been found fifty yards from the house. He compared the footprints to Keating's footwear and they matched exactly.

It was also revealed by a policeman that a key found near Carroll's door, unlocked the door to Keating's house.

The father of the accused Maurice Keating Senior was then called. He started by saying how he had reared his son well and taught him to be honest. Keating claimed the key found was missing with over two months. Then he relented admitting since the key went missing his son let himself in and out of the house.

The Friday before his son returned home drunk and the old man struck him on the face with the bellows for the fire. He said the day before the murder his son received about two shilling from selling rabbits. The father could not recall when his son last worked saying he drank every penny he could get. He even admitted his son would take his money and drink all that he could get his hands on it.

Dr Walsh was recalled and asked about the blood stains on Keating's clothes. He said Maurice had a cut on his face but that would not have produced the quantity of blood required. The blood stains were spatters and he found it difficult to see how a mere cut would do that. One blood stain looked as if a hand covered in blood came in to contact with the clothes.

Both William Roche and the young boy Barrett were recalled and both said Keating's clothes were not bloodstained when they say him that Saturday. The questioning of Barrett continued and again he said his father had told him to tell lies. The coroner remarked that his father's behaviour was shameful and that he should be in custody. He asked the resident magistrate Captain Coote to take charge of Mr Barrett for interfering with his son's evidence.

The boy then confirmed after some assistance that he saw Maurice Keating standing at the corner of Mrs Carroll's house that Saturday.

Coroner Daly told the jury that Keating's clothes had been sent to Dublin for analysis on the blood and the results would take some time. The jury however was satisfied with the evidence given over the two days and were ready to make a verdict. The coroner gave a long speech to the jury but reminded them their decision was not final that would be made at an Assize court.

After only a few minutes the jury returned a verdict of murder against Maurice Keating. He was removed from the room and taken back to jail to await a trial before another jury.

Months later in July Maurice Keating was charged with murder at the Cork Summer Assizes before Justice Morris. The prosecution was led by Colman O'Loughlan and Keating was defended by Michael O'Loughlan.

Colman O'Loughlan opened for the prosecution saying how this was not a case where the charge could be reduced to manslaughter. He admitted the jury would either have to convict on the circumstantial evidence or acquit him of the charges.

Norry Hayes described finding the body of her sister and the dreadful scene in the house. Henry Carroll gave evidence and recalled being in police custody for two days at the time.

Ned Roche who was the first person to meet Mrs Hayes that night was also called. He was working in a field all that day only two fields away from Carroll's house. He claimed he did not see anyone approach the house that day. William Roche who was out hunting with Keating was his son.

Twelve year old James Barrett, the son of a baker from Buttevant was then questioned. At first he was asked about the lies he told at the inquest and what his father had told him to say. He was out searching for a goat that day near Carroll's house. Barrett confirmed he did in fact see Maurice Keating at the corner of Carroll's house that day after leaving the house. He had spent half an hour with Mrs Carroll who was washing clothes at the time.

When he left Keating walked with him towards Buttevant but they parted and Maurice Keating headed back towards Carroll's house. Barrett arrived home in Buttevant about two that day.

Dr James Emerson Reynolds from Dublin described the items he had analyzed for blood stains. The iron bar was stained with blood and human hair. The hairs on the bar and those found on Keating by Inspector Barry were very similar. The doctor confirmed the stains on Keating's clothes were blood. There were fourteen blood stains on one shirt and twelve another. On the trousers he found six stains but none on the coat. Under cross examination the doctor agreed the blood stains could have come from a rabbit thrown over his shoulder.

The prosecution did not call William Roche to give evidence that day, they obviously felt he could not be trusted and was friendly with Keating. The defence also saw no benefit in calling Roche.

So it was just circumstantial evidence alone, Barrett saw him at the house, the key was found nearby, his clothes were spattered with blood and Keating bought a lot of drink that night.

On the other hand nobody had seen him do it nor heard the murder occur. Could the blood have come from rabbits and the money as well?

Michael O'Loughlan addressed the jury and explained to them the dangers of finding Keating guilty on such circumstantial evidence alone.

The jury left for only ten minutes and found Maurice Keating not guilty and he was acquitted. With the chief witness being a boy of twelve who had admitted telling lies it was not enough to hang a man on.

What made him murder my boy?
Gurteen wood, Ballyhooly, Fermoy 1835

Early March 1835 McKenzie the master tailor of the 94th regiment garrisoned at Fermoy worried about his son who had disappeared days before. The weather at the time was not at all conducive to a young lad sleeping rough. A huge thunderstorm swept across the Fermoy area followed by north westerly storms the likes of which had not been seen in years.

The master tailor made frantic enquiries about the whereabouts of his son who he had last seen on the morning of Shrove Tuesday the 3rd of March. Also missing from the house was a watch and 9 or 10 shillings. The only clue to his disappearance was that a private in the same regiment had deserted the night before.

It was later in the week when the tailor received the news that he was seen in the direction of Ballyhooly. On Friday a man working in the Gurteen Wood near Ballyhooly discovered the body of a boy in a saw pit. The workmen not knowing what to do sent for Lord Enniscrone at nearby Convamore. Later that day Duncan McKenzie arrived with a sergeant to the scene and saw his teenage son thrown there.

The body had just one injury which seemed to be a stab wound in the chest. He had boots and trousers on but no cap or coat that he had left home with.

The missing private from the same regiment was now the chief suspect. Several locals near to Gurteen Wood recalled seeing a soldier and a boy nearby on Shrove Tuesday. Now the search was on for the missing soldier from the 94th regiment. His name was John McCarthy aged about thirty four and originally from Charleville. Worse still for the father was the fact that he would most likely have known McCarthy.

Word was sent to police stations in the area - Castletownroche, Fermoy, Buttevant, Doneraile and Charleville. It was thought he may head for Charleville where his father was believed to be living. Police in those places were searching actively for a soldier fitting McCarthy's description. As a result John McCarthy was arrested in a pawn shop in Buttevant, in the process of pawning a watch.

Before the inquest early on the morning of the Saturday 7th of March doctor John Peard Edgar carried out an examination on the body. He found one triangular wound in the chest which had been the result of a sharp instrument. There were no other signs of violence on the body and the doctor thought he had died instantly.

The inquest took place in Ballyhooly by coroner Richard Jones. Several witnesses again could place McCarthy and the boy in the area of Gurteen Woods on Shrove Tuesday. There were more who later that day saw McCarthy leaving the general area with a bundle of clothes on a stick over his shoulder.

The inquest was adjourned until a week later by which time more investigations had been made. By now they had more on McCarthy. The watch he was pawning was NOT the tailor's. McCarthy had exchanged watches with a man called Horrigan near Doneraile. It was Horrigan's watch he was pawning but none the less the connection was made.

On the second day of the inquest breaking for the normal legal process Duncan McKenzie tried to get some answers from the accused directly. He asked "What made him murder my boy? Why did he not rob him and take all he could and not murder him?" McCarthy replied "I could not help it, the boy did it to himself, and I could not get rid of him any other way". To make it worse he went on "it can't be helped now; I know I shall be hanged for it and that's all they can do". The father asked "what did you do with the remainder of the clothes" and McCarthy replied "they were at Murphy's house in Castletownroche"

After this the jury had no doubt at all in their minds of the guilt of John McCarthy and duly they found a verdict to that effect. He was taken to Cork Gaol to await a trial before a jury in court. For John McCarthy it was a bad time of the year to commit such an act, the Cork Spring Assizes were imminent and justice was swift for people like him. He could be dangling from a rope within weeks.

Not many miles away in Cork at that time the aftermath of a massacre near Rathcormac was playing out. In comparison to this case it showed how the legal system was designed to protect its own (see Murder Most Local, East Cork).

Nowadays it can take years before cases come before the Criminal Courts, back then it happened faster well as we discussed in some cases at least.

John McCarthy found himself before Justice Crampton at the Assizes in Cork on Wednesday the 1st of April. He had made no arrangements for legal representation and from what he said at the inquest he felt it was pointless and was resigned to his fate. Two men stepped forward in court Mr Scannell and Mr Coppinger and took on the thankless task of being McCarthy's defence.

McCarthy was described in court as a short disagreeable man but didn't appear at all like a man one expected, given the brutality of the crime. He appeared in court dressed plainly in a blue coat but seemed intelligent and aware of what was going on.

He now though stood charged with the murder of Daniel McKenzie by stabbing him with a bayonet on the 3rd of March but pleaded not guilty.

Duncan McKenzie was the first examined that day in court. He told how he had not seen his son since he got up on Shrove Tuesday morning until he saw him dead in Gurteen Wood the following Friday. Once he noticed he was missing he also realised money, clothes and a watch were also gone. Duncan said he found his son's cap in a house in Castletownroche, as McCarthy had told him at the inquest. His watch he found with a publican called Horrigan in Carker Pike near Doneraile. The master tailor told how his son was his apprentice tailor. He had never seen his son keeping company with John McCarty on any occasion before.

The next witness was a man called Patrick Connors who lived in Ballymacallen, on the Fermoy side of Gurteen Wood. He told how on the morning of Shrove Tuesday, a boy and a soldier called to his house. While his wife prepared breakfast for them, the boy pulled out a bayonet and began marching around with it. Connors said this made the soldier cross and he told the boy to put away the bayonet. On leaving the soldier enquired could they get lodgings in Ballyhooly.

John Smith a Police sergeant told the court how he had arrested John McCarthy in the act of pawning a watch in Ryan's pawn shop Buttevant. He asked him his name but McCarthy replied "butter and cream". McCarthy still found this amusing and burst out laughing in front of the court. Smith then searched the suspect and found printed on his shirt J McCarthy 94th Regiment. It could very well have been Duncan McKenzie who had made the shirt. The sergeant went on saying how he took the soldier to Buttevant barracks where he got a statement from him.

The soldier admitted young Daniel had stolen from his father before running off with him. McCarthy said when the young fella followed him into the wood he became worried about his father, saying he would murder him. The soldier claimed it was Daniel that drew out the bayonet from the scabbard. According to McCarthy he either stabbed himself or fell on it. He then pulled out the bayonet from his body.

The sergeant asked him that day why he took his coat and cap. McCarthy said he may as well have them as someone else. The soldier said he got civilian clothes from Murphy in Castletownroche who promised to burn his regimental uniform but kept the bayonet.

John Horrigan recalled being in bed Shrove Tuesday night when McCarthy came to his house in Carker Pike near Doneraile. There were three other men with him that night and they stayed until noon on Friday. During that time McCarthy asked him to swap his watch with the one he had. Horrigan said on Friday he swopped watches with McCarthy and also gave him ten half crowns as part of the deal. McCarthy had admitted to Horrigan he was a deserter and could not return to Fermoy.   The witness told how he had given up the watch to the police and could identify both watches that were produced in court

Again Dr John Peard Edgar gave medical evidence. He told how by the time he examined the body the wound had nearly closed over. It was a triangular wound three inches left of the boy's navel. The wound though was deep he said travelling upwards in the body penetrating the intestines and even the heart. The doctor felt it was impossible for Daniel to have inflicted such a wound on himself. However under cross examination by Scannell the doctor admitted if the boy threw himself onto the bayonet he could have done it himself.

Daniel Duggan told the court that he met John McCarthy on Shrove Tuesday on the road going to Castletownroche. McCarthy told him he had a 21 day pass from his regiment and was going to see his father in Charleville. He enquired of Duggan how far it was to the next pub. Duggan said he went with him to Connor's public house where McCarthy bought him several glasses of whiskey. The soldier then made him a present of a cap which he since found out was belonged to the dead boy. Duggan parted company with McCarthy in Castletownroche that day outside Lombard's house.

Gurteen Wood as it is nowadays.

As at the inquest many more witnesses had seen McCarthy both with the boy heading towards Gurteen and alone heading towards Castletownroche on Shrove Tuesday.

A corporal Thomas Carney of the 94th regiment recalled finding a bayonet in the river at Castletownroche on the 23rd of March. He had since given the bayonet to the police and it was now produced in court.

Also called from the regiment was Sergeant Major Thomas Wade. He confirmed that McCarthy had no leave of absence but absconded on the 2nd of March. Wade said he had identified the body at the inquest and also could identify the bayonet. He described examining the bayonet and seeing marks of blood on it. He had also examined the wound on young Daniel and believed the bayonet had been driven right into him right up to the hilt or handle. McCarthy hearing this laughed in satisfaction as if he had done something to be proud of.

There were no witnesses called for the defence. Scannell or Coppinger didn't make a speech for him. How could they have anything prepared having only taken on the case that very day.

After only one hour of deliberation the jury entered the room and the verdict of guilty was read out aloud for all to hear.

Now having been found guilty by the jury the judge addressed McCarthy directly "You seduced that boy, the son of your comrade a man of your own regiment.You caused that boy to rob his own father and become your companion when you disgracefully deserted your colours, your king and your country. This unfortunate youth you induced to travel with you."

The judge told him because of the seriousness of his crime there was only one option open to him. The judge began "you John McCarthy be taken from the place on which you now stand to the place from whence you came, the common gaol, there your irons to be struck off and from thence you be taken on Friday the 3rd April to the common place of execution and there be hanged by the neck until you be dead"

The following Friday John McCarthy was duly executed outside the county Gaol for all to see. On the scaffold in his last moments he admitted his guilt saying he killed the boy but denied having any part in other murders which it had been rumoured he had. His body was afterwards buried on the grounds of the gaol. Just a few years before murderers would not have been allowed a Christian burial and their remains would have most likely been sent for dissection.

No tithes
Castlepook Doneraile 1832

Before the Catholic Emancipation act was passed, Catholics could not own land, vote in any election or even practice their own religion. Daniel O'Connell started a campaign for Catholic Emancipation in the 1820's and it was passed in 1829.

Following this Catholic farmers were required to pay a tithe which was ten percent of their farm produce. Anyone who worked over one acre was liable to pay a tithe. Up to 1823 grazing was exempt from tithes but afterwards it made many more liable to pay and raised much more money. The exemption on grazing though had mostly been advantageous to the landlords rather than the small farmer.

What was most insulting was the tithe was paid to the clergy of the Protestant Church of Ireland. The fact that the protestant clergymen who benefited from the tithes often didn't even live in the area caused even more resentment. Some absent clergymen even sold their right to collect a tithe to another. In the early 1830's the situation led to the Tithe war where many Irish farmers started a passive campaign of resistance to the paying of tithes. With more and more refusing to pay the tithe some protestant clergymen found themselves deprived of their income. They were not going to give up their income so easy and saw it as their right and way of life. More and more defaulted on their payments until it almost became the norm. It wasn't just common people not paying; some landlords also took advantage of the situation and defaulted even though they could well afford to pay.

Lists of defaulters were drawn up and orders issued to confiscate goods and property.

Tithe proctors or valuations were sent out around the countryside by the clergymen to calculate the fees that were due and later to collect payment or goods. The position of tithe valuator was not a popular role as they were seen as enabling the system. For men taking on such a role it was a dangerous occupation and they could be visited by the Whiteboys in the middle of the night.

The whole countryside would have been out to prevent the tithe valuators from doing their job. It's easy to see people hiding produce from the valuators to reduce the sum due. Those that tried to be diligent in their duties would have come in for even more harsh treatment.

Not all owners of tithes were clergy, in some cases it was payable to what was known as a lay impropriator. In the area near Doneraile that right was exercised by the Giles family of Youghal. They seem to have an annual income from tithes of over £1000, an absolute fortune in that time. As a result Giles, actively tries to secure the family income and send out valuators to identify produce to tax.

At Wallstown near Doneraile in early September 1832 two valuators were escorted by several local magistrates, policemen and soldiers of the 43rd regiment. They entered on the land of a man called Blake to value the harvest. Despite their numbers and being armed they met with resistance from the locals.

After reading the riot act and threatening the mob to disperse they still refused to budge shouting "no tithes no tithes ". The mob was armed with pick forks and such implements. When stones began to be thrown the magistrates ordered the mob to be fired upon and the commanding officer complied. Twelve people were injured but worse four had been killed. The remainder of the protesters cleared the area. The dead men were William Doyle, James Roche, David Regan and Michael Horrigan, all suffered horrendous gunshot wounds.

At the inquest the coroner Richard Jones tried to make it fair by getting friends of the dead men to select the jurors. Several men were objected to being on the jury. The twelve men picked were all upper class with not an Irish surname featuring.

Witnesses for the military said the mob that day was over 300 and they were told by the magistrates to fire. One magistrate George Bond Lowe asked who gave the orders. The reply he received was "as well as I can recollect sir from you".

While on the other side several locals also gave evidence. They reckoned the mob was only 100 mostly women and children. Only twelve were armed and they thought they would not fire upon them because the magistrates were local. They said the stones were thrown pitifully and had no chance of doing harm.

After sitting for two days the inquest into the four deaths found a verdict of justifiable homicide. Their claim was that the magistrate's lives were endangered that day.

About a week later the valuators were at work in the Doneraile area now unescorted. For several days the two valuators visited several farms in the area without any repeat of the trouble. On the fifth day which was the 19th of September the valuators Francis Canning and Thomas Cummins were at Castlepook about a mile and a half from Doneraile.

In the afternoon their work came to an abrupt and sudden end. A man walking along the bank of a stream noticed the stream ran red and then came across a body face down in the stream. Not a few yards away there was another body in a similar position.

He ran to raise the alarm but there was nobody else about the place. The authorities were informed. They realised quickly that a doctor was not required. Soon after a posse similar to the day of the shooting at Wallstown, headed for the murder scene at Castlepook. Magistrates George Bond Lowe, Admiral Evans and George Creagh were present. They were the very men who ordered the shooting and were armed again with police and military. It was three in the afternoon when Chief Constable Dames arrived from Doneraile.

Once on the scene the bodies were taken from the stream and they discovered the men had sustained a beating before being thrown into the stream. Canning's skull had been badly broken in and his face was barely recognisable. Cummins had suffered a little less but still his skull was fractured in several places.

The magistrates and the police then began making door to door enquires to find witnesses to the crime. Nobody in the countryside was going to admit seeing valuators being killed and soon they realised the people were silent. Only one woman admitted to being home that day but said she was in bed with a child and knew nothing about it. There was about eight houses close by with the nearest only fifty yards away. Yet there was nobody to be seen only two old women and some children. No men were working in the fields nearby. At one house though a young girl of eight did mention hearing something but her father stopped her from going further. Dames seized the opportunity and took the child into custody away from her family.

The bodies of the two men were then taken to Doneraile to await an inquest.

One of the first rumours that circulated was that the murders had been carried out by eight men dressed as women. Dressing as women or turning clothes inside out was often done by Whiteboys but they normally operated by night. In this case the valuators were easier targets during the day as they went from place to place.

The inquest was held on Friday the 21st by coroner Richard Jones. George Bond Lowe asked the coroner that as no one had yet been arrested that the inquest should be conducted in secret. The coroner replied that it was unnecessary but assured him no suspected party would be mentioned before the public.

As there was no direct evidence the inquest had little witnesses to call. The valuators employer Richard Giles was called. He had agreed to pay them £10 each for valuation of the area. He also explained how he was not the lay proprietor of the tithes but had made an arrangement with his brother Nicholas who was.

Doctor James Wall told of the injuries on both men. He described in detail the fractures to the skull saying they were caused by a blunt instrument. In both cases he found the lungs to be healthy and head injuries sufficient to cause death.

During William Hill's testimony the public were excluded but it seems he didn't implicate any person in the crime.

The jury duly found a verdict of wilful murder against a person or persons unknown.

About this time it also became public knowledge that an eight year old girl who lived near the scene was being held by the police in Doneraile. All communication with her family was denied and the police felt she would give information.

The funerals of the men took place after the inquest. Such were the feelings against the tithe system that Cummins brother could not get a horse in Doneraile to take the body to Buttevant for burial. The chief constable Dames was forced to lend his own horse for the purpose. When his widow returned to Doneraile from the funeral that day a few had gathered calling out "no tithes".

Up to becoming a valuator Canning had been a painter who lived in Buttevant. Before that he had been a sergeant in the south Cork militia. Cummins from Doneraile was a process server, the other most hated role in the countryside. He left behind a widow and seven children.

After the inquest the magistrates met and agreed to put up money as a reward for the apprehension of the killers. A subscription fund was set up for the families of the victims and quickly had £20 subscribed.

Over the next few days the authorities were very active in the area and confident that those responsible would be brought to justice. Eleven women and five men were arrested and lodged in Doneraile on suspicion of being involved. The police now revealed they knew the names of the remaining suspects who would soon be in custody also.

Daniel O'Connell wrote publically to the papers about the matter. He said of the Wallstown massacre that "these were committed under the sanction of, there is little prospect of justice." This was defeatist of O'Connell, the man who was described at the time of being the only man in Ireland who could save someone from the noose in court.

He went on the blame the injustice of the tithe system for the violence. It was highly unreasonable for the three thousand and sixty three Catholics in the Castlepook area to pay out a tenth of their produce each year to Mr Giles for nothing in return. Not only that he said but Giles insisted on valuing everything to ensure he got what he thought he had a right to. O'Connell the leading barrister in the country argued that there was no legal right to value the crop before it was harvested.

He did not deny though that Canning and Cummins had been butchered but blamed the tithe system. He called for reform by the government. No matter what O'Connell said reform of the tithe system was a few years away and many more would die before then.

When reform did come in 1838 the tithe was merged into the rent and landlords made the payment to the ruling clergy. By this time O'Connell was in an alliance with the Whigs and now rejected calls for a total abolishment of tithes. The ordinary man continued to support the protestant clergy but just paid indirectly by higher rent.

In Doneraile twelve men were arrested for having been part of the mob at Wallstown in early September. On Saturday the men were being taken from Doneraile to Mallow Barracks. Along the way another mob gathered and tried to rescue the men from their captors but failed. The police managed to make their way back to the town and called for military reinforcements from Buttevant.

The Cork Assizes that year were unusually opened in late October and seem to be running late. The number of cases before the court showed the great unrest in the countryside at that time. Of a total of 174 cases in the county, 70 were either murder or related to the tithe system. Most likely some of the murders were connected to unrest connected to tithes.

Several of those arrested for the murders of Canning and Cummins were taken to Mallow and charged under oath with being involved. Those were John Heaffy Senior and Junior, David Heaffy, Jeremiah Shine, John Hartnett, Mary Heaffy, Johanna Heaffy, Ellen Heaffy and Edmond Heaffy. About two weeks later chief constable Dames was out again at Castlepook, he arrested another seven men and two women. In total those in custody for the double murder was almost thirty. Surely Daniel O'Connell would appear and defend these when they appeared before a jury.

As the Assizes were running late that year the case was called in early November. The defendant's legal counsel argued for a postponement as they had not sufficient time to prepare. It was allowed until the next Assizes which would be the spring of the following year. While it bought time for them it also allowed the crown prosecution more opportunity to prepare.

At the Spring Assizes in late March of 1833 four people from a total of twenty six were called to court. Despite fines for non attendance there were not enough jurors present to charge four that day allowing for challenges by each of the accused. So they quickly improvised and only David Heaffy a well dressed young man was charged.

In court a ten year old boy William Herbert told how he lived with his mother in a house belonging to Michael Haly. It was Haly's yard that was closest to the scene of the crime.

William went on to say how on that day he was cutting ferns when he saw several people near the castle. The men encouraged the women to hit a man with stones and set a dog on him.

The boy named two women who then joined in the stoning as Ellen Duff and Mary Dennehy. One of the men being stoned was kneeling in Haly's yard begging to be set free. But William said the stoning continued and the man attempted to escape by leaping into the stream. There he was stoned again until he lay face down in the stream. The boy was clear he knew the accused David Heaffy and saw him throwing stones at the man in the stream. Then he said their attention turned to the other man who was standing at the other side of the river.

The boy heard a conversation amongst the group, one said let the second man go but the other said if they did they would all hang. Several people then pursued him knowing they had to kill him or they would get it.

William Herbert told that it was David Heaffy who struck the man with a stone; he fell down but managed to get up again. The man ran up the boreen towards Ned Heaffy's house. The boy was clear and said it was David Heaffy who then struck him with stones and killed him.

Mary McCarthy the eight year old girl who had been taken from her family by the police was next called in court. She swore an oath and informed the court how she understood what she was about to do. She recalled hearing men throwing stones near the castle one day in September. She heard them from her father's yard and watched the crowd come closer. David Heaffy was there that day and Mary saw him throwing stones in Haly's yard. Afterwards she witnessed a man running up Jack Heaffy's boreen. He was chased by a few men who struck him with stones until he was dead. Mary told how it was the women who then dragged the body to the stream.

Several more witnesses were produced that day including chief constable Dames and Magistrate George Bond Lowe. The judge seemed to have heard enough and proceeded to charge the jury.

After going over all the evidence again he let it to the jury to decide if they felt Heaffy was involved or not. Mr Twiss who represented the accused then addressed the judge and said he had witnesses to produce for the defence.

The judge allowed him to call those he had in turn. First was John McNamara who recalled seeing Heaffy going to the mountain at eight that morning. He did not see him again until the following day. The witness admitted to a juror that Heaffy could have returned without him seeing.

William Donovan told how he saw the accused on the mountain between eleven and three that day. Donovan recalled his brother being with him and they had a load of turf about three miles from Castlepook. He estimated when asked that it would take two hours for them to get home that day.

Cornelius Dennehy added to what the last witness had said. He admitted being there stacking turf with them until sometime between three and four that day.

Mary Herbert told the court how on the day of the killing she sent her son William to the mountain and he did not return until four. She had heard of the killing long before her son returned that day.

The last witness Daniel Linehan recalled seeing William Herbert on the mountain that day between three and four.

Twiss then addressed the court and asked that they consider this evidence rather than that of George Bond Lowe and Constable Dames. There was much more he could have said, some of what was heard questioned how David Heaffy was there at all, another witness doubted whether young William Herbert was there.

There was now a great doubt about what had occurred that day. Despite this the jury were in no doubt at all. They returned after only ten minutes and read out a verdict of guilty. The jury obviously did not believe the defence witnesses as they were friends and relations of the accused. It was strange Mary Herbert appeared for the defence and seemed to dispute what her own son had said for the prosecution.

Regardless the jury had decided and the judge then proceeded to read out a long speech addressed to David Heaffy who was now deemed the guilty party. There was no time for appealing and was told to abandon all hope. He was sentenced to be hung in two days time, the following Friday and his body to be given up for dissection afterwards.

On the 29th of March David Heaffy a condemned man was taken from his cell and led to the scaffold at the front of the county gaol. That day he called for the governor and made a statement to him.

Heaffy claimed at the last minute to have taken no part in the murder saying he returned from the mountain that day to find a crowd throwing stones at a man. Once he realised they were going to kill him, he left, going to his own house.

Before climbing the scaffold that day Heaffy spent several minutes praying. Then he took his last steps and seemed unafraid of what was about to happen. Given the opportunity he made no public declaration of his claimed innocence. Once the bolt was pulled he died instantly without any struggle.

That left twenty five more to be brought to court and charged. Some had been allowed out on bail but it's hard to imagine anyone affording the £50 to £100 required. They knew now that if brought before a court what fate they would meet even if they had alibis. They had months of agony waiting for a trial date.

It was Friday 16th August before the case came before Baron Pennefather at the Cork Summer Assizes. Now it was four who were charged on the capital crime of murder, Elizabeth Heaffy, Darby Shine, Thomas Ryan and Mary Dennehy. The four were indicted on several counts for killing Cummins and Canning and also aiding and abetting.

Between them they must have known their fate and how little their chance of being acquitted was. David Heaffy was sentenced to death despite a few witnesses saying he could not have been there. In most murder cases the accused had nobody to call for them. What now could save the four from the hangman?

Again the chief witnesses were eight year old Mary McCarthy and ten year old William Herbert. The accused women were lined up with others before young Herbert and the boy picked out Mary Dennehy. He described seeing Elizabeth Heaffy hold a large stone with two hands. Canning lay in the river and she struck him on the face with the stone. He also identified Shine and Ryan as being present when Cummins was killed. The boy then said that the two accused women also pelted Cummins with stones before he died.

Mary McCarthy explained to the court how she knew all of the accused. She was sure that she saw them killing the men that day and could recount many details.

The only witness called for the defence that day was Rev James Daly. He could not give them an alibi but said all four were hard working and sober. It was nowhere enough to save them now.

The jury were in some dispute over one of the accused. The foreman discussed at length with the judge but at last returned a verdict of guilty. Mary Dennehy they recommended to mercy and one of the jurors asked for mercy for Shine. It was then asked why they had found this verdict. The foreman explained because Mary seemed sorry afterwards and Shine did not seem as intent to kill.

The judge proceeded and addressed all four, they were sentenced to death the following Monday. This left them with just the weekend to reconcile themselves with their fate. The four were said to have been unmoved when being taken away but their friends and relations cried out.

On the day of execution, the 19th of August Mary Dennehy was given somewhat of a reprieve. The jury's plea for mercy for her had worked at last; her sentence was changed to transportation for life.

At three O'clock the others were taken to the drop outside the county gaol. A priest asked them had they anything to say, he warned they must tell the truth or face eternal death. Darby Shine's last words were that he had nothing to do with the killing that day. He claimed he only went to see what all the shouting was about. It was McCarthy's wife he said who told him what was happening, he went into a house alone to get away but never threw a stone that day. Shine admitted saying "what brought them there? Sure they ought to have known they would get something". But finally he forgave the world for what was about to occur to him and replied on God for mercy.

Thomas Ryan on the other hand admitted his part throwing the stones but claimed he did not intend to kill. He now felt guilty and asked God for forgiveness for what he had done. Elizabeth Heaffy also gave in and admitted her guilt and part in the killings.

On the scaffold, the executioner made the last minute adjustments to the rope for each of the three. At about three O'clock, a large crowd had assembled to see the morbid sight. The three condemned fell together, Shine and Ryan died in an instant. Elizabeth Heaffy was seen violently struggling on the end of the rope for several minutes.

Later in that month John Barrett, Anne Barrett, Ellen Duff, John Sullivan and John Harnett appeared before Baron Pennefather.

An arrangement was made in court that Harnett's trial should be postponed and the remaining four all changed their plea to guilty. The judge admitted it saved him going through with a trial and hearing all the evidence for a third time. He explained he could no longer interfere with the case. The prosecution now applied to the Attorney General to save the lives of those who admitted their guilt and face imprisonment instead. It was also agreed that day to let the remainder out on bail with the exception of John Harnett who would be tried at the winter Assizes.

Hartnett was held in custody until the following year and made several appearances in court. Several more were discharged at this stage and no more were executed for the murders.

Attacked on the way home
Shandrum, Charleville 1830

On the 31st of July 1830, Andrew Cloghane went to Charleville to sell two sheep. In town that day he didn't sell the sheep but he met Honora Quill. She had been sent seven miles to town with a message from the mistress. The pair arranged to travel home together.

As they were passing Shandrum that evening on their walk home with the sheep several men jumped out and attacked Andrew. The men beat him with sticks and stones and left him at the side of the road. The four men fled the scene as quickly as they appeared. Luckily Andrew's sister and neighbours came on the scene. They thought he was dead as he had been beaten unconscious.

With help they managed to take him the last few miles home and get medical help for him. He had cuts and bruises all over his body and head, his condition did not improve much.

For weeks Andrew remained in a weak state and was unable to do much.

Doctors could do nothing for him but monitor his condition. Finally three months later Andrew Cloghane died from head injuries inflicted on him. Before he died, he had identified two of the four men who had attacked him.

The police were now investigating a murder. A man called Callaghan was arrested and taken into custody but was released again without charge due to lack of evidence.

The other man Andrew named was also found, he was twenty year old David Lillis. He was described as an athletic powerful man who was known for fighting and troublemaking at fairs and markets in the locality. Lillis was held in jail to face a trial on the capital charge of murder. It was known back then that if he was found guilty he would surely hang. The law did not allow time for appeals or the like, once a jury decided that was it. Had Lillis even intended to kill Andrew Cloghane at all or just assault him? There was also talk that Cloghane's house had been attacked a few weeks before.

At the Cork Spring Assizes David Lillis was charged with the capital crime on the 1st April. As it fell on Good Friday the court did not sit until the afternoon to allow the judge and jury attend to their religious duties first. When Justice Jebb sat in court that day this was the last case of the Assizes.

Honora Quill was first to be questioned that day as she was the chief witness. She was a servant and related to Andrew Cloghane. That day she said Andrew did not have any argument with anyone in town nor did he go to a public house. On their way home, near Shandrum four men jumped out from behind a hedge and attacked Andrew. Honora was only able to identify one of those men and pointed out the accused David Lillis. She was sure it was him saying how she had met Lillis several times before that day.

She witnessed Andrew get six or eight blows with sticks and stones and was clear she had seen David Lillis strike him with a stone on the head as he lay on the road.

Honora told the court how she gave evidence to the inquest against Lillis the day after Andrew died. She claimed to have heard Callaghan was arrested but the police never came to her for information.

The brother of the deceased, John Cloghane was next before the court. John said his brother sent for him the day he died. On that occasion the dying man told him it was David Lillis and a man by the name of Callaghan that attacked him.

John also told how several weeks before that attack, men came to Andrew's house and fired shots. He claimed that David Lillis was amongst that gang. On that occasion the men shot a dog and mutilated a pig almost cutting it in two.

Dr Ahern was called to prove medical evidence as to the cause of death of Andrew Cloghane. The doctor told how it was a month after the attack before he attended to Andrew. From then on he saw him twice a week to monitor his condition. A week before he died his condition improved and Ahern prescribed gentle exercise, but Andrew had not been able for work since the attack. The doctor said he was of the opinion that Andrew died as a result of compression of the brain due to fracture of the skull. This he said was as a result of the blows he received from a blunt object. Under cross examination the doctor admitted that Andrew may not have died if he had been seen sooner by a doctor.

The only witness called for the defence that day was Patrick Tracy who tried to prove an alibi for Lillis. Patrick's father was a shoemaker in Charleville. He claimed that on the 31st of July David Lillis came to his father's about getting new shoes made and stayed from early morning until half seven that evening. When he left that night, Patrick said he took away his new shoes.

The prosecution revealed Tracy had been released from gaol after being charged with assault. The witness claimed it was his first offence and he had never broken the law before. Patrick still maintained that he recalled David Lillis actually still being at his father's house when he heard there had been an attack near Shandrum. He was positive that David Lillis could not have been at the scene of the crime.

The judge summed up the evidence which cannot have taken long as there were so few witnesses. He seemed to be of the opinion that the crime could not be reduced to manslaughter as evidence of premeditation existed.

When the jury deliberated, they took even less time and returned in less than five minutes with the verdict of guilty.

The judge then proceeded to address the convicted man "David Lillis you have been convicted upon the clearest of testimony of a foul and cruel murder". The judge went on telling Lillis he had better repent for his crimes. He began with the sentencing "David Lillis be taken from the place where you now stand. To that whence you came, the gaol and on Monday next the 4th April be taken to the common place of execution where....." The condemned man then interrupted the judge throwing his hands in the air and protesting to the sentence. Lillis began "My Lord and gentlemen tis now all over, I know I must die yes gentlemen all around me. I know I have but a few days to live but my lord I own to God and I say it now in his presence and your presence my lord and gentlemen of the jury, that I am a murdered man. I own to God I never was present at the murder of that man, and that my lord I am as innocent of it as you are. My life is taken from me."

Lillis calmed down and the judge continued where he had been interrupted "you are to be hanged by the body until dead, your body to be afterwards delivered over for dissection and may almighty God have mercy on you". David Lillis was then taken from the courtroom; he had the weekend to live.

On Monday the 4th of April minutes before the appointed time Lillis admitted getting people to attack Cloghane but denied being there himself. A huge crowd had gathered outside the county gaol to witness the execution. The executioner made the final preparations and David Lillis climbed the scaffold and the rope was placed around his neck.

Once the bolt was pulled and Lillis fell, he died in an instant without a hitch. After hanging for an hour David Lillis' body was taken down and removed from the jail. His remains were then brought to the School of Medicine in the South Infirmary Hospital for dissection.

Robbery, revenge or jealousy?
Knockanevin Mitchelstown 1871

In the townland of Knockanevin close to the Limerick border James O'Brien lived with his wife Anne and four children. They lived near Kilclooney Wood where not four years before Fenian Peter O'Neill Crowley was shot.

Some said O'Brien was a quiet man while others reckoned he drank a lot and treated his wife badly. The result of this was the couple were not living in the best of terms.

On Friday November 4th 1871 the children went off to school as normal. That day O'Brien had several labourers working for him on the farm. The three farm workers got their dinner in the middle of the day on Friday. As they went back to work, O'Brien was sitting by the fire reading a book. His wife was in the dairy, a room off the kitchen churning butter. The three labourers were digging potatoes in a field near the farm house.

Sometime in the afternoon, the workers heard the farmhouse door slam and O'Brien was seen leaving. Someone tried the door but as it was locked left again.

The children returned from school but were unable to get into their own house; normally their mother would have been home. One of the children climbed up and peeked through a crack in the door. Inside he saw something that terrified him and did not know what to do. They could have climbed in an open window but having seen blood inside ran off to tell the labourers.

Nothing more was done that Friday evening, the children stayed at a neighbour's house which they had never done before.

Early on Saturday morning people went to O'Brien's house and grew worried when the door was still locked from inside. The police were called and when they arrived a constable forced the door in. The door had been held from the inside by a crowbar.

Inside on the floor Anne O'Brien lay in a pool of her own blood. Not only was her head beaten in but her throat also appeared to have been cut. Found nearby were what was presumed to be the murder weapons a spade and a bloody razor.

While the police looked over the scene James O'Brien arrived home having spent the night away. The police were immediately suspicious of him, his trousers seemed to have been recently washed, yet there was a dark stain still visible. They arrested him as he walked up the boreen towards his house on suspicion of being involved in his wife's death.

Even before the inquest, newspapers announced his guilt saying he nearly cut his wife's head off with the razor. Nobody else was in the house at the time so it seemed like a safe assumption to make. Rumours in the area confirmed the motive; O'Brien had accused his wife of cheating on him. On several occasions in the past he had put her out of the house for the night but there seemed to be no foundation to his belief.

An inquest was held on Monday by Coroner Moore at Knockanevin and a jury of twelve local men.

Hanora Sweeney told how she and her husband were working for O'Brien digging potatoes that day. It was she who had made the dinner in the farmhouse. While boiling the potatoes for the dinner she said Anne O'Brien was making butter.

In the afternoon they worked only sixty yards from the farmhouse. Mrs Sweeney came back to the house to warm her child who was with her but found the door locked. She thought no more of it and went back to work. She heard nobody inside but thought they were still making butter.

Knockanevin near the scene of the crime.

Mrs Sweeney said there was nothing happened between the couple that day but she was aware for quite a while that there was a jealousy between them. Her husband also gave evidence.

Dr Rodgers gave medical evidence that day, saying the injuries could not have been self inflicted. A police constable proved how it was possible for someone to secure the door and leave the house through a window.

The inquest returned an open verdict "wilful murder against some person or persons unknown". Despite this resident magistrate Mr Eaton said they intended to keep O'Brien in custody.

O'Brien did not come before the Spring Assizes in Cork and by July 1871 was in custody for eight months. On the capital charge of murder especially the violent nature of it there was no question of bail.

The ones that must have suffered the most during this time were the four children. From that Friday in November when they returned from school they no longer had either a mother or father. Now with their father on the capital charge he could very likely not have long to live. The four children were under ten years old.

Tuesday the 22nd of July 1872 James O'Brien was brought before Justice Morris and charged with the murder of his wife. When called O'Brien pleaded not guilty to the charges.

Colman O'Loughlan led the crown prosecution while Mr P O'Brien represented his namesake.

O'Loughlan opened by stating the case for the prosecution. He admitted no human eye had witnessed the crime and all evidence heard would be circumstantial. O'Loughlan assured the jury though that circumstantial evidence could prove to be conclusive. He said the murder was committed in a fit of mad jealousy because he thought his wife was unfaithful.

He asked the jury did the accused do it and if he did not who did? There was no motive for someone else to kill her and no sign of a break in or robbery.

O'Brien's farmhouse was described in court as a low thatched cottage forty feet long with three rooms, kitchen, bedroom and a dairy. A surveyor told how the road led directly from O'Brien's house to Marshalstown where he stayed that night. The route through the fields was much longer and needed to cross two streams.

Dr Rodgers who was the medical officer at Kildorrey was called again to give the medical evidence. He had found the body of Anne O'Brien on the bedroom floor between a dresser and the fireplace. He said her throat was cut from ear to ear and the windpipe badly severed. The jagged nature of the wound led him to believe there was a struggle. Further evidence of the struggle was her cut hand possibly in an attempt to grasp the sharp instrument. Her face was bruised in several places like she had received a beating.

On the back of her head he found a skull fracture caused by a tremendous blow from behind. He said the razor did not cause this it was a much blunter object like the spade found nearby. The doctor concluded saying these injuries resulted in death and were not self inflicted.

Hanora Sweeney again told how she had been at O'Brien's farm that day. She explained how her husband had taken a patch of land from O'Brien and was that day digging potatoes. She had a young child with her that day, her husband and their servant James O'Brien.

Hanora recalled how the O'Brien's had welcomed her to their house that day. While she boiled potatoes for the dinner the couple were talking to each other. Under cross examination Hanora revealed she heard one of the children say their mother was dead on that Friday. She also admitted to being arrested and questioned by the police.

Her husband John Sweeney was then called and gave a similar story to that of his wife. He had seen nobody approach the O'Brien's house that day except the accused. The boys John and Jerry came to him in the field saying they were afraid and had seen a body on the floor in their house. Sweeney said that he did not go to the house and look inside, thinking nothing bad had happened. Instead he sent his servant boy to go with the brothers. It was the following morning before he found out that Mrs O'Brien was dead.

The servant boy James O'Brien said he was a second cousin to the accused his namesake. That afternoon he went to the house to light his pipe and found the door locked. He said later the children arrived home and could not get in. He took them to Sweeney's for the night. James claimed the boys had not told him that afternoon they had seen their mother on the floor. Nor did he think of looking in the window. At the time he thought the couple had gone to sell butter.

The local school mistress Miss Ryan was called by the prosecution. She told how she had lived at O'Brien's for three years up to 1870 with her mother. James O'Brien was a cousin of hers. She then went on to why she left O'Brien's house in November on 1870. It was because one day O'Brien came home and accused his wife of being unfaithful. He wanted her out of the house, Miss Ryan and her mother threatened to go as well. She said James O'Brien was highly agitated and excited and replied "do then". They left the house and stayed in the school that night with Anne O'Brien and her two young girls. Ryan and her mother never went back to O'Brien's again but Anne returned to her husband the following day.

Another woman Johanna Pine a neighbour gave a similar story. One night the August before Anne O'Brien came to her in a torn night dress. Anne stayed at her house that night and Johanna went back with her the following morning. That morning Anne's husband was standing at the door and still wanted his wife out of the house. He did let her in to retrieve some of her clothes so she could go to mass as it was Sunday.

As the prosecution relied entirely on circumstantial evidence they needed to build the case. Another neighbour was called, Thomas Roche who lived half a mile from O'Brien's. Thomas recalled a conversation with James O'Brien two weeks before Anne was killed. On that occasion O'Brien told him he suspected his wife of having an affair. One day he was on the hill and saw a man called O'Callaghan in the haggard with Anne. Roche tried to tell him his wife was an honest woman and would not do such a thing. O'Brien revealed to him "I nearly killed her one night only for the children".

William Fitzgibbon next gave evidence, explaining how he was married to James O'Brien's sister. A month before Anne was killed his wife took ill and Fitzgibbon sent for O'Brien to visit his sister. It had been about eighteen months since they had seen him. William said on the 3rd of November he was out in Glanworth until nine and O'Brien was there when he arrived home. He never mentioned his wife Anne that night and stayed until the following morning.

A servant of Fitzgibbon's Margaret Gurney told how she was out that evening and returned about dusk to find O'Brien sitting by the fire. O'Brien told her his trousers got wet when he slipped into the mill stream near Carroll's house. She told how O'Brien went to the room to see his sister who was confined to bed. Later she described O'Brien as being at his ease smoking by the fireside that evening.

Several constables gave evidence of arresting O'Brien and how he pleaded his innocence to them. Constable Bergin said for O'Brien to go to Fitzgibbons by Carroll's mill was not the direct route. It would have been miles longer and he had to cross several streams.

Hannah Barry said she met the accused on the road by Marshalstown on the morning of 4th of November. She walked a mile with O'Brien who was going home. He told her how he had been to see his sister but also said his wife had been sick.

As they met James Rea, O'Brien stopped to talk to him but Hannah walked on ahead. Rea told him to run home as fast as he could because the police were breaking in. Hannah told though that O'Brien didn't run he merely caught up with her and walked along with her again. Hannah asked him why would the police be there but O'Brien said one of the children might have got burned.

Along the way they met a boy with a load of corn who told them O'Brien's wife had been murdered. Hannah reckoned he didn't seem to pay much heed to it and they walked on again. On the road they met another boy who said "Jimmy the police are at the house, don't go down". O'Brien asked Hannah what was the boy getting at saying that and again they walked on. Afterwards Hannah parted with O'Brien on the road and he went on home. Under cross examination she confirmed that O'Brien never ran that day when he heard either the police were at his house or that his wife had been murdered.

When the case for the prosecution finished, Colman O'Loughlan said he had no objection to either of the sons John or Jeremiah O'Brien being examined for the defence.

John O'Brien a boy of nine or ten years was called to the stand. The father up to now had kept his composure but now seeing his son, he became quite upset. He was asked "did you before the coroner say I told John Sweeney and Jimmy O'Brien on Friday that there was a body in the house?" The boy replied he did but this was not what they had said. Did you tell James O'Brien who was working in the field that your mother was dead? Again the boy replied he had told them that Friday he saw a body on the floor.

The defence then made their closing speech in an attempt to save their client from the hangman. Men had been convicted in the past on circumstantial evidence.

The defence claimed it was impossible that the three in the field had not heard the screams of Anne O'Brien. Then again neither of the men even looked in the window that night.

The defence went on saying O'Brien had gone to see his sister and someone else may have come and killed her. He even suggested the man to whom she was alleged to be having an affair may have killed her out of passion and even claimed she was raped.

They pointed the finger at the three working in the field that day, saying they had a better opportunity than anyone to kill her. Their motive he suggested was robbery because people knew O'Brien had money in the house. The defence were confident that the jury would have to acquit O'Brien on lack of evidence.

Of course when the prosecution got their chance they were sure that O'Brien had done it and urged the jury to find him guilty.

When the jury left the room that day it only took them twenty minutes to reach a decision. They returned with the verdict of not guilty. The judge then asked was there any other charges against O'Brien. When told there was nothing he could be charged with the judge ordered him to be released from custody.

What had changed?
Meentinny Rockchapel 1928

Warning: Involves the death of very young infant which some may find upsetting

On the 13th of February 1928 Benjamin Quinlan, a young man in his twenties was walking to a neighbour when he spotted something off the road. His attention was drawn to what appeared to be a baby face down in a bog hole. The land where it was found belonged to his father.

Instead of running to the nearest house he turned back and headed home to tell his father who he lived with at Meentinny near Rockchapel. The guards from Newmarket were called and also Dr Arthur Verling.

When Dr Verling removed a female baby's body from the bog hole he realised it had been there for some time. A cord had been found in the grass which was attached to the body. He carried out a superficial examination and found a circular wound under one of the shoulder blades and another wound behind the ear. He then organized a post mortem to be carried out assisted by Dr Ryan. The county coroner was also notified to arrange an inquest once the doctors were finished.

The guards focused their suspicions on the house nearest the bog hole. They made an arrest the next day. Chief Superintendent Brennan and Superintendent Devine Kanturk arrested eighteen year old Hannah Lenihan who lived with her grandparents not four hundred yards from where the baby was found. As the guards took her away the grandmother Mary Lenihan pleaded with a sergeant to make it as easy for her as possible and tried to press a pound note into his hand for his trouble.

At first Hannah denied any knowledge of the baby, she did admit to being sick last June. Later in custody Hannah revealed she was the mother of the baby. She claimed to have been going to the well for water on New Year's Day when the baby was born suddenly. The baby she said was dead so she wrapped it up and threw it into the bog hole.

Dr Verling from Newmarket however had made an examination of the new born baby and what he found did not fit with her story at all.

Of all days the inquest was held on the 14th of February by county coroner Michael Ryan.

At the inquest the doctors gave the evidence from the post mortem. They disclosed that the right lung, liver and heart had been removed from the baby's body. The doctor told that the left lung was intact and this proved to him that the baby had lived for some time. The organs he said had been removed with great skill through the wound under the shoulder blade. This wound he described as being about the size of a shilling coin which was less than an inch diameter. Dr Verling thought death was as a result of the wound behind the ear. There they had found the base of the skull severely fractured.

The jury found their verdict in agreement with the medical evidence "wilful murder against some person or persons unknown". The same day Hannah Lenihan appeared before a magistrate and was remanded to the next sitting of Kanturk Court.

Hannah was born in 1909 to her mother who was also called Hannah. Her mother was not married so the child was brought up by the grandparents Mary and Thomas Lenihan. Young Hannah's mother married widower William Fitzgerald from Ballydesmond years later. Young Hannah remained with her grandparents. Thomas Lenihan had married Mary Cosgrove in 1884 and the couple had reared thirteen children of their own.

The barren landscape near Rockchapel.

At Kanturk Court on the 29th of February 1928 eighteen year old Hannah Lenihan was brought before District Justice Gallagher. State Solicitor David Casey led the prosecution while Hannah was defended by Solicitor Lenihan from Kanturk.

Sergeant Duffy gave evidence of arrest and told how Hannah had at first denied being the mother of the baby. He said later she relented and said the baby was born near the well but was dead. She wrapped it in her shawl and threw it into the bog hole.

Dr Verling and Dr Michael Ryan from Glounthane again gave medical evidence.

Dr Verling described finding the body in the bog hole and went on to the results of the post mortem. The doctor told how he had also examined Hannah and found evidence that she had recently given birth. Dr Ryan reiterated the fact he believed the baby was born alive, it was a normally developed full term baby.

Casey questioned the doctor as to how the organs could have been removed. The doctor said it took great skill and the person must have had knowledge of the organs locations inside the tiny body. He thought it would almost have required a surgeon even to locate the lung. The doctor said there was no other way but the organs had been removed through the wound under the shoulder blade.

The defence asked the doctor did he think Hannah Lenihan a young woman of eighteen was capable of doing such a thing. The doctor replied "in my opinion, she would not be either competent or capable of doing so". He went on to say even under instruction from another person Hannah could not have done it.

Solicitor Lenihan argued that there was no evidence to prove the baby Hannah Lenihan had given birth to was the one found in the bog. He said no jury could find her guilty on lack of evidence.

Despite the fact the doctors thought Hannah incapable of removing the organs; the judge proceeded with the charge. He decided a prima facie case existed against Hannah Lenihan based on her own statement. Also he said both doctors proved the baby was born alive.

Hannah then asked to make a statement, but despite being warned it would be written down she still wanted desperately to get something off her chest.

"The baby was born inside at home on New Year's Night and it was only just born when my grandmother killed it. It was just born when she choked it. She told me never to own it was she killed the baby and to say it was myself did all. The baby was born at twenty minutes to twelve on New Year's night in the kitchen and nobody was present but myself and the grandmother. She put the baby into a box in another room where no one was sleeping and turned the box upside down on the baby. She told me to stay in bed and to pretend I had a pain in the head. A couple of nights afterwards she buried the baby. I did not know where she put it at all until I saw the Guards on the hill. That was about six weeks after the birth of the baby and I told my grandmother the guards were on the hill and she then told me it was there she put the baby. We were both looking at the Guards and she said to me she would go down that night and see if they found the baby but she was afraid to do so. My grandmother gave me £1 note that evening and told me not to ever own it was herself killed the baby but to say myself did it. I told this to the Governor and the Wardress of Cork Jail and they told me to tell the court the truth if she did it. I would not beat a baby not to mind killing it."

It was now too late the judge had found a prima facie case against her and had to return the case for trial at the Central Criminal Court on the capital charge of murder.

On the 5th of July at the Central Criminal Court in Green Street in Dublin, Justice Hanna and a jury heard the case. Hannah Lenihan pleaded not guilty to the charge of murder of her own baby. Solicitor Carrigan led the prosecution while Art O'Connor was assigned to the defence.

Mr Carrigan opened for the prosecution saying how gruesome and shocking the killing was. The prosecution produced no evidence that day that had not been heard already. The Quinlan's, Benjamin and his father told of the discovery of the body. Both the doctors' medical evidence was heard.

When the prosecution was finished, O'Connor questioned Hannah Lenihan. She said her grandmother had told her what to say and at first she lied. Then she had told the story the baby was born alive but died shortly after. Now Hannah admitted it was her grandmother who took the baby, she never knew the baby was in the bog until the guards arrived.

Carrigan asked her "what will you do if your grandmother denies all this?" Hannah replied that she was willing to serve any imprisonment she might get. The young girl was maybe unaware the punishment for murder was still the death sentence. The judge asked her was she aware it would require her giving evidence against her own grandmother but Hannah accepted this.

Art O'Connor then addressed the jury saying how the doctors had made it clear Hannah was not capable of such an act. He said if they were still unsure the jury must acquit her.

When the judge summed up he also seemed to lean towards Hannah's version of events. He admitted it seemed the girl was dominated by her grandmother.

After this the jury took just a few minutes to reach their verdict of not guilty. It was obvious enough that Hannah could not go home to her grandmother's house even though her grandmother would not be there. Art O'Connor her legal counsel informed the judge he had made arrangements for her. Hannah was to be taken to the Daughters of Charity convent in Henrietta Street.

The following day sixty seven year old Mary Lenihan was arrested at her house near Rockchapel. She was due to appear before the next sitting of the Kanturk District Court.

A week later Mary Lenihan appeared in court charged with the murder of her infant great granddaughter. Again David Casey state solicitor prosecuted and John Guiney solicitor Kanturk appeared for Mary Lenihan.

The evidence was heard from the same witnesses and Hannah Lenihan was also now a witness. Hannah told how on New Year's night she was in bed. Her grandmother told her to get up and she gave birth in the kitchen. Hannah heard the baby crying on the floor but got back into bed and her grandmother got into bed with her. A while after her grandmother told her she had choked the baby and not to tell her aunts about it.

Hannah when questioned by Casey told that her grandmother put the baby in a box and hid it in another room. It was two or three days later her grandmother told her she had buried the baby.

On the 13th Hannah returning home with a cousin saw the guards searching near her house. She said it was only then she knew her grandmother had dumped the baby in the bog hole.

The judge asked the doctors was there any other way the organs could have been removed after weeks in the bog. Doctor Ryan was sure it had to have been carried out by a human hand. He thought someone used to killing poultry would have knowledge of the location of organs. Dr Ryan told the court he still believed that Hannah was not capable of doing it.

None of the witnesses were cross examined and the defence reserved its case. The judge returned Mary Lenihan for trial at the next Criminal Court and she was sent back to jail until then.

It was over four months later before Mary Lenihan found herself in Green Street courthouse at the Criminal Court. Before Justice O'Sullivan the sixty seven year old pleaded not guilty to the killing of her new born great granddaughter. Mr Carrigan again led the prosecution while Mary Lenihan had been assigned Mr Howe but JJ Lenihan, Kanturk was also present.

Carrigan opened the case by telling the jury how he would prove it was murder. He asked the jury to "steel their nerves" for the story they were about to hear was too terrible to sound real. The person who carried it out had knowledge of midwifery and locations of internal organs. He was certain it was an attempt to prevent doctors of knowing whether the baby was born alive or not. He said evidence would show it had to have been carried out by a human hand. The accused tried to bribe her granddaughter and even the guards. He also ruled out the possibility of the charge being reduced to concealment of birth, saying it must be wilful murder or not.

That day Hannah Lenihan gave evidence against her grandmother. She admitted telling lies at first but explained her grandmother had told her what to say.

Dr Verling was again examined and still of the opinion that the baby was born alive. Under cross examination every detail and possibility was looked into but the doctor still felt it was done with such skill it must be a human hand.

On the second day in court the 30th of November Mary Lenihan was questioned. She denied the baby had been born in her house. Mary explained giving money to the sergeant saying "because I thought I should pay them for their troubles". She also denied giving money to Hannah when she was arrested on the Valentine's Day.

Carrigan cross examined Mary who claimed Hannah was sick in bed on the 1st January and even denied knowing her granddaughter was pregnant. Mary told how she herself had given birth to thirteen children, eleven of whom were still alive.

Sergeant Duffy gave evidence of arresting Hannah on the 14th of February; he told how Mary tried to give him a pound note saying "make it easy for her anyhow". He turned down her offer and afterwards saw the old woman give the note to Hannah. Duffy also arrested Mary Lenihan in July, but said she made no statement to him at the time.

Superintendent Devine gave similar evidence to the sergeant. He recalled when arresting Hannah, her grandmother became violent and shouted abuse at Hannah calling her names.

The jury found Mary Lenihan guilty of murder but pleaded mercy for her on account of her age. Mary was asked had she any statement to make but only again denied any knowledge of the baby being born.

Justice O'Sullivan said he would forward the juries plead for mercy to the relevant quarters but proceeded with sentencing. He shocked the courtroom announcing that Mary Lenihan would be sentenced to death on the 27th of December. O'Sullivan refused the application for leave to appeal the sentence.

Mary Lenihan seemed more shocked than anyone and was in disbelief of what had just happened. Being removed from the court she waved at her granddaughter Hannah but was not noticed. Hannah at the time had her face in her hands in floods of tears.

Mary Lenihan's legal team didn't stop there, they applied to the court of Criminal Appeal for a hearing but they had to work fast with Christmas approaching. It was very possible Mary would get the death sentence. She would not be the first woman hanged under the legal system of the Irish Free State. Three years before Anne Walsh from Fedamore Co Limerick had been hanged for the murder of her husband.

On the 19th of December, the Court of Criminal Appeal was presided over by Chief Justice Kennedy, Justice Hanna and Justice O'Byrne. Mr Howe laid out the grounds for appeal which were mostly against the trial judge O'Sullivan.

One of the grounds for appeal was that Hannah Lenihan was an accomplice to the murder or a person with guilty knowledge. The defence now claimed that O'Sullivan had misdirected the jury by expressing his opinion that Hannah was not an accessory at the trial.

Howe also argued that there was no evidence except that Hannah had given birth to a child. Also that O'Sullivan should have warned the jury about Hannah's evidence and the fact it was not corroborated by anything.

Joseph Healy representing the Attorney General argued the opposite saying the trial was conducted properly and fairly by the trial judge. He claimed O'Sullivan could not have warned the jury about Hannah's evidence. Healy said Mr Howe had now changed his opinion where at the trial he left it to the jury to decide.

On the second day of the appeal Chief Justice Kennedy came to a decision. At first the chief justice went over the evidence saying how Hannah had been acquitted. Then he said Hannah had turned on her grandmother and become the chief witness against her. He agreed that under the law Hannah was in fact an accomplice. Kennedy also was of the opinion that the failure of O'Sullivan to warn the jury of Hannah's evidence could have changed the verdict.

The chief justice quashed the finding of the trial and Mary's death sentence.

Under Section five (additional powers of the Court of Criminal Appeal) of the Courts of Justice Act 1928, he ordered a new trial. It would be again held at the Criminal Court the following year.

The chief Justice made it clear Mary Lenihan was to be held in custody until the next trial.

In early March Mary was back in Green Street Courthouse for the start of another trial before Justice Johnson. She still pleaded not guilty to the charges against her.

There was no new evidence and Hannah was still the chief witness.

Doctors Ryan and Verling were again in the witness box answering questions on their findings having done so several times before.

Howe for the defence asked Dr Ryan about how easy it was to smother a baby and leave no marks. Dr Ryan replied saying "I'm afraid this often occurs nowadays". Howe asked then why would an old woman go to such trouble removing organs when it was so easy. Ryan however could not give an opinion to why it was done.

Superintendent Devine told that when he arrested Hannah, Mary let on she had heard nothing of a baby until then. She became violent and called Hannah a ruffian.

The defence now argued that there was nothing to connect Mary Lenihan to the crime only Hannah's testimony. That evidence they could claim since the appeal was completely uncorroborated. The medical evidence could not even prove the baby was Hannah's and could only prove Hannah had given birth.

Mary Lenihan was then called and told how Hannah was the illegitimate daughter of her own daughter. Mary said she had reared her since she was a few days old. She completely denied knowing Hannah was pregnant or that she had a baby. The old woman became upset as she pleaded her innocence and burst out crying before the courtroom.

The old woman regained her composure and went on saying how over Christmas Hannah stayed in bed a lot. She thought Hannah was suffering from a head ache or toothache back then. Several times Mary claimed to have had no hand or knowledge at all of the crime. She was the only witness the defence called that day.

After an hour the jury returned saying they could not all agree a verdict that day. Justice Johnson could do nothing. A century before the judge may have coached or coaxed the jury to a decision. Now Mary Lenihan was put back into custody to face yet another trial and a few months in jail waiting.

In early June of that year she was back again in Green Street Courthouse this time before Justice O'Byrne. Even before a jury was sworn in that day Mr Howe for the defence addressed the judge. He argued that under the Court of Justice Act 1928 the Court of Criminal Appeal could only order one retrial. That retrial he said had occurred in March and the jury disagreed. Howe now applied for an order of Habeas Corpus to determine if his client should be released from custody.

Justice O'Byrne refused the application and proceeded with the trial. The case for the prosecution was then opened by Mr Lavery. He went over the sordid details of the case one more time for the jury before calling witnesses.

For the prosecution the doctors and the arresting guards gave evidence. Hannah the chief witness gave evidence against her grandmother yet again.

Mary Lenihan was again called by the defence and this time she went a little further. The old woman now said Hannah had invented the whole story of her involvement. Mary tried again to deny even knowing her granddaughter was expecting a baby. She even denied knowing the baby was born at all until the guards came to her house in February. Mary did admit to trying to give the sergeant a pound note but could not explain why she did this.

Howe asked the jury what possible motive could the old woman have had to commit the crime. He also argued the same case he did at the appeal, that Hannah's testimony could not be trusted as she herself was an accomplice to the crime. Howe was confident that based on the evidence the jury could not convict her for the murder.

When the jury did leave the courtroom they only took an hour to reach a verdict. When the jury returned a verdict of not guilty was read out and the judge announced that Mary Lenihan was to be discharged.

So who did kill the baby and with surgical skill remove internal organs? Mary denied all knowledge of the baby; surely she knew something of it. When Hannah was tried, even the judge was convinced she was not capable of disembowelling her own baby.

It goes to show how in Catholic Ireland the lengths somebody was willing to go to hide an illegitimate baby. Yet Hannah herself was an illegitimate baby born to her mother Hannah in 1909 and she was reared by her grandmother. So what had changed in less than twenty years that a baby born in 1928 could not be given the same chance in life?

THE CEMETERY, ROCKCHAPEL

The graveyard near Rockchapel back then.

Supernatural or just a shooting
Glenamuckla Newmarket 1888

On the Saturday morning 28th July 1888, James Rourke went to work for a farmer called David McAuliffe in the townland of Glenamuckla. He was going to McAuliffe's to help cut the hay. The two men were only a few minutes mowing the hay when they noticed a man approaching.

As the man came closer, it became obvious he was disguised with a white cloth over his face. His jacket was also turned inside out, these were often the calling cards of the moonlighters but they normally operated under the cover of darkness.

The man was armed with a double barrelled shotgun which he seemed intent on using. Rourke asked "who is it" but being disguised he was hardly going to answer to that. The gunman got up on the ditch and called the pair over.

He asked them to identify themselves McAuliffe told him his name but Rourke gave his name as John Fleming a nearby farmer. Rourke was acting like he had been expecting someone and he was now standing behind McAuliffe.

David had nothing to hide and stepped forward took off his hat and told the man how he had never done anything to make trouble. Then Rourke approached the man, the man took aim and shot Rourke at close range. He fell to the ground and the man discharged the other shot into him as he lay there.

The man then pulled out a revolver and fired more shots while David McAuliffe ran off to his house which was not far away. He sent his servant Ellen O'Sullivan to nearby farmer John Fleming to get help.

Meanwhile Rourke lay in the field in drastic pain from the shots he had received but still clung on to life. The gunman had fled as fast as he appeared in a southerly direction.

David McAuliffe regained his composure and returned to the scene and took Rourke in a horse and cart. They headed towards Rourke's house which was about three miles away, as Rourke wanted to see his wife. He was asked that day did he know who had shot him but he did not. James survived for less than three hours and died at home.

Later that evening a young man Cornelius O'Keeffe was arrested for the murder but David McAuliffe was not able to identify him.

The inquest was held in Rourke's house on Monday the 30th of July by Coroner Byrne to inquire into the circumstance surrounding the death. The jury was comprised of respectable farmers from the surrounding district.

The chief witness was farmer David McAuliffe who recalled Rourke coming to his house the Saturday morning before. David said they were only cutting the hay a few minutes when the disguised man turned up. He was less than six yards from them when he asked them their names. More than once the gunman asked the farmer to stand aside from Rourke but he did not budge.

He said it was when Rourke stepped forward the man took aim and shot Rourke. He heard him announce that he was hit and saw him fall. Another shot was fired and McAuliffe said he heard Rourke groan as he was hit again.

McAuliffe then heard the gunman say "if that would not do you would get this" and pulled out a revolver. The witness said he fled when he got the chance towards his house and the gunman ran off in a southerly direction. The only description McAuliffe gave of the killer was in answer to a question by a juror. The farmer described the man as being tall but could not identify who the man was.

The next witness called that day was Ellen Sullivan who was a servant of McAuliffe's. She also recalled Rourke coming to the house that morning and said McAuliffe came running back only a few minutes after leaving the house.

She followed her master to the scene of the crime to find Rourke lying there telling her he was shot. He asked her to get a drink for him which she did. Ellen told how she had not heard any shots fired that morning despite the house not being far away.

Dr O'Riordan from Boherbue was called to give evidence of the post-mortem he had carried out on the body with Dr Verling. He found a lot of shot in Rourke's body, the gunshot wound was on the left side above the hip. The intestines and kidneys had been hit which caused a large haemorrhage of blood in the stomach. He concluded that death was due to loss of blood as a result of the gunshot wounds. Dr Walter Verling of Newmarket concurred with the evidence of Dr O'Riordan.

The coroner James Byrne then addressed the jury and was of the opinion they should have no difficulty finding a verdict. He assumed they would find a verdict that James Rourke met his death by gunshot inflicted by some person unknown. The jury concurred with the coroner and found the verdict accordingly.

Directly after the inquest James O'Rourke's funeral took place as was usual back then. A large crowd had gathered and the funeral cortege headed towards Clonfert graveyard where he was buried.

Initially the rumour was James Rourke worked for a local farmer called Patrick Twomey who was not liked in the area, but surely it was not enough to kill him for.

Twomey it seems had lent money to a brother in law of his Timothy Shine years before.

Like many money transactions in families it was not paid back in the time agreed and led to a dispute. Later in 1886 Twomey got his brother in law evicted so he could recover part of the debt.

Near the scene of the crime and the "footprints" at Glenamuckla.

One month before being shot a notice was supposed to have been posted on Rourke's door. It threatened him that he would meet a similar fate to James Quinn who had been shot near Cullen in May of that year. The notice threatened he had to stop working for Patrick Twomey who reportedly had police protection. Rourke it seems ignored the notice and continued working for Twomey.

Another rumour was that Rourke was himself involved with the moonlighters and they suspected he was giving information to the police. There was no evidence to support these rumours.

There was also no evidence to connect Cornelius O'Keeffe with the shooting. All the police had found was gunpowder and shot in his father's house.

O'Keeffe appeared before a magistrate on Friday 10th of August in Kanturk. No evidence was given that day because the police had little to go on. They merely applied for a remand until the next Newmarket Petty sessions in a week's time. The application for the remand was granted, while the application for bail was refused.

A week later at Newmarket Petty sessions it was Timothy O'Keeffe father of Cornelius who was first charged by the magistrates. Under the Peace Preservation Act 1881 he was charged with having ammunition in his house without the relevant license.

A Constable Brophy told how he searched the house on the 28th when Con was arrested. He found the powder and shot under a bed in the house.

His defence solicitor argued that it was not evidence against them and he was only liable for it being in his house. The magistrates came to a swift decision and sentenced the old man to a month in jail.

His son Con was then called and charged with the much more serious charge of murder.

District Inspector Yates represented the police and prosecution while solicitors Barry and Beytagh the defence.

Yates applied to the magistrate for yet another remand of eight days but needed to give some indication new evidence would be found against O'Keeffe. Head Constable Connelly from Kingwilliamstown claimed he was investigating information that connected O'Keeffe with the murder. He agreed a remand of eight days would give him enough time.

Typical scene at a Petty Sessions back then.

Several more times in August the case was again remanded and young O'Keeffe sent back to jail in Cork. Finally on the 30th of August at Kanturk Courthouse the case was dealt with.

The defence argued that it was unfair to continually hold his client without evidence; during August he had been remanded at least six times. Now District Inspector agreed that he should be discharged as they had failed to find any case against him.

James Rourke was a forty six year old labourer living in Glennakeel. He had one daughter Ellen who was then 10 years old by his first wife Johanna Cahill. She had died when Ellen was barely a year old and James remarried to Julia Flynn who was fourteen years younger than him. Despite this in eight years of marriage up to his death no more children were born to the couple.

Aged eighteen Ellen left Ireland for Massachusetts in America in 1896 with her first cousin Timothy Guinee from Kiskeam. There she met and married a local man John O'Connell who had originally come from Rathmore.

Con O'Keeffe was reputed to have left the area sometime after and emigrated to America. Nobody was ever proved to have been the gunman who killed Rourke, either nobody knew him or were scared to give evidence as they might meet a similar fate.

Locally many stories have lived on about the murder and who done it. Some say the murderer was a local called Con Barry, who also left the area only days after the shooting. It is presumed that there was no connection to moonlighters or Twomey. It was supposedly just a family dispute over money.

As murders go it would have been long forgotten except for the appearance near the murder spot in 1920 of two marks on the ditch now know as the footprints. It was thirty two years later and folklore in the area connected these to the murder. It even goes further and claims that the murderer died in America in 1920 and these footprints appeared in the field afterwards.

Over the years many versions of the story have evolved and connect the footprints to the supernatural. Supposedly several attempts have been made over the years to clear them but they remain.

Whether the footprints are somehow connected to a man standing on a ditch over thirty years before their appearance I leave it up to you to decide.

Quinn, the Bog Ranger
Laghtsigh Nohovaldaly near Rathmore 1888

James Quinn 64, widow, lived alone and worked as a rent warner to Mr Longfield of Longueville House near Mallow. As if that would not make him unpopular enough, he was also a bog ranger who rented rights to the bog for the Shine Lawlor estate. His wife had died many years before and his children were all reared, with several gone to America.

You could ask yourself why he was out doing such a job at that hour of his life especially in such turbulent times. Even more so as for some time he had been getting threatening letters telling him not to go bog letting anymore.

The first Sunday in May notices were placed in the village of Cullen warning Quinn not to go to Nohoval Daly bog. The following day Quinn ignored all threats and left his home to go to the same bog for the purpose of letting it out to tenants. Rent warner's, agents and anyone who was involved in evictions were receiving threats all over the countryside and had to be tough in their dangerous predicament.

That evening Andrew Quinn became worried about his brother when he did not return home. He asked the neighbours had they seen him but they had not seen him since morning. James Quinn's grandson normally slept in his grandfather's house to keep him company. But that night when he went to the door it was locked and no one was home.

The next morning the family searched for Quinn, one would suppose at first not fearing the worst but still worried. Nohoval bog had a history of trouble, the bog ranger before Quinn was a man called Carroll. He gave information which led to a man being convicted of being a moonlighter. This led to the bog being boycotted and as a result Carroll had to relinquish his post.

The bog was without a ranger for several years and locals continued cutting their turf. They had what is called turbary a right to cut turf for their own use in a patch of bog. This did not give them the right to sell any surplus turf over and above what they needed themselves. The landlord however could let portions of the bog to those that had no turbary and it could be a lucrative business. With no bog ranger for several years there was no one to keep the situation in check and the tenants were free to do as they pleased.

It was into this situation that Quinn took up the role. He had no trouble for at least two years. Then the Shine Lawlor estate was sold to O'Connell's of Derrynane. Some say it was about this time that Quinn no longer turned a blind eye to what had been going on. For this reason he came under the attention of those who issued the threats.

Quinn had reported the threats he received to the police. They asked to be informed when he went to the bog and on at least one occasion he was escorted to the bog. But that Monday he set out alone to the bog.

On that Tuesday some of his relations formed a search party and got others to help. They sought the help of John Connors as he knew the bog better than any other. Connors was barely searching ten minutes that day when he came on old Quinn lying on his back in a drain. People were cutting turf only one hundred yards away oblivious to the fact a man had been killed and his body was so close. It was not a remote area and there were houses nearby.

His throat had been cut and one of his hands was in his pocket. The men ran off for the police without interfering with the body. Doctors were informed to carry out a post mortem and the body was taken to the village of Cullen. In Cullen the body was kept in an outhouse of Mahony's Pub to await the inquest.

The general area of Nohoval bog as it is today.

The police began an investigation but knew it was near impossible to find out who had killed Quinn. Even if somebody saw or heard something the day before, no one was willing to talk for fear of being boycotted or meeting a similar fate.

A large party of police descended on the village of Cullen to investigate the brutal murder as there was not a shred of evidence. No witnesses were willing to come forward; several had heard a gunshot about noon on Monday but at the time thought nothing of it. It was claimed that despite his occupation, James Quinn was popular in the area.

Rumours in the area claimed that it was someone who wanted Quinn's position as bog ranger that killed him. This though seems unlikely as despite possibly being lucrative very few wanted such a job being well aware of possible repercussions.

An inquest was held in the village of Cullen at noon on Thursday the 10th May by county coroner Mr Byrne. As it happened that day was a holiday, Ascension Thursday and a large crowd gathered in the village to attend mass.

A boycotted farmer called O'Keeffe came for mass under Police protection. When the locals saw him enter the church they all left, such was the feelings on the area against him. He was told that if he wanted to attend mass he would have to walk to Millstreet five miles away. A notice was found outside the National School that morning that anyone cutting on the bog would regret it.

There was tension in Cullen that day ever before the inquest. Shortly after noon the jury comprising of local respectable men was sworn in. Robert Dunne was foreman. Other jury members were shopkeepers Jeremiah Vaughan and Timothy Riordan, publican Cornelius Goulding all from Cullen.

John Connors was the first witness called as he had found Quinn. He recalled Tuesday as he was planting cabbages for a neighbour when his sister said he was needed at the house. There he found two men Mike Quinn and another 'John Connors' who said their uncle was missing. They came for him as he knew the bog better than they did. When they got to the bog that morning they met John Quinn and Thade Bradley. Between them they spread out to cover the bog. Connors came on the body of

James Quinn lying on his back after only 10 minutes searching. The left hand was in his trousers pocket and his right hand on his chest. Connors called the others and then sent for the police straight away. He had last seen Quinn alive the Sunday before when they chatted at the chapel gate.

Thade Bradley and the other John Connors both gave similar evidence of seeing the body in the bog the Tuesday before.

Sergeant Owen Geoghan told that he was stationed nearby at Lisnaboy. He said Michael Quinn nephew of the deceased man came to the hut at four on Tuesday. Geoghan explained that he was in Lisnaboy as protection of the boycotted estate of Archdeacon Bland.

The Sergeant with a constable left their post and set out for the bog and found Quinn in a drain. The hands were as Connors had described but he also found the throat had been cut. The scene he thought did not give him the impression that the old man had put up any struggle. The Sergeant then told how when he turned over the body he found a bullet wound on the left shoulder and the left hand was also broken.

The sergeant told how when he searched the body he found a small slip of paper in Quinn's trouser pocket. The coroner had the slip of paper and read it out "take notice that any person found cutting turf on Nohoval Bog will be shot at like a mad dog by the captain who never failed". The sergeant concluded his evidence by saying he arranged to have the body taken from the bog and removed to Cullen.

A juror stated that he wanted it to be known that the murder had not taken place in the parish of Cullen. It was clear the people of Cullen wanted to distance themselves from the crime; they had enough trouble closer to home.

The medical evidence was given that day by Dr Thomas Ryan who described carrying out the post mortem with Dr James O'Riordan. He first spoke of the gunshot wound in the shoulder. The bullet he found passed right through and also fractured the humerus bone of his upper left arm. He located more of the shot in the chest wall and lungs. The doctor found the shot was very large and had been fired from a very close range. The throat had been slit; the doctor said this was an incised wound under the jaw several inches long. At the back of the head he found a large fracture of the skull that pressed into the brain. The police believed this was the result of a blow from the butt of a gun while Quinn lay on the ground.

Ryan finished by saying that any of the wounds inflicted on Quinn would have resulted in death. The cause of death was as a result of shock and haemorrhage as a result of the wounds.

Dr O'Riordan concurred with Ryan and gave no new evidence.

The coroner suggested to the jury that they should have no trouble coming to a verdict. He even went as far as saying that Quinn died as a result of wounds inflicted by a person or persons unknown. The jury agreed with him and found their verdict accordingly.

The inquest was now complete but the police were no nearer to finding the killer and had no witnesses. One thing was clear, whoever wanted Quinn dead was not afraid of being seen firing a gun in the middle of the day. They didn't just shoot and flee; they made certain he was dead before leaving.

On the evening of Wednesday the 30th of May the police made their move on a suspect in Rathmore. The man arrested was Daniel Kelly who was supposed to be on the run since Quinn was killed. Had he not gone on the run he may not have been suspected at all.

About the same time it was heard that the relations of Quinn were intending to make a case before the Grand Jury of County Cork for compensation. Their claim was for £1000 which at that time was a hell of a lot of money.

Not much more is heard of Daniel Kelly indicating he was most likely released for lack of evidence against him. It does seem that this turbulent time in Ireland captain moonlight or those imitating him were free to kill who they chose. They seemed to be safe in the knowledge that the countryside would remain silent and keep out of it.

Save your soul
Killinane Banteer 1825

On Sunday morning 25th of September 1825 in the townland of Killinane west of Banteer a body was found in a dyke. The body was covered in water but once fished out it was obvious a murder had occurred. Not only had the throat been cut but the body was slashed in several places. The trouble was nobody in the area could identify the body. On the body a scrap of paper was found with "Ardfinnan" scribbled on it. The initial presumption was a motive of robbery and that the man was travelling to Kerry to buy cattle.

The only clue they had was the man had been seen in a public house in Banteer the evening before. Two other strangers were with him where he had paid for drinks with a note.

The dead man was about forty years of age and five foot seven inches tall.

It was Tuesday before the coroner James Daltera arrived in town for the inquest. A jury was quickly sworn in made up of respectable men from the area, mostly shopkeepers.

The man still had not been identified at this point and all the inquest could do was describe him. It emerged he had been wearing a blue body coat with a striped vest inside and corduroy trousers. He had a large pair of unusual heavy shoes and wool socks. It was hoped someone would recognise the shoes.

As a post mortem had not been yet carried out it was decided to postpone the inquest until Friday.

At the inquest on Friday Doctor Michael Cahill gave the results of the examination. The jury had already viewed the body and were well aware of what he was about to say. He described the many injuries which resulted in the man's death. He had found the skull fractured in four places and the left temple also smashed to pieces. The face and cheeks had been cut and stabbed several times and the throat slit in two places. The right palm was extremely badly beaten and the left arm was broken. The legs also bore the signs of having been slashed all over with a sharp instrument.

With no actual witnesses there was not much more the inquest could do but find a verdict. They went with what evidence the doctor gave and returned a verdict of wilful murder against persons unknown. At this point the deceased also remained unknown to them.

There were no clues as to who had done it. Signs of blood had been traced from the scene to the main road. Subscriptions amounting to over £200 were collected as a reward for information leading to an arrest of a suspect. Despite the little evidence the magistrates were confident someone would be apprehended. Within weeks the subscriptions had gone up to £263 and a magistrate Major Carter offered another £50 but it was to no avail.

Despite the reward being such a huge sum of money, no person came forward until May of the following year. Owen Callaghan claimed he had seen the deceased man in the public house where he worked that night in September. He said there was a man and woman with him and identified the man as John Purdon whom he knew. He claimed to have followed them that night and actually witnessed the killing. Purdon's wife was also suspected with having been involved in the killing but it seems she was not arrested.

On the strength of this evidence John Purdon was tracked down and arrested. Purdon was a married man in his thirties with several young children. He was to be tried before a jury at the next Assizes and if Callaghan was believed, would meet his doom.

It was worse for Purdon though, further investigation revealed the dead man as Thomas Stammers. Purdon was also under suspicion for another lesser known murder in the area around the same time of a man whose identity is not known.

At the Cork Assizes presided over by Baron Pennefather, on Saturday 5th of August 1826 John Purdon who was also known as John Ford was charged with the wilful murder of Thomas Stammers at Killinane the September before. He was also charged with the second murder but no evidence was produced in this case if there was though he was sure to die for it.

In the first case the chief witness was Owen Callaghan and it was strange that now he had plenty to say, having for months not said a word. Callaghan recalled well the night of Saturday 24th of September. He worked and lived at McAuliffe's public house in Banteer where he saw the accused man. There was a man and woman with him and they were drinking porter. When they got up to leave it was Purdon who paid. He had seen the man had a knife hidden in the sleeve of his coat while in the pub. While Purdon settled the bill the witness said he spoke to the other man outside the door. That man showed him his shoes which were unusual and he could remember them well. He then described the clothes that man wore a blue coat, soldier's jacket and corduroy trousers. Callaghan saw the body in Kanturk afterwards in the same clothes.

When the three left the pub that night Callaghan did not follow at first. He had heard where Purdon's father lived and headed towards Coolclough. He told the court he decided to follow them but not till they were out of sight.

Despite being dark the witness caught up and could see the three ahead who were no longer walking together. Near Lisnacon Colliery they turned up a small road and went into a field. He saw Purdon approach the other man and strike him on the back of the head with something he held with two hands. The man fell and the woman came and tried to help keep the man down. Against the two of them he managed to struggle to his feet, Callaghan saw Purdon strike him on the head again. This time the man and woman were again on top of him but managed now to keep him down. Callaghan also saw about this time some boys approach across the fields having heard the cries. Purdon also saw them approaching. Both he and the woman dragged the body out of sight and fled.

Under cross examination the witness admitted how he had not come forward until he was obliged to do so. Referring to the reward he claimed it was small and did not come for that reason but would gladly accept the money. He revealed that on the night he ran away but with hindsight could have got assistance and reported the murder. When questioned Callaghan said a strange curiosity drove him to following the three that night. Callaghan knew that Purdon had a bad reputation and thought he was going out stealing sheep that night, he had no idea a man would be killed.

He had told his master the publican that he was going to a dance. Afterwards Owen did in fact go to a dance after witnessing the murder. He told the court how he was not a very good dancer.

He even told how he had been to the inquest but had not come forward and told what he knew. That day he did tell Mrs McAuliffe that the dead man had been drinking in the pub that night. He now tried to claim he had made no secret of this fact back then but said Mrs McAuliffe warned him not to mention it or he himself could be blamed. Callaghan told how he left his employment in McAuliffe's shortly afterwards. The defence asked how he could go to a dance after witnessing a murder. Owen said he would go to a dance after seeing fifty men murdered and even told he would go to a dance after seeing his father killed.

John Healy described how he had found the body covered in water that Sunday morning.

Father and son, Daniel and Phillip Scully both said they had heard unusual noises the Saturday night before the body was found. What they had heard seemed like the groans of a man. Daniel's two sons went to investigate that night and found nothing.

Michael Kelly had seen the accused with four pound notes on the Sunday after the murder. He had never seen John with a note before then. Several more witnesses were produced who had seen Purdon with money the day after the murder.

A police constable read out a statement the accused had made to him. In it Purdon claimed that school master called Sullivan carried out the murder. He had admitted to having been forced to go with him and give the man a blow to the head with a stone. That statement the policeman said was given by Purdon in the hope of becoming an approver for the prosecution and possibly even getting a reward.

The prosecution case came to an end and the defence had no witness to call. Why did Purdon's wife not give her husband an alibi? Maybe it was better as she may have implicated herself.

The judge then summed up at length and the jury took about an hour to decide the fate of Purdon. The jury returned the verdict of guilty of murder.

Pennefather proceeded to address the now guilty man reminding the court of the terrible deeds he had carried out. He even blamed Purdon for involving his wife in the murder but there was never a mention of her being charged. Maybe it was felt that for the family to lose their father was justice enough and the children needed their mother. The sentence he was to receive was in no doubt at all, it was to cost him his life as he had taken a life.

Baron Pennefather concluded his address to the guilty man saying "prepare for death for you have but a short time to live".

Purdon appeared shocked and tormented by the verdict and sentence. He replied to the judge saying "a long day, I pray a long day". Pennefather quickly explained to him that it was not in his power to grant longer time till the execution. Under the law he had to be executed within forty eight hours unless it fell on a Sunday. The judge told him not to waste his time and instead to repent for his dreadful crimes.

The execution was set for the following Monday and nothing could be done to change that. The condemned man had little time to consider his predicament. By Sunday though it was said he had become resigned to his fate and knew he could not be saved.

That Monday morning Purdon was taken to Gallow's Green in Cork where a large crowd had gathered to see him die. It possibly was the last execution carried out at Gallow's Green and from the following year all executions were done outside the county gaol.

At noon on Monday he was separated from his wife and it was a dreadful spectacle to see. His wife begged him "if it were of service to his soul to declare everything regarding the murder". She told him not to mind the disgrace it brought her and the children but to save his soul.

Purdon heeded his wife's advice and before taking the steps to the scaffold he made his confession. He now not only tried to save his soul but also to save his wife from suspicion. The soon to be dead man claimed that he alone was responsible for the murder and neither his wife nor any other person was present at the time.

Then when the time came Purdon seemed petrified as he took his final steps up to the scaffold. He was heard to cry out and ask god for mercy with his last breaths. The drop fell and Purdon hung on the end of a rope and struggled for a minute in front of the crowd who had come to see the execution. He would have been left hanging there for some time to make sure he was dead and justice was served.

A day at the fair
Newmarket 1943

Back in the day fairs would have been the highlight of the year. They were a day out for everyone young and old not just for farmers and horse or cattle dealers. Aside from the business side there was also entertainment and amusements.

On the negative side many over indulged in the pubs and trouble sometimes spilled out onto the streets. Some young fellas were well known for attending fairs with the intention of causing trouble. In most cases simple disagreements were sparked off after drink.

In the north west of Cork Newmarket Horse fair was no different. It was held biannually in February and October. In 1943 the horse fair was held on the14th of October. At four in the afternoon that day a hackney driver Daniel O'Sullivan was called to convey a man to Dr Verling urgently. It soon became obvious that the man was in a bad way. He had been stabbed in the chest. He managed to walk to the car but getting in said "oh I'm dying". On the way to the doctors he repeated the words and said nothing else.

The stabbed man John Maurice Lane was taken into Dr Verling's surgery but the doctor knew he could do little. There was blood everywhere but the doctor suspected the internal bleed was much worse. The doctor decided to send for the priest. Verling could not find a pulse, yet the injured man was still alive and was telling the doctor he was dying. When Fr Bowles arrived he suggested taking the man to the hospital.

Back in the hackney Lane repeated the words "I'm dying". At the hospital the driver asked who had done this to him and Lane replied "Mahony". Within half an hour forty two year old farmer John Maurice Lane was dead.

This was the deadly fallout of the fair but Lane wasn't the only man to be stabbed that day. The other man however was not in a life threatening condition. Was this going to be a simple case of murder as Lane had named the man who had stabbed him.

It turned out the two men who had been stabbed were both from the Ballydesmond area as was the third man Geoffrey O'Mahony whom the dying man had named. O'Mahony was a farmer from Meendurragha, while John Lane lived a little further north in Glenlahan.

O'Mahony was arrested that very day and on Friday appeared before a magistrate. The case was remanded to Kanturk District Court on the following Friday the 22nd when the inquest would have reached a verdict. Dr McGrath the state pathologist arrived in the town on Friday to carry out the post mortem.

The inquest was held on Saturday the 16th of October by coroner Michael Ryan in the Kanturk Hospital. Superintendent Holland from Kanturk represented the state and William O'Keeffe was the foreman of the jury.

John Maurice Lane's remains were identified by his sister Bridget Carroll. Bridget said she had met her brother at the fair on the day he died. He was his usual self and in good health.

The state pathologist Dr McGrath carried out the post-mortem assisted by Dr Geoffrey Collins from Kanturk Hospital and Dr Verling. He described Lane as a powerfully built man who had several recent scrapes and cuts on hands and face. He found a slit like puncture wound on the front of the chest. The wound was deep and passed through the chest wall and lung. He also found the wound had cut the superior vena cava, the blood vessel which returns blood from the upper body to the heart. As a result of this the chest was full of blood and clots. In total the pathologist told he had found nine pints of blood in the chest. He found a similar wound on the left shoulder which did not penetrate as deep as the chest wound. He had no trouble coming to the conclusion that Lane died as a result of the internal haemorrhage and loss of blood from the stab wound.

Dr Verling also gave evidence as he had attempted to treat Lane the day he died. Verling recalled receiving a call that Matthew Jones had been stabbed. It was John Lane though he said turned up in a car at his surgery. Lane's clothes were covered in blood and he knew he has dying. The doctor told Lane was losing consciousness due to blood loss and he sent for the priest.

Dr Collins from Kanturk Hospital also gave evidence of how Lane was dying when he first saw him. He said Lane died twenty minutes after arriving in hospital.

After this coroner Ryan, adjourned the proceeding sine die meaning there was no future date set.

Several times during October and November the case was remanded many times. The prosecution was responsible for the delay waiting for direction in the case from the Attorney General. Finally a date was set to begin hearing evidence November 19th in Mallow Courthouse.

That day in court the prosecution was represented by David Casey state solicitor and Superintendent Holland. O'Mahony's legal counsel comprised of Timothy Linehan a solicitor who was also TD for Cork North.

Linehan began that day by complaining how badly his client had been treated in prison. He had been arrested in working clothes and despite clothes being sent to him he had not been allowed to wear them. The judge asked for the matter to be looked into saying "in our eyes the man is innocent so far".

As at the inquest Dr McGrath and Dr Verling told of the injuries Lane had sustained and the reasons why he died. That day McGrath's evidence alone took well over thirty minutes going over the post mortem in detail. Verling recalled Lane saying "I'm dying" and asked who had stabbed him. Immediately Linehan objected knowing his client would be named.

The objection was noted by District Justice Connor but overruled. He was satisfied that Lane knew he was dying therefore the evidence was admissible as a dying declaration. The doctor was allowed to repeat what Lane told him that day "I am dying Geoffrey Mahony stabbed me".

Verling told how he had examined O'Mahony on the 15th of October. He described minor injuries to his hands and dressed an abrasion on his nose.

A nurse and the matron from the hospital were also produced. Both said they asked Lane who knew he was dying "who did it". He replied to both of them on more than one occasion "O'Mahony". According to them he even told them O'Mahony was from Kingwilliamstown.

Several times during their account Linehan objected but was overruled.

Matthew Jones farmer from Glentanefinnane was called to give evidence, having been drinking with Lane on the 14th. That morning he left home at five thirty on a horse heading for Newmarket. On the way there between Clashkinleen Creamery and Newmarket he passed the accused O'Mahony who was walking with Michael Jones.

He claimed that O'Mahony shouted at him "you crooked nosed murderer come right off here on the ground and fight". Matthew however said he ignored him and rode on to the fair.

Later that day at two in the afternoon he met up with John Lane and together they went to Sheehan's pub. In the pub a scuffle broke out between Lane and O'Mahony, the crowd scattered when a glass was broken. He saw O'Mahony trying to raise his stick and threaten Lane. He heard Lane say something like "you dirty thing you are not worth hitting". Such was the extent of the scuffle that a guard was called and both men were put out of Sheehan's.

Centre of Newmarket as it is nowadays.

At this point the witness said he went off about his business and bumped into Lane again. They then went into Quinlan's Pub with David Jones. They parted afterwards at the town cross and he saw Lane walk away up the other side of the street.

Jones said in the distance he witnessed O'Mahony make a dash for Lane and strike him on the chest. He said Lane had his hands in his pockets at the time but recovered himself and pursued O'Mahony. A crowd then gathered around them and Jones said he ran to the action. As he approached

O'Mahony emerged from the crowd and attacked him on the face. A guard was quickly on the scene and took O'Mahony away. It was only then Jones realised he was bleeding and saw O'Mahony with a knife in his hand as he left. He tried to call out to warn the guard that he had a knife.

Linehan questioned Jones and asked how many drinks had they that day. He tried to make out both he and Lane were drunk asking had they twenty pints each. Jones could not tell how much they had drank that day but thought it was no more than five.

Next called was Michael Jones a farmer's son from Knockdown Cordal, County Kerry near the county border. He had gone to town with O'Mahony that day. He recalled O'Mahony saying something to Matthew Jones that morning. He reluctantly recalled the words O'Mahony used which were similar to what was heard before. Michael said early that morning in Newmarket O'Mahony emerged from a pub and told him Matthew Jones and Lane had made a go for him inside.

Publican Katherine Sheehan and her daughter Mary Josephine told their version of the trouble in their pub at the fair. Katherine said she separated the two men and ordered them out of her pub. At the same time Mary collected the glasses and revealed Lane drank stout while O'Mahony only drank a mineral.

After a day in court and hearing from several witnesses the judge adjourned until November 30th. At this point they were no nearer to knowing what exactly had occurred that day. More detail was needed to reach a verdict for if it could be proved Lane had provoked O'Mahony that day his counsel would argue the charge to be reduced to manslaughter.

The next day in court Patrick Loughlin a farm labourer began by recalling people rushing into Sheehan's pub on the day of the fair. Afterwards he saw O'Mahony emerge with Garda Murphy. Later that day he heard O'Mahony shout at Lane "come here you big bully" and Lane replied "is it me you want O'Mahony". The witness said O'Mahony struck Lane on the chest who fell backwards. Lane attempted to recover himself but fell forward on his face and hands. Lane then tried to get up and pursue his opponent managing to strike him with a stick he had. Loughlin caught a glimpse of a blade in O'Mahony's hand and claimed he called out to the approaching guard to warn him.

The witness then told how he tried to help Lane and opened his clothes knowing he had been stabbed. Once he exposed the chest he described finding blood gushing from the wound.

He then took Lane to O'Sullivan's garage to get a car to take him to hospital. On the way there he assisted Lane who was struggling. Lane told him "I'm dying now anyway".

Several more witnesses were called that had been at the fair and saw the fight that day. Daniel Foley revealed that he was with Lane in Sheehan's and involved in the trouble but did not know O'Mahony. Lane had told him to go with Matthew Jones and hit O'Mahony.

Patrick Casey from Kiskeam was also in Sheehan's pub he heard O'Mahony shouting "you tried to kill me before. Do you remember the morning going to the creamery when you tried to kill me with the iron bar"

Statements taken from the accused were read out by a Garda. He denied even having a knife that day despite what several witnesses had said. O'Mahony also claimed that Garda Murphy who was on the scene quickly did not find a knife on him that day. The accused did admit that Matthew Jones passed him that morning but denied there were words between them.

After hearing several witness statements it certainly left one thinking there was a history of trouble between the men. Lane and Jones were not completely innocent and had pursued O'Mahony in town on the day of the fair. All the same there was never any doubt about what O'Mahony had done.

The judge had no option but to return him for trial before the Central Criminal Court on the capital charge of murder. He was also to appear before the Cork county Court on the charge of wounding Matthew Jones. David Casey indicated he intended to apply to have both cases heard together in Dublin and Linehan agreed on behalf of his client to this.

Five months later Geoffrey O'Mahony was before Justice Conor Maguire at Green Street Courthouse. The charge against him was still one of murder. The prosecution maintained Lane had died of injuries inflicted by O'Mahony in Newmarket on 14th October.

The defence claimed that their client had been held by the throat earlier that day by Lane. They claimed O'Mahony was afraid of both

Matthew Jones and John Lane and had tried to avoid them. They also claimed that John Lane struck O'Mahony on the head with a stick before Lane fell that day. The defence still maintained that O'Mahony did not have a knife on him that day at all. They told that O'Mahony had sustained an injury to his right hand years before in New York which prevented him from fully closing his right hand. Despite an intensive search the knife had never been found but could easily have been picked up by one of the large crowd.

Over several more days in court the evidence was heard again. Matthew Jones still maintained he had seen a knife in O'Mahony's hand that day. When cross examined his evidence was seen in a different light. He denied going to town that day to organise a beating of O'Mahony. He could not deny though that he had previously been charged with striking O'Mahony with an iron bar. Jones argued this was in self-defence. The county court had ordered him to pay O'Mahony £30 but he admitted that day in court he had never paid it.

Denis O'Mahony a cousin of the accused told how Geoffrey was followed through the streets that day by Lane and Jones. His version was that his cousin was in dread of them and tried to avoid them.

Having heard the conflicting evidence from several more witnesses, the jury felt it was not possible to find him guilty on the charge of murder. The jury found O'Mahony guilty on the charge of manslaughter under provocation.

When sentencing Justice Maguire felt the jury had taken a lenient view of the case. He did concede there was provocation and that O'Mahony was normally a sober farmer not often in trouble. He sentenced Geoffrey O'Mahony to twelve months hard labour.

I'm done for
Marshalstown, Kildorrery 1829

On the 20th of January three friends Thomas Casey, Daniel Moylan and John Roche returned home from the fair of Ahercross near Kildorrery. They were on their way to Tipperary having conducted some business at the fair. They had a few drinks before they departed. Casey had purchased a colt that day.

The three had not got very far when approached by two men and one of them struck the mare on which Moylan was riding. Moylan gave out to the man and only got cheek from him saying he would soon get the same. Still Moylan was having none of it and got down from the horse to confront the man. The man lashed him with the handle of a whip. He gave as good as he got and lashed out with such force he knocked the man down. A struggle broke out on the road between the men.

Thomas Casey intervened and broke them up and got Moylan to move on. When they did one of the pair produced a pistol from his pocket and took aim. He was aiming for Casey. Only one shot was fired and it was enough for it struck Casey in his side. The two attackers disappeared as quickly as they had come upon the three friends.

It was the following day that Thomas Casey died from the injuries he had sustained from the shot. Back then doctors could do little to stop internal bleeding or prevent infection from spreading.

Soon word spread throughout the countryside who the killers were. One had been recognised as Patrick Duggan, a known outlaw who had deserted from the army about two years before. The other man was known as Denis McAuliffe. They had been terrorising the countryside since and suspected of being involved in all sorts of crime. They were threatening people at gunpoint for money.

An inquest was held on Thursday the 22nd by Coroner Richard Jones. Over the course of three days the inquest heard from Roche, Moylan and doctors.

The jury found that Thomas Casey had died as a result of wilful murder by Duggan and McAuliffe. Normally the inquest was not interested in who committed the crime, but how the victim died. In this case the pair were known to be notorious outlaws wanted for a while.

The search for the outlaws intensified especially as the charges against them would put an end to their rampage. A warrant for their arrest was issued by the Earl of Kingston and their description sent out around the area.

A few weeks later in early March the police in county Limerick tracked down the pair to a house where a wake was being held. Despite the crowd in the house the two outlaws used their guns. In the siege McAuliffe shot several times from the house and managed to shoot and seriously wound one of the police. Duggan on the other hand shot his way out of trouble and made his escape to the nearby mountains. The shooting died down and the police held back to prevent more bloodshed. They waited until the following morning and when they entered the house McAuliffe gave himself up.

Denis McAuliffe was convicted of shooting the police at the next Limerick Assizes and duly found guilty. He was sentenced to death but later got a reprieve. Instead he received a sentence of transportation for life most likely to Australia. By May he was on board a hulk ship in Cobh awaiting his journey to the other side of the world.

Duggan was still at large and if apprehended would face a fate worse than transportation. The police had to get clever to find him and started watching his regular haunts. They knew where his father lived and suspected he would turn up there at some stage.

In late May Duggan was arrested in Kilbeheny near the Cork border, his father lived nearby. This was only seven miles from where Casey had been shot. Duggan told that he was intending to abscond to America and was calling to see his father one last time before leaving.

Despite being arrested in May of 1839 it was not until the Cork Spring Assizes 1840 that Duggan came before a judge and jury. It was Thursday the 25th of March when the case was called before Baron Pennefather.

Typical scene at the Assizes.

Daniel Moylan recalled returning from the fair that day. He said it was McAuliffe that struck his mare. It was after the scuffle he saw Duggan pull out the pistol and load it with powder. Casey had gone on ahead about thirty yards. Moylan witnessed Duggan go after him and heard the shot but did not actually see him shoot.

Moylan then ran to his friend and found him bleeding and falling about the road in agony. Casey called out to him "I'm done for, I'm done for".

Under cross examination by the defence, Moylan denied being drunk that day saying he had a few pints of port and a glass or two of whiskey, but would often have had more. He admitted striking McAuliffe with such force to knock him down but denied kicking him in the face when on the ground.

John Roche gave similar evidence and swore that the only part Casey took that day was to pacify the situation. Moylan swore he never set eyes upon McAuliffe before the attack, yet Roche swore he didn't know Duggan before the day in question.

Dr O'Neill confirmed that Thomas Casey died as a result of the gunshot wound he received.

Policeman Charles McCarthy gave evidence of arresting Duggan and told how he had been hunting for him the past three years. He had often watched Duggan's father's house for him during that time. When he finally came on him in Kilbeheny, Duggan gave himself up without any resistance.

When the evidence was heard the accused asked if he could say a few words and the judge granted him his request. Duggan addressed the court in a most convincing way. His intelligent manner was not expected from a man on the run.

"My lord not withstanding the able manner in which Mr Freeman has advocated my cause, it will be a consolation to myself to say a few words. It has been sworn that I had a pistol, in my hand on the fair day and shot Casey with it. I here protest in the face of heaven and before men that I am not guilty of that crime nor do I know who committed it. Besides I solemnly declare that I have never been guilty of any house breaking or robbery nor was I in the habit of crimes that would call down upon me the severe punishment of the law which I am threatened with here today. But if it pleases the court to convict me I am ready to hear my condemnation with patience and undergo my sentence with resignation."

Baron Pennefather then addressed the jury and went back over all the evidence that had been heard that day. The jury left the court room for a mere fifteen minutes and returned with the verdict of guilty. From his own words it was clear Duggan was a capable man and understood the charges against him and the punishment he would now face. The judge then addressed Duggan at length before sentencing. He began "Patrick Duggan you have been found guilty of the crime of murder after the most minute inquiry". He then reminded him that there was now no hope at all saying "entertain no hopes of pardon". Duggan was told he was to be hung the following Saturday and his body given up for dissection.

Duggan must have naively thought he would only have got jail for he called out "then I am doomed to die". He was taken from the court with just two days to live.

By Saturday it was only a miracle could save Duggan, in the 1830's there was no such thing as an appeal. A priest, magistrate or respectable person would have to arrive swearing new information and this was never going to happen. Duggan had terrorised the district for several years and they wanted him gone.

Little is known of the execution that Saturday morning but it was in public and a crowd would have gathered to see the spectacle. As the judge had said his body was given up for dissection afterwards as at the time a murderer could not be allowed a Christian burial.

Outside the newly built county gaol that the execution took place.

Two strange men
Castletownroche 1848

Catherine McCarthy ran a small grocery shop in the village of Castletownroche around the time of the famine. She also let out rooms above the shop to lodgers passing through the village for a little extra income. Her husband had died some years before and she was left to run the business on her own. In late 1847 her health began to fail her so a young niece Mary Reynolds came to live with her and help her with the shop. The old woman was known to have money and people said she was always careful with her business and very hardworking.

On Tuesday the 4th of January night two men took a room there. One of the men had been seen in the village before but the other was a stranger. The next morning neither the old woman nor the niece opened the shop. At first the neighbours thought nothing of it saying the old woman was independent and liked to manage her own affairs. Maybe she had gone off for the day to buy supplies without telling anyone.

After several days, the neighbours noticed that no sign had been seen of the old woman or her niece. The little shop they normally ran had not been opened on Wednesday or Thursday. Smoke had not been seen coming from the chimney or any lodgers seen coming or going. On Thursday evening the neighbours finally informed the police who took the drastic step of forcing in the backdoor which was bolted from the inside. The front door was also locked but there was no sign of the key in the house.

What they found inside was shocking, the old woman and her niece dead in the same bed. Catherine had a cord around her neck by which they thought she must have been strangled. Young Mary also had marks on her neck where she was held by a murderer's hand. The police could clearly see the finger and thumb marks and could tell that she had put up a great struggle.

There was not a penny to be found in the house or shop and the police discovered several strong boxes broken open.

The two women were found in a bedroom downstairs off the kitchen. The police found that a bed upstairs seemed to have been recently slept in by two people. Locals reckoned the old woman had about £60, which there was no sign of in the house. The killers had even taken a cloak and coats belonging to the old woman. Clothes belonging to her dead husband were also missing. An old pair of trousers which had gotten wet was the only shred of evidence left behind but could have been anyone's.

The inquest was held the following day on Friday the 7th January by the county coroner Richard Jones. The police were represented by Sub inspector McLeod who was investigating the case and a jury of respectable local men were sworn in.

Michael Troy who lived right next door told how he had been in Mrs McCarthy's on the Tuesday night before. That night he recalled seeing two strange men there who had taken a room for the night. He had seen them sitting by the fire chatting to the woman of the house in a perfectly normal way. That night he noticed that one of the men though kept his head down as if to hide his identity.

Dr Tuckey who had examined the bodies concluded that both had died from strangulation. He had found young Margaret Reynolds naked in the bed with the bed clothes pulled over her. Tuckey had found her mouth full of froth and blood due to the terrible struggle with her killer. He told the inquest how finger nail marks could clearly be identified on her neck.

The doctor found the aunt with a cord around her neck pulled tightly. She had not put up the struggle her niece had. He surmised both were dead at least a day as the bodies were cold and stiff when he examined them.

The jury agreed with the medical evidence that both women were strangled by a person or persons unknown.

The motive of the murder seems to have been robbery which was thought to have been premeditated. Their only reason for staying there that night seems to be just to rob the old woman of everything she had. Why they could not have crept around the house and found her money and left her sleeping in bed is a mystery. It was not like either of the women came on the men rifling through their stuff as they were killed in their beds. Most likely the old woman was killed first and quickly. Young Margaret on the other hand put up a fight.

It seems though that nobody was ever caught for the terrible deed despite the best efforts of the police. If it was the two men who stayed there that night they moved on undetected and having gotten away with it done likewise in other parts of the country. At the time it was difficult to connect crimes in different parts of the country without the help of fingerprints and modern day forensics.

Crime was rampant in the country as people starving were driven to petty crime in order to just survive. Punishments were harsh. Yet this was a crime much more depraved than the ordinary man stealing to feed his family from someone who he thought had enough. There is no doubt that poor people in the area at the time had little. A few weeks later the parish priest appeals for aid as children have given up attending school "owing to their want of clothing and food".

Castletownroche a few decades later, image courtesy of the National Library of Ireland.

A man came in and killed her
Horgan's Cross Kiskeam 1922

The year 1922 was unusual for the ordinary people of the Irish countryside and strange things were happening.

On Saturday morning the 9th of September sometime after nine, Dan Cronin walked past Horgan's cross halfway between Kiskeam and Boherbue. Suddenly he heard a woman break the morning silence screaming "Nora Nora Nora Fitz, will you come to me" in a frightened voice. At the same time he met a servant boy Jeremiah Dennehy and told him someone was calling Nora Fitzgerald.

Cronin headed towards the source of the voice which he had recognised and it took him to Horgan's farmhouse. Inside the house it was now silent and he called out "Mary where are you".

What came next was a shock to him "I'm in here and Nora is dead". Nora was not an old woman, she was only married seven years and was about forty years old, and it was strange that she was dead. He found Mary on the scullery floor holding Nora Horgan close to her chest. To him Nora appeared to be dead and was covered in blood, especially her head.

Cronin asked what had happened and Mary frantically replied "Oh lord a man came in and killed her". There was no one else in the house at the time, Nora's husband Jeremiah was out working. Knowing there was nothing he could do Cronin ran out and raised the alarm. A man on horseback was passing and sent for a priest. It was also almost noon when a doctor arrived and there was nothing he could do, Cronin's initial thoughts were right, she was dead.

Hearing the news neighbours searched the countryside but no trace of a strange man could be found. All they had to go on was the servant Mary Moynihan's description, a big tall young man wearing brown clothes who appeared rough, a tramp she said.

On Monday the 11th of September the inquest was held by Coroner Ryan from Lombardstown before a jury of twelve local men in Horgans's farmhouse. Mr D O'Carroll was the foreman and when the jury inspected the body the hearing of witnesses began.

It was obvious the first witness called that day was servant Mary Moynihan who worked for the Horgan's for the last five years. She said that morning she milked the cows with Nora Horgan and finished about half eight. Dennehy went to the creamery with the milk and the women had breakfast about nine. She said Nora then fed the chickens in the haggard. At about half nine on the morning she was washing ware in the kitchen. The woman of the house Nora Horgan was in the scullery off the kitchen plucking a chicken. She heard voices in the scullery but at first took no notice. When she heard Nora's screams, she knew something was wrong. She ran to see and found a man in the scullery. Both women were then screaming and Mary said she ended up on the floor.

When Mary got up the man struck her with his fist on the head and she fell again. Mary then said the man got her on her knees and threatened to kill her if she raised the alarm. He fled and Mary did what she could for Nora but found she was dead. It was then that Mary screamed out for help. A juror asked her had he something in his hand but Mary said she did not see it.

Dan Cronin then told of how he came on the dreadful scene, he said Nora Horgan was covered in blood and appeared dead. He asked Mary what had occurred and she said a man. He asked where the man was, Mary said "Oh, god a big tall man, with wild eyes and brown clothes".

Horgan's Cross where a woman was heard screaming.

Husband of the dead woman, farmer Jeremiah Horgan told how on the morning in question he had left home at half four. He was up early to take pigs to Kanturk and then on to Cork. It was Saturday evening when he returned to Kanturk and heard his wife was dead.

Jeremiah told the inquest how he came home and saw his wife laid out dead. He asked the servant what had occurred. He questioned her did the dogs not bark when a strange man approached the farmhouse but now couldn't recall what she had said. A juror questioned him about the dogs and Jeremiah said he had five dogs and they normally barked when seeing strangers.

Medical evidence was then given by Dr James O'Riordan from Boherbue. He had attended Horgan's house on the 9th and carried out an examination on the body. He had found many injuries to her head, three wounds on the left side 2-3 inches long. On the right side of the head he found another six wounds cut right to the bone of the skull. The skull was fractured and pressed in the brain, medically called a depressed fracture. Death he said was as a result of the fracture, which resulted in shock and great haemorrhage of blood. He felt the wounds were not done with great force but rather with a sharp instrument.

Coroner Ryan regretted to say that there was no evidence of who had caused the terrible crime. The jury duly returned a verdict of murder by some person or persons unknown.

Both the foreman and the coroner expressed their sympathy to the husband and family of the dead woman. The coroner hoped that whoever had committed the crime would soon be brought to justice.

After the inquest the funeral took place. Nora Horgan was buried at the family plot in Cullen and the procession was one of the biggest in the locality for a long time. This showed that the family were greatly respected in the area but also that people were shocked by such a mysterious murder of an innocent woman. Mary Moynihan left the employment of the Horgan's after working there for several years.

Once a few days had passed there was little hope the man would be found in the area, he would be long gone. With all that was going on in Ireland at the time was there anyone to investigate?

The Civic Guards as they were called had been set up earlier in the year but there had been a seven week mutiny. It was only September of that year when the first of the new recruits were dispatched around the country. The Civil War had started which was one of the bloodiest parts of Irish history. Maybe this was why the murder of a farmer's wife in rural North Cork went unnoticed as there was no law and order. It cannot have been easy for people in the area to accept that the killer was still out there and could strike again.

Especially frightening to people, was the complete lack of obvious motive, there had been no family disputes over land or otherwise which usually resulted in such things. The only safe assumption that could be made was theft and when Nora called for her servant he panicked and fled afterwards. Strange though that the man had gotten away in the morning without being seen at all.

It was a year later in August of 1923 that the Civic Guard was renamed the Garda Síochána and some semblance of normality returned to the countryside. For the new force it would take time to work through a backlog. Was the murder of Nora Horgan just one such crime that had fallen between the cracks or was there just no evidence?

Rumours were obviously going about and some felt they knew who had done it. In August 1923 around the time of the General Election Jeremiah Horgan was told the name of the man who killed his wife. He went to Moynihan's and asked Mary was there any truth to the rumours that Dan Kiely had murdered his wife. Dan Kiely would have been well known to Mary but also to Mrs Horgan. Mary confirmed to him she had heard the rumours also. She also didn't deny it but said the man that done it looked like Kiely. Mary said on the day of the murder the man had a cap pulled down over his face and she couldn't tell if it was him or not for sure. Was this ever reported to the authorities at the time or was there any point?

More than once that year Jeremiah Horgan went round to Moynihan's and questioned Mary for more detail but she didn't give it. He warned her that time would come again when there was a law in the countryside and she would have to answer the questions then.

It was not forgotten by the authorities at all, it just took time. In October 1923 questions began to be asked. Superintendent Peter Fahy and a sergeant made several trips to the area. Horgan's house was inspected but it was over a year later. Fahy called to Mary Moynihan where she now lived with her father in Lisrobin. He managed to get a statement from her and probably a better account of what she had given before.

On Thursday the 17th of January 1924 Superintendent Peter Fahy left his temporary headquarters at Moore's hotel in Cork and travelled towards the Kanturk again. He had been investigating the case for several weeks and was now ready to make an arrest.

Later that day he tracked down Mary Moynihan and took her into custody for the murder. She was charged before a magistrate in Kanturk that on the 9th of September 1922 at Tooreenavuscaun she wilfully murdered Nora Horgan. A remand was applied for eight days and arrangements made to hear the case again before Kanturk District court. Afterwards she was transferred to custody in Cork Jail.

It was Thursday the 31st of January before evidence was heard in court at Kanturk before District Justice Cahill. State Solicitor Daniel Casey led the prosecution for the state with Superintendent Fahy. The accused had employed Mr Ferguson from Kanturk and Jeremiah Horgan was represented by solicitor Mr Lenehan. There was great public interest in the case and crowds gathered to hear the proceedings.

Daniel Casey opened the case saying it occurred at a time when there was no law and order in the countryside. He admitted this may cause some difficulty but was still confident a prima facie case could be proved against Mary Moynihan.

First called to take the stand that day was Jeremiah Horgan. He told how he was happily married to Nora since 1915. Mary Moynihan was employed since 1917 helping out on the farm until when his wife was killed. One of her duties was to clean the milk tanks and Nora would scold her when the milk was sour.

He then detailed the morning of the murder, his wife called Mary Moynihan early that day. At 3:30 am Jeremiah and his wife had tea brought to their bed by their servant, the accused. Outside he heard Denis Herlihy and Patrick Dineen in the yard taking the pigs to Kanturk.

Jeremiah got up as he was going to Cork to sell fat pigs. His breakfast was served by Moynihan and before leaving he asked Mary to take another cup of tea to his wife who was still in bed. After breakfast he had a conversation with his wife who was still in bed while he dressed. He left home at half four and that was the last time he had seen his wife alive.

When he left that morning the only people in the house were his wife, Mary Moynihan and Jeremiah Dennehy. It was Dennehy's job every morning to take the milk to Kiskeam creamery. He normally left about eight and returned about two hours later.

That morning Horgan said he caught up with the men taking the pigs to Kanturk. There they were loaded onto a lorry and he travelled to Cork. It was six that evening when he returned in the lorry to Kanturk.

In Kanturk he heard something had happened to his wife and he went straight home. Several neighbours had gathered around his yard. He found his wife upstairs in bed as she had been that morning but now she was dead.

Jeremiah said at the other end of the house he found Mary Moynihan in her bedroom. She was lying in bed crying at the time. He asked Mary several questions. What is the cause of it? Who killed my wife?

Jeremiah told the court how he searched the scullery the day after the murder; he explained how the house had three sculleries. That day the lower scullery had blood all over it but he said there was also blood in the middle scullery. The slasher was missing from the scullery window and also a cart leaf spring was missing. He said that on the window in the lower scullery wrenches and bolts were kept and that day though they were thrown about on the floor stained in blood. A few days later he found the slasher in a closet under the dresser in the kitchen, the leaf spring was found under a bin in the lower scullery.

The judge asked him about the layout of the sculleries and Jeremiah told him that the lower scullery had no door to the yard.

He then related how on the day after the funeral, Mary Moynihan's father arrived at his house and Mary left with him. She did not work for him since then. At that time he admitted owing her £17 7s in wages which they left without asking for. Horgan told how he later sent for Mr Moynihan and settled the wage bill.

The next witness called that day arrived at Horgan's house that morning having heard the screaming. It was not Dan Cronin though; it was a farmer John James O'Connor who had gone for the priest that day.

John recalled that morning halfway between the crossroads and Horgan's house he saw Dan Cronin from Knocknamucklagh on the road with a scythe. Cronin threw down the scythe and ran towards Horgan's house. John said as he approached he heard a woman's screams coming from Horgan's.

He soon recognised the voice as that of Mary Moynihan. Asked in court John replied that the screaming seemed to come from outside the front of Horgan's house. He rode on to Horgan's house and when he got there Dan Cronin was in the field at the back of the house calling to raise the alarm.

John entered the house by the back door and heard Mary Moynihan's voice in the back or lower scullery. He heard her say "oh dear god, what will I do". When he went to the lower scullery Mary Moynihan was sitting with Nora Horgan stretched on the floor her head resting on Mary's chest. Mary said to him "oh dear god Jack and I alone". He told the court how Nora had wounds on her head but they were not bleeding. Instead he said the wounds appeared to be "crusted over"

O'Connor said he took hold of Nora's arms and pressed hard to check if she was dead. She felt slightly warm but he assumed that she was dead. He asked Mary what happened and she said "wisha I don't know".

He then left for the priest in Boherbue and it was almost two hours before he returned to Horgan's house. John told how when he returned that day he met Mary at the back door and questioned her about what had happened. He said she gave the story of a man in brown clothes but was slow to answer and to give any detail. He noticed that day that Mary had a clump of hair missing from her forehead. She had loose hair on her head and also a finger print of blood on the bare patch.

He then told how in the afternoon that day with Dan Cronin, they inspected the sculleries.

In the first scullery inside the back door he found one patch of blood on the floor, he said about an egg cup full. In the middle scullery he saw spots of blood on one wall. In the lower scullery though there were big splashes of blood. Solicitor Ferguson suggested that a visit should be made to see the layout of Horgan's sculleries. Mr Lenehan found this completely unnecessary and would not hear of it.

Finally that day Superintendent Peter Fahy took the stand. He told of arresting Moynihan and having previously got a statement from her. He would not read it out that day, saying the investigation was still ongoing. He was confident more evidence would connect the accused to the murder. She was then remanded to custody for eight days to appear again at Kanturk District court.

It seems Superintendent Fahy and his team were slower finding the evidence against her than he hoped, several times throughout February Moynihan was called to court and the state merely sought a remand.

Finally at the end of February the prosecution was ready to resume the case against her. With 1924 being a leap year the court sat on Friday the 29th of February.

Medical Evidence was given again by Dr James O'Riordan who was the medical officer for Boherbue district. When he arrived that day at noon Nora's head was still resting on Mary Moynihan's lap. He had the body moved to the kitchen where there was more light to work on her. He found her dead and the body cold; he thought she might be dead from three or four to eight hours. On arrival he found clotted blood on her head wounds. The wound over her eye he felt was received while she was standing but the others while she was lying down.

He told the court how death from her injuries would have been instantaneous. The slasher and leaf spring were produced and O'Riordan reckoned they could produce the injuries.

Nora's brother Cornelius Herlihy also gave evidence having gone to Horgan's after hearing his sister had been killed.

Sergeant Jeremiah Sullivan told how he went to Moynihan's in Lisrobin last October with Superintendent Fahy. That day they took a statement from Mary Moynihan and he still wished to keep that statement till a later date. He then told how he got another statement from her while in Kanturk Barracks on the 29th February that year. Her solicitor Mr Ferguson was also present that day. He read out the statement, Mary said she heard a man's voice in the scullery that morning at first she thought it was young

Mick Sullivan or Mick the cottage as he was known. While washing the dishes Nora called her from the scullery.

Seeing a strange man there she said "I put my hand about her neck to save her". The man she said caught both of them and pulled them down to the third scullery. Mary claimed the man struck her on the head and then threw her against the wall. She could not recall how long she was there but the man then threatened her not to raise the alarm. Once the man left she called for help and Dan Cronin was the first to arrive.

Sullivan told how it was Mr Ferguson who encouraged Mary to reveal a man's name that day. She mentioned the name Dan Kiely and later told that he was the postman in Kiskeam and his brother was the shoe maker. He told how he heard Mary whisper to her father "that name is wrong, they will find it all out"; the father replied "sure they will".

The sergeant then announced that he didn't wish to produce any more evidence and applied for another remand. Mr Ferguson was pleased with the days proceeding, he knew once the name Dan Kiely was mentioned the prosecution would now be obliged to look into it. It would at the very least buy some time for his client.

The next day in court though Ferguson must have realised that the Dan Kiely story would do little for Mary Moynihan. On the 10th of March there was some damning evidence despite the fact nobody had actually witnessed the murder.

Coroner Michael Ryan told the court how he had conducted the inquest on the 11th of September 1922. He explained how the evidence received from Mary at the inquest was voluntary and he had cautioned her before. He then read for the court the statement Mary had given at the inquest. Ryan said it was strange that Mary described the man as having his cap pulled down over his face. Yet when he asked her did the man have a moustache or not she could not answer.

When cross examined Ferguson asked "were the irregulars present at the inquest". Ryan confirmed they were. He also told that fifty men were present and some were armed.

Mrs Ellen Clifford a widow from nearby townland Urraghil Beg told how she had known Nora for the last twenty years. On the 9th of September 1922 she went to Horgan's after hearing Nora was dead. Ellen told the court how she questioned Mary Moynihan that day in the scullery but Mary said "put no more questions to me, I have enough trouble". Ellen told her to get up from under Nora as she was dead but Mary was said she could not leave her.

Ellen said she again questioned Mary in the Kitchen, asking how Nora was killed while she was there. Mary told her the man put her out of the scullery and bolted the door from the inside. Ellen then asked Mary what did she do while locked out of the lower scullery and she said she just stood there. Ellen said "you stood listening to the man killing Mrs Horgan inside, why didn't you fasten the door from the outside and run for help and you would have the man caught inside?" Mary claimed she was afraid to run for help.

Ellen told how she went back into the scullery at about quarter to twelve before the doctor arrived. Ellen said that Mary Moynihan was back in the same position with the dead woman's head in her lap. Ellen stayed in Horgan's that day and helped Con Herlihy wash the body. Several times that day she heard Mary say "oh my god how will I stand before Jerry Horgan".

Ellen told the court how she went back to Horgan's house the following Wednesday. That day she went to the lower scullery and examined the door. She found there was no bolt or lock on the inside of the door of the lower scullery. On the outside though she said there was a chain which could have been attached to a nail to secure the door. Ferguson declined the opportunity to cross examine Ellen Clifford.

Superintendent Fahy should have considered hiring Ellen Clifford as a detective but a woman was not hired by the Gardaí until 1959. This was the first real evidence that showed there were grave holes in Mary Moynihan's story. Not only that but it showed how Mary attempted to conceal it by looking concerned about her employer.

Daniel Cronin who had been one of the first on the murder scene took the stand. He described himself that day as a fireman in the Kiskeam Creamery who lived in Knocknamucklagh. Dan began by saying at the funeral Jeremiah Horgan asked him to remain in his house that day with three other men. While there Mary Moynihan issued orders to the men of what work was required on the farm. The three men went at their jobs but

Dan Cronin said he didn't do what Mary had told him. Instead he did as Mr Horgan had asked and remained watching Moynihan.

He followed her to the parlour and caught her putting a bottle into a press. He questioned her, what she was doing and found the bottle had a poison label on it. Afterwards Cronin gave the bottle to Jeremiah Horgan and told him about it.

After that day in court no more evidence was given for several weeks. Every eight days either Superintendent Fahy or Sergeant Sullivan applied for a further remand. It was not until the 11th of April that more witnesses were heard. Ferguson protested strongly that day that his client was now in custody for over three months. He said if she was to be sent for trial it should be done without delay but disagreed with the repeated adjournments.

Casey for the state said that either way she would be in custody as no assize courts had been setup since the foundation of the Free State. Later that month the Courts of Justice Act 1924 changed that situation by setting up the Criminal Court, Supreme Court and Criminal Court of Appeal. The year before Petty Sessions had been replaced by the District Court system. Now the English system Resident Magistrates and amateur magistrates was abolished. Under the Irish system all judges were employed by the state.

That day in court a niece and nephew of Mrs Horgan were called as witnesses, Maria Herlihy and Denis Sheehan. Both gave very similar evidence of attending the wake in Horgan's house on the day Nora had been killed. They were both present when Jeremiah Horgan returned to find people at his house for the wake. Both witnesses saw Horgan embrace Mary Moynihan and recalled them kissing. What were the prosecution trying to prove by calling these witnesses?

Next the prosecution tried to put to bed the story the accused had told, that Dan Kiely had done it. James Archdeacon said he slept in Dan Kiely's house in Kiskeam on the 9th of September. That morning Dan Kiely got up and left at nine.

A postman from Kiskeam Francis Cronin could tell more of Dan Kiely's movements that morning. He had seen Kiely return before ten with a load of turf. When the mail arrived from Banteer both he and Kiely sorted it in the post office and then set out on their rounds for the day.

Again Jeremiah Horgan was called and told Solicitor Casey about the poison bottle.

He also told how he wrote to Mary Moynihan and also called to see her asking her for more information about the death of his wife. Mary declined to say more and her written reply to him was read out in court.

When Ferguson got his chance he tried his best to involve Jeremiah Horgan in the crime but it would do little to prove his client's innocence. He asked some hard hitting questions to the widowed farmer.

Do you believe Mary Moynihan killed her? I don't know who killed her.

Before you left the house that morning did you arrange with anyone to kill your wife? No   I did not.

Did you ever suggest to Mary Moynihan that she should kill your wife? No.

Had Mary Moynihan any reason for killing your wife? No I don't think so.

Did Mary Moynihan kiss you on the night of the wake as deposed to by Denis Sheehan? No sir.

 Horgan admitted his wife's relations were cool with him since her death.

Did they ever accuse you of having a hand in the murder? I knew by them they had it in their nose against me, but they never accused me of it.

Were there ever any improper relations between you and Mary Moynihan? No Sir.

Do you believe Mary Moynihan killed your wife? No sir, I could not believe it until I see it sworn.

It was another month later on the 12th May before more evidence would be heard, it felt for weeks that something shocking would be found against Mary Moynihan but it was not to be. The prosecution spent months trying but could find little against her.

That day another witness was called who had met Dan Kiely returning with a load of turf on the morning of the 9th. No more evidence was called against the accused.

The remainder of the day was spent reviewing the evidence and each side making their speech. It was revealed that Dan Kiely would have given a statement of his movements but was interned in the Curragh at the time.

Fergusson stated that no jury would find Moynihan guilty and claimed it should be Jeremiah Horgan in the dock. Casey for the prosecution said the defence had changed their story, first a tall man, then Dan Kiely and now they accused Jeremiah Horgan.

Late that evening the judge went back over the evidence again and said he found that Moynihan could be connected to the murder. He returned her for trial at the next court in Dublin. When asked had she anything to say Moynihan had to consult her solicitor. She then said "I make no statement".

Now Mary Moynihan found herself back in jail waiting for a trial before a new legal system. She had now spent four months between jail and the district court, with repeated adjournments.

It was another eight months in custody before she appeared in Green Street Courthouse.

When the Criminal court sat in December 1924 the system was just months old. Despite the change in the legal system the death penalty remained for those found guilty of murder for men or women. Mary Moynihan must have faced Justice Sullivan knowing that in a few days time he could be putting on the black cap and sending her to the scaffold. She could be the first woman sentenced to death in the Irish Free State.

On Thursday the 11th of December 1924 Mary pleaded not guilty. She was now represented by Joseph Healy and the prosecution was led by a Mr Carrigan.

The same witnesses were called as at the district court and they told mostly the same story. Again some of the best evidence was given by Mrs Clifford even though she had actually seen nothing. The big difference now was it would take only two days, instead of the months in the District Court. The other difference was a jury of twelve men would now decide whether Mary Moynihan would live or die.

The final witness called on the second day was Daniel Kiely who had since been released. He stated that he had no part in the murder or Mrs Horgan and how could he with so many alibis.

Joseph Healy made a long speech for his client but again the defence had no witnesses to call. Healy said that Moynihan didn't always tell the truth but her story of the tall man was the truth. He claimed it was impossible that Mary could have overcome a strong woman such as Mrs Horgan. Healy hinted at the fact that Horgan was involved in his wife's murder. He read a line from Mary's letter to him saying how she would do him no harm, implying Mary could reveal what she knew.

Mr Carrigan on the other hand argued that there was no reason Mary Moynihan would shield Jeremiah Horgan and the jury must find her guilty of murder.

The judge finished his address to the jury at half four in the afternoon. The jury spent two hours debating their verdict and returned at half six. Their verdict was guilty but they strongly recommended mercy.

Mary Moynihan was then asked was there any reason why she should not face the death sentence. She said she was not guilty then "the man that is guilty I wish to tell the judge that he be arrested, he put me in a state that he tempted me with murder as well. He forced me into it and I shielded him at the time but I won't shield him now. I think it time for me to say that I won't shield him any longer and the man that will be arrested is Horgan that committed the murder on the morning"

Horgan was not arrested though it was far too late for this and far too late for Mary. She would have said anything now to save herself. Justice Sullivan carried on with the proceeding and put on the black cap before reading the sentence. He read out the sentence " it is ordered and adjudged that you Mary Moynihan be taken from the bar of the Court where you now stand to the prison from whence you last came and that on Tuesday the 13th of January you be taken to the common place of execution in the prison in which you shall then be confined, and that you be then hanged by the neck until you be dead and that your body be buried within the walls of the prison in which the aforesaid judgement of death shall be executed upon you". Mary was said to be calm while hearing this and was then removed from the courtroom.

A week later and the case was heard before the Criminal Court of Appeal in Dublin Castle with Chief Justice O'Shaughnessy. The Chief Justice admitted the urgency of the case but compared the situation to the English system. There he said the judge did not give the day of execution which allowed more time for an appeal.

The appeal needed to be heard before the 13th of January. With the Christmas period in the middle this seemed impossible. After much discussion the Chief Justice postponed the execution until 30th of January allowing more time for the appeal in the middle of January.

In the last few days of January 1924 the Governor General taking the advice of the Executive Council decided on a reprieve of the death sentence. Instead Mary Moynihan faced a life sentence of penal servitude.

Despite the reprieve though Mary Moynihan did not drop the appeal and accept her fate of a life in prison. Throughout January her legal team applied for leave to appeal and it was heard before the chief justice.

In early February the appeal was again before the Chief Justice. Joseph Healy outlined the grounds for appeal saying how some of the statements were obtained from Mary made them inadmissible. He also complained with the trial judge's charge to the jury and to a remark Mr Carrigan had said.

The chief justice ruled that no miscarriage of justice had occurred. He also remarked that no objections had been raised to these points during the trial. The chief justice ruled that the trial had been fair and impartial. This must have come as a blow to Mr Healy who was intending to call more evidence which he had failed to do during the trial. So Mary Moynihan remained in jail with little prospect of anything else.

The motive many suspected all along was that Mary Moynihan was having an affair with her employer. Did she harbour thoughts that she may become the woman of the house and took a drastic step to achieve that goal? Or did she just snap one day at her overbearing mistress and go too far?

If she had the opportunity to marry a man like Horgan she would have had a better life for herself and her children would have been well setup. She would have had servants of her own and somewhat of a say instead of her wages going to her father.

Mary Moynihan would have been attractive to Horgan as she was twenty years younger and gave him more chance of a child. He had been married for seven years or so and there seems to have been no sign of a baby. For a farmer like Horgan, Moynihan was of the labouring class and far beneath him, from a marriage point of view. It is possible Horgan could have told young Mary things he never had any intention of just to get his way. She may have believed him and found her own way of making it happen.

If Mary had those intentions, why then did she leave Horgan's after the murder at all? Surely even her father would have left her there if he thought there was a chance of her advancement in life. They certainly had plenty of time to let it cool off as there was little suspicion on Moynihan for a long time.

On the other hand if there was evidence of them having an affair surely some neighbour would have broken their silence sooner. In the 1920's it certainly would have been a taboo but after all it went on in many places. Somebody was bound to have told sooner when they saw Mary getting away scot free at the time.

Also if Jeremiah was involved with Moynihan would he himself not come forward sooner, knowing her to be a suspect when he got home that night to the wake? It wasn't worth covering up an affair for a woman who had killed - he could have been next.

Mary Moynihan does come close to getting away with it, and then comes close to being the first woman to be hung for murder in the Free State. However she never comes close to marriage if that was her goal.

All for money?
Knockanare, Buttevant 1859

Darby Rourke a thirty five year old farm labourer originally from Killavullen and for the last ten or so years had been working and living near Buttevant. He was a sober, reliable man who worked for local farmers. He needed little, for he got his living where he worked and the farmers held on to his wages until he needed it.

On Sunday the 10th of April 1859 Darby called to James Regan's house in Knockanare a mile and a half from Buttevant. He stayed for a few hours that day but said he was on his way to James Elliott's farm where he had worked a few weeks before. Darby told Regan that afternoon he was going to borrow a grub to till his garden but also to seek wages owed to him. As he left Regan's about seven that evening, he didn't have far to go but nobody would admit to seeing him alive again.

Nobody noticed Darby missing until his body was found the next morning. It was discovered in a field by a local man. His face was covered in blood and his head had been beaten in. It was obvious right from then that Darby Rourke had died as a result of tremendous violence and no attempt had been made to conceal the body.

The man ran off to get help and went to Regan's farm, strange that he did not go to Elliott's as it was nearer. James Regan then went to Buttevant to inform the police.

The police were immediately suspicious of James Elliott. Elliott was a thirty five year old farmer who rented thirty acres from Lord Doneraile near to where Darby was found. Elliott was arrested and taken into custody despite not a shred of evidence against him. The police at Buttevant, Doneraile and Charleville were actively investigating the case.

An inquest was held on Tuesday the 12th of April at Buttevant Courthouse by Coroner Charles Daly. James Elliott was brought to the inquest by the police and had been in custody since the day before. He listened intently to everything that was said that day but did not react or say a word.

Darby's brother, Owen Rourke from Killavullen, formally identified the body. He said the last time he saw his brother alive was at harvest time three years before.

Bryan Sweeney described finding the body on Monday morning in a field. He said at the time he was walking along a path on his way to James Regan's house, two fields from the road.

Sweeney knew straight away Darby was dead as the face was bloody and disfigured. The wounds were dry and crusted over. Sweeney said he found a man called Sheehan in the next field who was Lord Doneraile's shepherd. It was Sheehan that recognised the body and they went to Regan's farm house.

James Regan confirmed that Rourke was in good health when he left his house that Sunday. That afternoon Rourke told him several of the farmers in the area owed him money and he was going to Elliott's looking for the £8 10s he was owed. He also told him that Thomas Coughlan, Thomas Blake, Henry Langley and George Lowe also owed him for work he had done. James Regan told how he had seen the body on Monday in a field. He thought it was in a direct line between his house and Elliott's. Regan described a large flat stone he saw near the body which he thought had a blood stain on it.

Michael Regan, son of James Regan from Knockanare was talking to Darby that Sunday and several times the week before. Regan was aware that Darby was demanding money from Elliott but advised him not to push the farmer too much. As Darby was leaving his father's house he told him there was no fear of him and he would get the money from Elliott alright.

The doctor James Patrick Sheehan told the jury how he had examined the body the evening before. He described the wounds he found as being the result of extreme violence. Five wounds to the head, one was a straight clean wound. Another wound behind the left ear was triangular shaped and very deep, fracturing the skull. This wound alone he thought was enough to result in an instant death. The doctor made no mention on what sort of instrument was used to inflict such injuries.

As there was no more evidence it was decided to adjourn the inquest until the following week. It was hoped that by then the police would have more evidence against Elliott.

Not long after the inquest was adjourned Darby's clothes were searched. They found five shillings and six pence concealed in a small red purse despite the clothes being search by the police before.

The grub which Darby was going to borrow was missing but had been seen at Elliott's farm on Saturday. There were rumours it had been stolen as a plough belonging to another farmer had gone missing the same night. The police were actively searching the area for the grub or any other object which may have been the murder weapon. The Awbeg River flowed nearby and they thought it was likely the murderer threw their weapon into the river.

The inquest resumed again on the following Monday in Buttevant. The coroner inquired if the police had any further details. Head Constable O'Neill from Charleville said they had no more evidence nor were there any more witnesses to examine.

The coroner then suggested to the jury that an open verdict as there was no evidence to be found against James Elliott. The jury did not take long to come to their verdict "we find that the deceased Darby Rourke was found murdered on the morning of the 11th of April on the lands of Knockanare in this county but by whom we are not informed".

Mr Baily the resident magistrate who was present that day again refused the application for bail for James Elliott.

Despite the best efforts of the police there was never enough evidence to take James Elliott to trial. Eventually the magistrates had to give in and grant the release of their suspect but it was June before this occurred. James Elliott went back to his farm in Knockanare and continued on as before. Now at least he didn't have to pay the £8 10s to Rourke. It seemed like that would be the end of it and nobody would be caught for the murder.

The following April, over twelve months since the murder, the rumours of Elliott's involvement again were discussed. More evidence was said to have been found which could link Elliott to the killing.

James Elliott was nowhere to be seen after being at home for ten months. Did he flee for his own safety before the neighbours took the law into their own hands or was it a sign he was guilty after all. Word was sent out to police stations to be on the lookout for Elliott.

It was a constable McManus in Cork who found James Elliott at a boarding house on Patrick's Quay. He was arrested but the magistrates in Cork were in favour of releasing him again because they had no information of the charges against him. Inspector Brownrigg came to court and said he had reason to believe Elliott was involved and a remand was granted.

Elliott denied he fled Buttevant saying if he wanted to he could have left the country months ago. Clearly though Elliott was now feeling the pressure and was described as pale in court.

A few days later and another court appearance the only thing the magistrates in Cork could suggest was to have the prisoner transferred to Buttevant. The police were confident with new evidence this time round they could take James Elliott to trial.

It seems though that there was never any new evidence at all. There is no record of Elliott being investigated by a magistrate, never mind an Assizes Court. Sooner or later the police would have to release him from custody as magistrates could not keep remanding him.

Does Elliott go home again to the farm in Knockanare? This is very doubtful as the locals seemed to have turned on him. Years later the name Elliott had died out in the townland.

Glossary

Adze is a tool that dates back to the Stone Age, it is like an axe but the blade is turned at right angle to the handle. It is mostly used to shape wood and is often used in boat building.

Approver a person, who is suspected in a crime, confesses and then gives evidence against others.

Assizes periodic criminal courts held quarterly that heard the most serious cases before a jury.

Billhook large hooked blade fixed to a handle, used in farming since medieval times to cut shrubs and harvest crops.

Coroner is a person who conducts an inquest into the cause of death, is normally a magistrate or solicitor.

Emergencymen employed by the landlord to guard a property after an eviction.

Gibbets a gallows used to hang someone, gibbeting was the practice of hanging them in chains for display purposes.

Goulogue cutting tool like a bill hook

Governor General or Seanascal this role was created with the formation of the Free State in 1922.The role was to be the official representative of the sovereign in Ireland. The role was a controversial one as the sovereign was still the king. The duties included giving royal assent to legislation and dissolving the Dáil.

Graffawn or graffaun hand tool like a pick axe but with a much wider blade used for digging or grubbing soil. Similar shaped to an adze but blade wouldn't be sharpened like an adze.

Grain unit of measurement originally based on the weight of a grain of barley, was used for medicines and was equivalent to approximately 65 milligram's.

Grand Jury was normally made up of the largest local rate payers or put another way were the landlords. They acted as a form of local government as well as sitting as jury on more serious criminal cases. Members of a Grand Jury could also sit as magistrates judging lesser cases.

Griffiths valuation land survey carried out in mid 19th century Ireland. The maid reason was to value land and buildings to determine the tax liable.

Grub a heavy hoe used for digging soil and weeding.

Habeas Corpus is a writ to bring a person in custody before a judge and determine if their incarceration is legal or not.

Haggard is a small enclosed field or yard at the back of a farm cottage. Often used for storing winter supplies of hay, straw or fodder.

Inquest is a judicial inquiry held in public into the cause of death. A jury is required when the death is suspicious or a murder is suspected.

Nolle prosequi legal phrase used by the prosecutor to say the case is being dropped.

Martial Law usually a temporary measure where the military take over from the Government and impose law.

Oxters ones arm pits, often used in the phrase up to your oxters.

Pitch or tar was one time the primary waterproofing material especially on ships.

Penal Servitude or hard labour was introduced in the 1770's and could also include transportation to a distant colony. By the 1850's transportation had been abolished but hard labour remained the norm. Not all labour was productive some prisons used punitive exercise such as a treadmill. As a form of punishment penal servitude was abolished in Britain in the1950's but remained in Ireland until 1997 when the law was finally changed.

Petty Sessions local court of magistrates

Prima facie in simple terms legally means there is enough evidence for there to be a case to answer.

Provost Sergeant non commissioned officer who is responsible for the maintenance of order and discipline in the regiment.

Riot Act a British law from 1714 which gave powers to local authorities. Any group of 12 persons or more could be declared unlawful and required to disperse. If the group did not go within an hour they were likely to face punishment.

Scullery small traditional room, used for washing dishes or laundering clothes, could now be referred to in some form as a utility room.

Tithe a tax a tenth of all farm produce, collected in Ireland by the English clergy.

Tithe proctor men whose job it was to value farm produce and set the tithe value and then collect it. Was not a popular job in rural Ireland and a dangerous occupation.

Turbary is an ancient right to cut turf from a particular patch of bog. Normally attached to the tenancy of a dwelling house and for domestic purposes only.

Under Secretary of Ireland up till 1922 was the head of the civil service.

Whiteboys secret organisation in rural Ireland, which used any means including violence threats and boycotts to obtain rights for tenants.

Bibliography

Newspapers:
Belfast newsletter
Chutes Western Herald
Cork Constitution
Cork Examiner
Evening Herald
Freeman's Journal
Irish Daily Independent
Irish Independent
Irish Press
Kerry Champion
Kerry Evening Star
Kerry Reporter 1924-35
Limerick Leader
Munster Express
Skibbereen Eagle
Southern Star
The Cork Southern Reporter
The Kerry Evening Post

Websites:
www.jstor.org
www.corkgen.org
www.landedestates.nuigalway.ie
www.irishgenealogy.ie
www.nli.ie
www.nationalarchives.ie
www.ancestry.co.uk
www.dippam.ac.uk
www.historicgraves.com
www.findagrave.com
www.askaboutireland/Griffiths-valuation
www.timeanddate.com

Publications
O'Flanagan's Munster Circuit 1880
Ingenious Ireland by Mary Mulvihill
Thou Shalt Not Kill, Gill and MacMillan
Griffiths Valuation
Guys Almanac

Other Publications by the Author

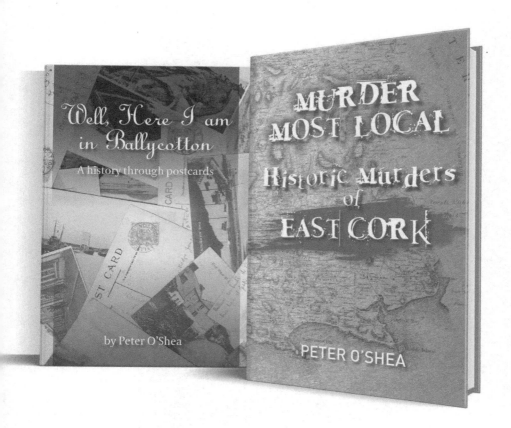

Coming Soon in 2020...

About the Author

Peter O'Shea is a native of Ballycotton. This is Peter's third book. His first book 'Well, Here I am in Ballycotton' combined his passion for postcards, his love of the sea and his appreciation for Ballycotton and its history. He wrote his second 'Murder Most Local, East Cork Historical Murders' following on from feedback he received about a local murder in his Ballycotton Book. Readers wanted to know more. Peter researched other local murders and wrote about 47 local East Cork murders. While researching the East Cork edition he found many other historical murders around Cork County.

Since January 2011 he has been Mechanic on the Ballycotton Lifeboat, he joined the Lifeboat as a volunteer many years before, when he was 18. During school and college Peter worked on local fishing boats and has always had a keen interest in all things maritime. Peter lives in Ballycotton with his partner Karen and their 3 sons James, Edward and Henry.

More information at www.facebook.com/ballycottonhistory